A World of Indigenous Languages

LINGUISTIC DIVERSITY AND LANGUAGE RIGHTS: 17

A World of Indigenous Languages

Politics, Pedagogies and Prospects for Language Reclamation

Edited by
**Teresa L. McCarty,
Sheilah E. Nicholas and
Gillian Wigglesworth**

MULTILINGUAL MATTERS
Bristol • Blue Ridge Summit

DOI https://doi.org/10.21832/MCCART3064

Library of Congress Cataloging in Publication Data
A catalog record for this book is available from the Library of Congress.
Names: McCarty, T.L., editor. | Nicholas, Sheilah E. (Sheilah Ernestine), editor. | Wigglesworth, Gillian, editor
Title: A World of Indigenous Languages: Politics, Pedagogies and Prospects for Language Reclamation/Edited by Teresa L. McCarty, Sheilah E. Nicholas and Gillian Wigglesworth.
Description: Bristol; Blue Ridge Summit, PA: Multilingual Matters, 2019. | Series: Linguistic Diversity and Language Rights: 17 | Includes bibliographical references and index.
Identifiers: LCCN 2018046180| ISBN 9781788923064 (hbk : alk. paper) | ISBN 9781788923057 (pbk : alk. paper) | ISBN 9781788923095 (kindle)
Subjects: LCSH: Language revival. | Linguistic minorities. | Language maintenance. | Language policy.
Classification: LCC P40.5.L357 W67 2019 | DDC 306.44/9—dc23 LC record available at https://lccn.loc.gov/2018046180

British Library Cataloguing in Publication Data
A catalogue entry for this book is available from the British Library.

ISBN-13: 978-1-78892-306-4 (hbk)
ISBN-13: 978-1-78892-305-7 (pbk)

Multilingual Matters
UK: St Nicholas House, 31–34 High Street, Bristol BS1 2AW, UK.
USA: NBN, Blue Ridge Summit, PA, USA.

Website: www.multilingual-matters.com
Twitter: Multi_Ling_Mat
Facebook: https://www.facebook.com/multilingualmatters
Blog: www.channelviewpublications.wordpress.com

The policy of Multilingual Matters/Channel View Publications is to use papers that are natural, renewable and recyclable products, made from wood grown in sustainable forests. In the manufacturing process of our books, and to further support our policy, preference is given to printers that have FSC and PEFC Chain of Custody certification. The FSC and/or PEFC logos will appear on those books where full certification has been granted to the printer concerned.

Typeset by Nova Techset Private Limited, Bengaluru and Chennai, India.
Printed and bound in the UK by Short Run Press Ltd.
Printed and bound in the US by Thomson-Shore, Inc.

To ancestors whose languages and voices have been carried to the present so that their descendants and those yet to come will receive the gifts—inheritance, birthright, history, and identity—that will guide them toward the future, and to all who work to sustain a world of Indigenous languages. Askwali. Ahéhee'. Thank you.

Front cover image: This photograph exemplifies how cultural understandings are passed on intergenerationally through the Indigenous language. Isaia Kealoha guides three kindergarten students as they learn how to work in the *māla 'uala*, or sweet potato garden, as he did as a child from his elders. Special appreciation goes to Isaia Kealoha, Kalāmanamana Harman, Paeaokalani Lavin and Kekuahiwi Woods; photograph courtesy of Ke Kula 'O Nāwahīokalani'ōpu'u Iki Lab Public Charter School, Kea'au, HI, USA.

Contents

Contributors

Pem Bird is a long-serving Māori educator and leader who has received several awards including the Queen's Service Medal in 2008. He became a Member of the New Zealand Order of Merit in 2017 and most recently won the Te Ururangi Award, all in recognition of his significant contribution to education. His influence stretches to asssisting with the development of Māori language strategies and serving on several Ministry of Education advisory and reference groups over the years. He held the position of president of the Māori Party for three years beginning in 2010, was the founding Chairperson of Ngā Kura ā Iwi o Aotearoa and is the Principal of Te Kura Kaupapa Māori Motuhake o Tāwhiiuau in his beloved Ngāti Manawa tribal area and home town, Murupara, in the Bay of Plenty.

Serafín M. Coronel-Molina is Associate Professor in the Department of Literacy, Culture, and Language Education at Indiana University, USA. His research appears in a number of book chapters published by prestigious European publishing houses, and in several international journals. He is the author of the *Quechua Phrasebook* (2014, 4th edition, Lonely Planet), and *Language Ideology, Policy and Planning in Peru*, 2015, Multilingual Matters), and co-editor with Teresa L. McCarty of *Indigenous Language Revitalization in the Americas* (2016, Routledge). His research is multi-, inter- and trans-disciplinary, drawing on fields as diverse as macro- and micro-sociolinguistics, educational linguistics/language education, applied linguistics, linguistic anthropology, Andean Studies, Indigenous Studies, Latin American Studies and Literacy Studies.

Elizabeth Marrkilyi Ellis is an Indigenous linguist and speaker of multiple Western Desert dialects. She has worked as an Ngaatjatjarra/Pitjantjatjara language teacher, interpreter/translator and dictionary worker over many decades. Having recently been awarded an Australian Research Council – Discovery Indigenous Fellowship she is now affiliated with the Centre of Excellence for the Dynamics of Language and the School of Literature, Languages and Linguistics at the Australian National University, documenting and analyzing the verbal arts of her speech community.

Ciprian-Virgil Gerstenberger is a computational linguist and programmer working with Giellatekno, the Center for Saami Language Technology, at the University of Tromsø – The Arctic University of Norway – since 2008. He received a degree as a Diplom-Linguist from the Institute for Natural Language Processing (Institut für Maschinelle Sprachverarbeitung, IMS), University of Stuttgart, Germany. In his current position he works not only with all Saami languages but also with Kven, Meänkieli, Komi and other minority languages. He assists both field linguists in language description and documentation and language activists in developing digital resources for language learning.

Mary (Fong) Hermes is a mixed heritage Indigenous person with 20 years of experience in Indigenous language revitalization. She holds a PhD in Curriculum and Instruction and is an Associate Professor at the University of Minnesota Twin Cities in the Culture and Teaching (CAT) and Second Language and Education (SLE) programs. Her research interests include improving the effectiveness of Indigenous language teaching and learning; culture and identity in education; Queer and Feminist theory; and activist research methods. Whatever else she is doing, she is continually speaking and learning Ojibwe, adding to the communities of Indigenous language speakers.

Nkonko M. Kamwangamalu is Professor of Linguistics in the Department of English at Howard University, Washington, DC. He has received a Fulbright Award and a Howard University Distinguished Faculty Research Award, and is internationally known for his publications on topics in language planning, multilingualism, codeswitching and African linguistics. His most recent book is titled *Language Policy and Economics: The Language Question in Africa* (Palgrave, 2016). He has edited special issues for *International Journal of the Sociology of Language* (2000, 2013), *Language Problems and Language Planning* (2004), *Multilingua* (1998) and *World Englishes* (2002), and is co-editor of the journal *Current Issues in Language Planning*.

Kendall A. King is a Professor of Second Language Education at the University of Minnesota. Her scholarship examines ideological, interactional, and policy perspectives on second language learning and bilingualism, with particular attention to educational practices impacting language use among Indigenous populations in Latin America and Spanish and Somali speakers in the US. She teaches graduate-level courses in sociolinguistics, language policy, language research methods, and language education and undergraduate courses in linguistics, and is incoming president of the American Association of Applied Linguistics.

Inge Kral is a linguistic anthropologist co-affiliated with the Centre for Aboriginal Economic Policy Research (CAEPR) and the ARC Centre of Excellence for the Dynamics of Language (CoEDL) at the Australian National University. Inge draws on some 30 years' experience in Indigenous education, language and literacy in remote Australia. Inge is currently a Co-Investigator with Elizabeth Ellis on an ARC-Discovery Indigenous project documenting and analyzing Western Desert Verbal Arts in the Ngaanyatjarra Lands region of Western Australia. Inge's research interests also include community-based out-of-school learning and literacy; youth, digital media and new literacies; and school-to-work transitions. Additionally, she is a co-researcher on a youth media and literacy project in an Orang Asli Indigenous village in Peninsular Malaysia.

Rosalva Mojica Lagunas is an Indigenous scholar and educator with family roots in Guerrero, Mexico. She earned her doctorate in Curriculum and Instruction with an emphasis in Language and Literacy at Arizona State University, USA. Rosalva's research and teaching focus on bilingualism and biliteracy, elementary education, Indigenous languages and education, language revitalization, and language planning and policy. She has explored these interests in the context of urban public schools in the US and Nahuatl heritage-language communities in Mexico. Her studies contribute to the larger fields of language education and sociolinguistics/applied linguistics, and to policy and practice.

Teresa L. McCarty is the G.F. Kneller Chair in Education and Anthropology and Faculty in American Indian Studies at the University of California, Los Angeles, USA. A Fellow of the American Educational Research Association, the Society for Applied Anthropology, and the International Centre for Language Revitalisation, her books include '*To Remain an Indian*' – *Lessons in Democracy from a Century of Native American Education* (with K.T. Lomawaima, 2006), *Ethnography and Language Policy* (2011), *Language Planning and Policy in Native America* (2013), *Indigenous Youth and Multilingualism* (with L.T. Wyman and S.E. Nicholas, 2014) and *Indigenous Language Revitalization in the Americas* (with S.M. Coronel-Molina, 2016). She is Principal Investigator on a US-wide study of Indigenous-language immersion schooling.

Barbra A. Meek, a Comanche citizen and professionally trained linguist and anthropologist, is Professor of Anthropology and Linguistics at the University of Michigan, Ann Arbor, USA. Her research focuses on language endangerment, revitalization and the interplay of language and ethno-racial differences in mainstream media. For almost 20 years, she has worked with Kaska language teachers and First Nations citizens (Yukon Territory Canada) on various projects aimed at heritage language sustainability. Most recently, she co-edited *Engaging Native American Publics* (2017, Routledge) with Paul Kroskrity.

Waimātao Murphy served as the inaugural CEO for Ngā Kura Iwi o Aoteroa and oversaw the development of its constitution and strategic plan. The number of membership schools grew under her watch as the organization spread nationally to support communities and their schools wishing to be more accountable and to service more directly their tribal groups. Waimātao served for many years as a Governor on the Board of Trustees for Te Kura Kaupapa Māori Motuhake o Tāwhiiuau located in Murupara in the Bay of Plenty, Aotearoa/New Zealand. Her influence has extended beyond Māori education to also include the health sector.

Sheilah E. Nicholas is a member of the Hopi Tribe, an Indigenous society located in the state of Arizona in the southwestern United States. She is an Associate Professor in the Department of Teaching, Learning and Sociocultural Studies at the University of Arizona. The focus of her scholarly work includes Indigenous/Hopi language maintenance and reclamation, Hopi language teacher education, and Hopi language ideologies and epistemologies. Her current research projects include a collaborative tri-university national study of Indigenous-language immersion schools and academic achievement, and engaging a community school to investigate the role of schools in Indigenous language reclamation in her home community of Hopi.

Marja-Liisa Olthuis is a university lecturer at University of Oulu, Finland. Her major interests are the Saami languages, Finnish, language revitalization, lexicology, second/foreign language teaching, translation studies and language technology. In 2015–2016, she collaborated with the Giellatekno group, the Center for Saami Language Technology, at the University of Tromsø – The Arctic University of Norway, in a machine translation (MT) project developing a rule-based MT system between North Saami and Aanaar Saami. She is the driving force behind the language revitalization project of her native language, Aanaar Saami.

Prem Phyak received his PhD in Second Language Studies from the University of Hawaii at Manoa, USA. Currently, he is an assistant professor at the Central Department of Education and the Head of the Department of English Language Education, University Campus, Tribhuvan University, Nepal. His areas of research include language policy, multilingualism across spaces, political economy of English language teaching, Indigenous knowledges and agency, and social justice in education. His recent publications include *Engaged Language Policy and Practices* (with Kathryn A. Davis, Routledge), and other articles in *Language Policy, Critical Inquiry in Language Studies* and *Language in Society*.

Cath Rau is a Māori medium specialist with over 30 years experience developing initiatives to support and strengthen Māori-mediun education in the compulsory schooling sector in Aotearoa/New Zealand. She leads a team of experienced educators under Kia Ata Mai Educational Trust whose work includes supporting Māori students and Māori teachers in schools nationwide to deliver quality programs in te reo Māori. She has been on several Ministry of Education advisory and working groups over the years, has authored numerous teacher resources and student materials and was also the lead facilitator and coordinator of professional learning and development and intervention programs for students in Ngā Kura ā Iwi o Aotearoa.

Gillian Wigglesworth has worked extensively with Indigenous children growing up in remote communities in Australia, largely in the Northern Territory. Her publications address issues in both first and second language acquisition, bilingualism and multilingualism. Her major research focus is on the languages Indigenous children living in these remote communities are learning, the complexity of their language ecology, and how these interact with English once they enter the formal school system. She is chief investigator in the Australian Research Council Centre of Excellence for the Dynamics of Language and leads one of its major programs, and a Redmond Barry Distinguished Professor at the University of Melbourne.

Acknowledgements

We express our sincere appreciation to Tim McNamara, Professor and Deputy Head of the School of Languages and Linguistics at the University of Melbourne, for providing the original impetus for this volume. We are also grateful to Kim Eggleton, former Commissioning Editor at Multilingual Matters, for encouraging the book proposal, and to Tommi Grover, Managing Director for Multilingual Matters, for his faith in the book project and seeing it through to completion. Thank you as well to Laura Longworth, Florence McClelland, Elinor Robertson and Sarah Williams for multifaceted support at Multilingual Matters.

We are deeply honored to have this volume included in the Linguistic Diversity and Language Rights series edited by Tove Skutnabb-Kangas, whose life work has been devoted to promoting Indigenous and minoritized languages and linguistic human rights. For their exceptional contributions to the book and the field, we thank each of the chapter authors; the book – and the language reclamation work it (re)presents – would not be possible without you. For extremely valuable reviews of earlier versions of the volume, we thank Beverly Baker, Samantha Disbray, Kathleen Heugh, Margie Hohepa, David Hough, Leena Huss, Leketi Makalela, John Mansfield, Jacqueline Messing, Susan Penfield and Tove Skutnabb-Kangas. To the esteemed Indigenous education scholars who took time to review the entire book manuscript and whose words appear on the back cover – Leena Huss, Tiffany S. Lee, and K. Tsianina Lomawaima – we express humble gratitude. We also express appreciation to UCLA doctoral candidate Lu (Priscilla) Liu for editorial assistance during the early stages of the project.

We extend special appreciation to Kauanoe Kamanā and William (Pila) Wilson of Ke Kula ‘O Nāwahīokalani‘ōpu‘u Iki (Nāwahī) Laboratory Public Charter School and the University of Hawaii‘i-Hilo, Keiki Kawai‘ae‘e of Ka Haka ‘Ula O Ke‘elikōlani College of Hawaiian Language at the University of Hawai‘i-Hilo, and Kupuna (Elder) Isaia Kealoha of Hilo, Hawai‘i, for their support of this volume and efforts to secure a fitting and inspiring cover image. Through their life’s work and commitment these leaders in the Hawaiian language movement teach and model for all of us what it takes – and means – to sustain a ‘world of Indigenous languages.’ We are honored to witness this work.

Teresa McCarty would like to acknowledge summer funding support from the George F. Kneller Endowment in Education and Anthropology. She also expresses gratitude to the Indigenous educators and communities with whom she has worked over many years, whose experiences and insights live and breathe with the language reclamation work presented in these pages. To editorial partners Sheilah Nicholas and Gillian Wigglesworth: a heartfelt *ahéhee'* for all the teamwork. And to my life partner, John Martin, thank you for your unwavering support through another lengthy editorial endeavor and for the wisdom of knowing when it is time to pause.

Sheilah Nicholas expresses her sincere appreciation to Teresa McCarty for the invitation to join her in recognizing the tremendous commitment of the contributors of this volume to the political, educational, ecological, and survival work of language reclamation throughout the world. The invitation also afforded her a place among the chapter authors whose work is uplifting, inspiring and empowering and attests to the fact that this work is not undertaken alone. She is most grateful to the participants of her study who entrusted her with telling their stories and from which she has gained an immense understanding of Hopi epistemology, the strength of culture and the role of language within oral tradition. This appreciation is extended to the late Emory Sekaquaptewa and Laura Nasetoynewa, to whom I look for daily guidance, and my parents who provided me with privileges and birthright to the Hopi world. Wholehearted thanks to Gillian Wigglesworth for keeping us on task throughout the duration of the editing process and for her invaluable ability to nudge us consistently but gently along the way. Finally, Sheilah would like to recognize her adult children, Sarah, Seth and Rachel LaMantia, as providing the aspiration for pursuing this work to reclaim responsibility in maintaining their connection to their heritage and community. Her gratitude extends to her husband, Joseph LaMantia, for his unconditional support throughout the years.

Gillian acknowledges the support of Australian Research Council funding to the Centre of Excellence for the Dynamics of Language (CE140100041) during the period in which this volume was conceived, written and edited. She is also immensely grateful to her colleagues, both Indigenous and non-Indigenous, in remote Australian communities for their support and friendship over many years. She also thanks her partner, Grant Cleary, for his support throughout the rather long period the collation of this volume required.

Finally, to all who do the work of language reclamation we express our collective admiration, thankfulness and honor.

Preface

Three-quarters of the known spoken languages in the world are Indigenous languages. All face an uncertain future due to colonization and ongoing raciolinguistic discrimination. Language endangerment is a global concern, reflected in a growing body of research and scholarship and a worldwide language reclamation movement. This book provides a comparative international perspective on that movement – its challenges, possibilities, and role in sustaining distinctive Indigenous ways of knowing and being. We use *reclamation* as an orienting framework to explore this movement. As Miami linguist Wesley Leonard (2017: 15) writes, a language reclamation paradigm 'moves beyond a focus on direct language measures such as creating new speakers (*language revitalization*) to incorporate community epistemologies such as how "language" is defined and given sociocultural meaning.'

The chapters herein have been specially prepared for this volume. Spanning Indigenous-language communities in Aotearoa/New Zealand, Australia, Canada, Finland, Latin America, Nepal, South Africa and the USA, the authors explore language reclamation at the local, national, and international levels, and the interstices between.

The book opens with a comprehensive introduction that situates the present moment of Indigenous-language scholarship and praxis historically and in the context of contemporary language reclamation efforts worldwide. The remainder of the volume is organized around three thematic strands. Part 1 takes up policies and politics, drawing on cases from Canada and South Africa. In Part 2, the authors examine the pedagogic dimensions of language reclamation, drawing on Māori, Quechua, Ngaanyatjarra, Ojibwe, and Aanaar Saami case examples. In the third section, the authors address the multi- and inter-generational prospects for language reclamation, with ethnographic case studies of Hopi, Limbu, and Nahuatl (also called Mexicano).

Addressing the construction of linguistic difference, identity and authenticity, and exploring innovative strategies for Indigenous-language learning, the chapters highlight multifaceted issues of politics, pedagogy and ideology in language reclamation work. In some cases, as in the Yukon Territory of Canada, the issues center on official language policies in settler states that reimagine citizenship in ways that transcend legacies of difference. In other cases, such as Māori in Aotearoa/New Zealand and in Australia and the USA, language reclamation has focused on curricular and pedagogical transformations carried out in schools, family homes and online communities. Some of these efforts, such as those for Quechua, Ngaanyatjarra and Ojibwe, involve the use of social media and conversational archives. Youth and young adults are key stakeholders in all of these processes, and the final chapters focus on the role of youth and intergenerational ties that are (re)activated through language reclamation projects. Taken together, the chapters foreground the myriad language reclamation approaches being adopted and adapted throughout the world.

Indigenous scholars have authored or coauthored every chapter. All the chapters emphasize language reclamation as a site of Indigenous self-(re)empowerment and self-determination.

The book is written with a broad readership in mind: undergraduate and graduate classes in applied linguistics, anthropology, education and Indigenous/Ethnic Studies; international scholars in those fields; a broader audience of policymakers and the public; and, most especially, Indigenous language educators, revitalizers, and activists and their allies. We offer the volume as testimony to this growing movement and its transformative potential for Indigenous peoples and the world.

Teresa L. McCarty
Los Angeles, California, USA

Sheilah E. Nicholas
Tucson, Arizona, USA

Gillian Wigglesworth
Melbourne, Victoria, Australia

A World of Indigenous Languages – Resurgence, Reclamation, Revitalization and Resilience

Teresa L. McCarty, Sheilah E. Nicholas and Gillian Wigglesworth

In titling this volume we foreground multilingualism as the global norm. We also foreground the prominence of Indigenous peoples as producers of global linguistic and cultural diversity. Of approximately 7000 known spoken languages, three-quarters are spoken by Indigenous peoples. We live in a world of Indigenous languages.

Yet, more than universal diversity, in this volume we valorize enduring traditions of Indigenous persistence in which linguistic and cultural diversity has always been valued as a reliable guide toward the future. Colonization and attempted genocide, linguicide and ethnocide have placed those traditions at risk. At least half the world's languages 'may no longer continue to exist after a few more generations as they are not being learnt by children as first languages' (Austin & Sallabank, 2011: 1). The majority of endangered languages are Indigenous languages (Skutnabb-Kangas & Dunbar, 2010).

In this volume we shift our gaze from what Maliseet anthropologist and language revitalizer Bernard Perley (2011: 3) calls 'the specter of language death' to the vital and growing Indigenous-language reclamation movement. In so doing, we decenter discourses of endangerment that often serve as a running tally of loss (Moore *et al.*, 2010; see also Duchêne & Heller, 2007; Moore, 2017). Instead, we focus on the forward-looking work of the survivors of linguistic assimilation and what we call the four Rs: resurgence, reclamation, revitalization and resilience. We also shift the focus from language as a bounded, abstract entity – a formulation that privileges imagined 'pure' forms of ancestral languages – exploring instead the dynamic, multi-sited, multi-vocalic language practices within contemporary Indigenous communities (see also Webster & Peterson, 2011). Here we are interested in what people actually *do* with their language practices.

We cannot address the present moment without confronting historic and ongoing inequities that lead to language endangerment in the first place. Power and authority must be at the center of any analysis of Indigenous and minoritized language issues. Language reclamation is linguistic work; it is educational work. As Haley De Korne and Wesley Leonard note (2017: 7), it is also political work in which people 'negotiate control over linguistic authority, knowledge production and self-definition through their linguistic practices.' But most importantly it is *survival* work that finds its purpose in the stewardship of distinctive Indigenous linguistic, sociocultural and physical home places and ecologies. This perspective places language reclamation squarely in the context of the settler colonial state and 'erase and replace' settler logics: 'Erase Native languages, replace with English. Erase Native religions, replace with Christianity,' and so on (Lomawaima & McCarty, 2006: xxii). In this sense language reclamation can be seen as a practice of decolonization that 'links language work with the underlying causes of language shift' (Leonard, 2017: 17; see also López, 2017).

Pre-eminent among those causes is colonial schooling, which has banned, restricted and exacted punishment for speaking the mother tongue. Language-restrictive policies are associated with myriad educational, economic and social disparities. These include low rates of educational attainment and high rates of poverty, clinical depression and teen suicide (Castagno & Brayboy, 2008). As a consequence, many language reclamation efforts are closely tied to educational self-determination, as illustrated in this volume by Nkonko Kamwangamalu's analysis of South African language policy (Chapter 2), Cath Rau and colleagues' examination of Māori-medium schooling in Aotearoa/New Zealand (Chapter 3), Inge Kral and Elizabeth Ellis's analysis of Ngaanyatjarra language vitality in and out of school in Western Australia (Chapter 5), and Prem Phyak's discussion of Limbu youth activism in Nepal's language education policies (Chapter 9).

We use the term reclamation to encompass this linguistic-educational-political-survival work, applying myaamia[1] (Miami) linguist Wesley Leonard's definition of language reclamation as 'a larger effort by a community to claim its right to speak a language and to set associated goals in response to community needs and perspectives' (2012: 359; see also Leonard, 2011: 141). Leonard elaborates:

> Reclamation … begins with community histories and contemporary needs, which are determined by community agents, and uses this background as a basis to design and develop language work. … Reclamation … calls for an ecological approach to language work, one that recognizes how language is never independent from the environment in which its speakers (and potential future speakers) live. Language work thus must be produced in a way that integrates 'non-linguistic' factors. (2017: 19–20)

We emphasize reclamation as a paradigmatic covering concept because it highlights the decolonizing aims of contemporary language movements (Leonard & De Korne, 2017; López, 2017), and the self-(re)empowerment of Indigenous peoples in the continuance of their languages, lands and life-ways (Leonard & De Korne, 2017; see also Lee & McCarty, 2017; López, 2017; McCarty, 2013a). Within a reclamation framework the terms language resurgence, revival, revitalization, regeneration and reversal of language shift reference specific language planning activities and goals. By *resurgence* we refer to the growing wave of social movement with language at the heart. As we see in the chapters that follow, this is a healing movement: 'Language reclamation is about community building and healing from the past,' says myaamia language revitalizer Daryl Baldwin (2003: 15–16). This resurgence engages both youth and adults as second language learners who are bringing ancestral languages into new uses and domains. As Indigenous scholars Mary Hermes, Megan Bang and Ananda Marin write, the movement is 'passionate, political and deeply personal, particularly for many Native people who are acutely aware that the [settler colonial state's] attempted genocide was the direct cause of Indigenous language loss' (2012: 383).

Revival refers to activities designed to restore oral and/or written uses for a language with no living first-language speakers, sometimes called 'sleeping' or 'dormant' languages (Hinton, 2001b, 2011; Leonard, 2008). In such cases, the language is no longer spoken, but the potential for its 'awakening' exists by virtue of documentary sources (written texts, audio recordings) and a heritage-language community with the desire to learn it (Hinton, 2001b, 2011; Indigenous Language Institute, 2004; Leonard, 2011). Wôpanâak, a language indigenous to what is now the northeastern United States, is one such example, which, after more than 150 years of being silenced, has been revived by community members using written documentary sources (little doe baird, 2013). Kaurna, from the Adelaide region of South Australia, is a further example of a revived language that has benefited over the past 30 years – a period corresponding to an intergenerational process – from a collaboration between the Kaurna community and the University of Adelaide, with the language's revival based largely on historical documents (Amery, 2016).

Revitalization refers to activities designed to cultivate new speakers in situations in which intergenerational transmission has been severely disrupted and children are no longer acquiring their ancestral language as a first language (Hinton, 2011). *Regeneration*, says Māori scholar Margie Kahukura Hohepa (2006: 294), speaks of 'growth and regrowth, development and redeveloping,' acknowledging that nothing 'regrows in exactly the same shape that it had previously, or in exactly the same direction.' *Reversal of language shift* (RLS), a concept developed by the sociolinguist Joshua Fishman (1991, 2001), refers to deliberate re-engineering of the social mechanisms and contexts that support language transmission from generation to generation – restoring and buttressing the family-community nexus in which intergenerational language transmission and acquisition take place. While each of these terms is often defined and used independently, in practice all refer to overlapping sociolinguistic, sociocultural and socio-political processes, as illustrated by the chapters in this volume.

With this as an overarching framework, we take as a foundational premise the inherent human right to learn, use and transmit a language of heritage and birth. We further proceed on the assumption that linguistic and cultural diversity is an intrinsically enabling condition for individuals, families and societies. To expand upon Richard Ruiz's (1984) notion of language-as-resource, linguistic systems and practices represent an infinite reservoir of human intellectual, cultural and scientific effort (see also Hale, 1997).

But, more than universalist notions of linguistic resources and rights, we highlight Indigenous community-based efforts to (re)claim and sustain vital links to communal heritage and identity through language reclamation work. 'We believe that First Nations, Inuit and Métis languages are sacred and are gifts from the Creator,' the Task Force on Aboriginal Languages and Cultures affirms (2005: 3). '[W]hen we stake ourselves to the defense of ... our languages,' writes Cheyenne scholar-educator-activist Richard Littlebear, 'we are not going to relent' (2013: xvi). Centering Indigenous experiences also illuminates broader lessons about the role of language in individual and communal well-being and social, educational and linguistic justice.

In the remainder of this introductory chapter, we position the present moment of Indigenous-language scholarship, practice and activism historically in the context of Indigenous sovereignties and macro-level policies intended to protect linguistic human rights. We then provide key examples of Indigenous-language reclamation movements around the world. This is followed by a preview of the chapters within the three focal areas that organize this book: (1) language policies and politics; (2) language pedagogies and teaching-learning processes; and (3) the present and future prospects for research and praxis in language reclamation work. We conclude with some synthetic, forward-looking reflections on this work.

A Sociohistoric Perspective on Indigenous Language Reclamation

To appreciate the distinctive qualities of Indigenous language reclamation, we need to situate this work socially and historically. Indigenous language reclamation has been most widely implemented in Aotearoa/ New Zealand, Australia, Canada and the Americas, including Hawai'i – all parts of the world characterized by settler colonialism. As Aleut scholar Eve Tuck and K. Wayne Yang explain, the settler state is a distinctive form of colonization in which 'the colonizers arrive at a place ("discovering" it) and make it a permanent home ("claiming" it)… . The settler colonial nation-state is dependent on destroying and erasing Indigenous inhabitants in order to clear them from valuable land' (2014: 224). The Australian anthropologist Patrick Wolfe sums up settler colonialism this way: 'The colonizers came to stay,' making invasion 'a structure not an event' (1999: 2).

In addition to military force, colonial schooling and 'conscious acts of language liquidation' (wa Thiong'o, 2009: 17) have been primary instruments in the construction of settler-colonial societies. 'All of us now inherit the legacy of this … genocidal history,' say Tlingit scholar-activist Nora Dauenhauer and Richard Dauenhauer of the situation for Alaska Native communities (1998: 60). Extreme language shift (Ó hIfearnáin, 2015) is one consequence of these state-level formations.

Key to the analyses of Indigenous language reclamation in this volume is recognition of the inherent sovereignty of Indigenous peoples. This is more than a legal-political relationship with the colonizer; Indigenous sovereignty entails a deep and abiding connection of people to place and others in that place over time. Mother languages embody and are central to these connections. Kanaka Maōli (Native Hawaiian) scholar Noelani Goodyear-Ka'ōpua (2014) explains sovereignty with the Native Hawaiian term ea – life and breath. 'Unlike Euro-American … notions of sovereignty,' she states, 'ea is based on the experiences of people on the land, relationships forged through the process of remembering and caring for wahi pana, storied places' (2014: 4).

Indigenous sovereignties predate the colonial invasion but are also recognized constitutionally in many settler states and in myriad treaties, legislation and case law. In the United States and Canada – two national contexts addressed in this volume – tribal sovereignty entails a singular, legally and morally binding government-to-government relationship between Indigenous nations and federal, state/provincial and territorial governments (Wilkins & Lomawaima, 2001). In the Nordic countries, also examined in this volume, the Finnmark Act recognizes 'Saami ownership of most of the land in Finnmark' (Magga, 2015: 298); the Sámi Act and Saami (Sámi) Parliament in Norway constitute official recognition of inherent Indigenous sovereignties. In Aotearoa/New Zealand, a national context explored in Chapter 3, the 1840 Te Tiritio Waitangi (Treaty of Waitangi), signed between Māori leaders and the British Crown, established a 'mutual framework by which colonization could proceed' while guaranteeing Māori 'possession of their lands, their homes and all their treasured possessions (tonga)' (May, 2012: 303).

International recognition of Indigenous sovereignty and linguistic rights has been sporadic and has come relatively late. In 1919 the International Labour Organization (ILO) was created through the Treaty of Versailles that ended World War I, with the goal of fostering universal peace and social justice (ILO, 1996–2018: para. 1). A key component of the ILO's mission is to protect the rights of minoritized ethnicities. Nearly four decades later, in 1957, the ILO adopted Convention No. 107, the first international instrument setting forth the rights of Indigenous peoples. It would take another 50 years of activism by Indigenous peoples and allies before the United Nations General Assembly adopted the *Declaration on the Rights of Indigenous Peoples* (UNDRIP) in 2007. Among its provisions is the 'right to revitalize, use, develop and transmit to future generations their histories, languages, oral traditions, philosophies, writing systems and literatures ... Indigenous peoples have the right to establish and control their educational systems and institutions providing education in their own languages, in a manner appropriate to their cultural methods of teaching and learning' (United Nations General Assembly, 2007: Articles 13, 14).

While important in establishing a legal-political framework for Indigenous language reclamation and human rights, international declarations are nonbinding and international conventions are often laced with escape clauses. As Amy Tsui and James Tollefson note, 'Qualifications such as "appropriate," "wherever possible" and "adequate opportunities" allow the state to adopt a minimalist approach' (2004: 6; see also Skutnabb-Kangas, 2000). In this sense these policies illustrate Ruiz's distinction between language and voice: As an abstract entity, language can exist 'even when it is suppressed,' Ruiz states. In contrast, 'when voice is suppressed, it is not heard – it does not exist. To deny people their language is, to be sure, to deny them voice,' Ruiz adds, 'but to allow them "their" language ... is not really to allow them voice. Indeed, this may be the most evil form of colonialism, because everyone, even the colonizers, recognizes it as just the opposite' (1991: 220).

Ruiz equates voice with agency – the power to act with positive effect. Further, he insists that empowerment is not 'a gift from those in power to those out,' but is people realizing their own power – self-(re)empowerment) such that individual voices can be joined 'to effect social action on behalf of the community' (1991: 222, 224). It is exactly these qualities – voice, agency and self-(re)empowerment – that characterize contemporary Indigenous-language reclamation movements. We turn now to a closer examination of those movements.

A Global Perspective on Indigenous Language Reclamation

By definition Indigenous languages are autochthonous to their originary peoples and places. Unlike speakers of colonial and immigrant languages, Indigenous communities do not have an external 'pool' of speakers and language resources (Dauenhauer & Dauenhauer, 1998: 94). Most non-Native observers 'cannot properly imagine the finality of losing an indigenous language in which much of the associated cultural knowledge is stored…, with which living people connect to their ancestors and to their cultural sense of spirituality,' linguistic anthropologist Paul Kroskrity explains (2012: 12). This means that efforts to reclaim and revitalize Indigenous languages tend to be local, organic and grassroots – sometimes as 'local' as a single individual or family (Linn & Oberly, 2016: 49; see also Hinton, 2013). Yet these small-scale efforts take on tremendous responsibility in planting the seeds of intergenerational linguistic and cultural transformation. From the viewpoint of many revitalizers, it often seems that their local, on-the-ground efforts stand alone in this tremendous undertaking. Thus, it becomes empowering to realize that others are engaged in the same fight. As we see in the chapters that follow, in all these efforts a core concern is with 'an *indigenous* plan of self-determination that includes language and culture regeneration' (Hohepa, 2006: 299; emphasis in original).

As examples of this, two prominent, coterminous language reclamation movements emerged in the US state of Hawai'i and Aotearoa/New Zealand during the 1970s and 1980s. Closely related Eastern Polynesian languages, Hawaiian and Māori were severely threatened by more than 100 years of colonization that decimated Native population numbers, dispossessed survivors from their lands and banned Indigenous languages in the schools (May, 2005; Warner, 1999; Wilson, 2014). In Hawai'i, says William Wilson, a cofounder of the Hawaiian-language 'Renaissance,' by the mid-1970s 'there were fewer than 50 children under the age of 19 who were fluent in the [Hawaiian] language' (2014: 221).

Parallel Indigenous resurgence movements led to the co-officialization of Hawaiian and English in the state constitution in 1978, and, nine years later, the officialization of Māori (and later, New Zealand Sign Language) in Aotearoa/New Zealand.[2] A parent-led movement in both Aotearoa/New Zealand and Hawai'i established Māori Kōhanga Reo and Hawaiian Pūnana Leo ('language nest') preschools in which all learning and teaching takes place in the Indigenous language. The preschool movement spread horizontally to other communities and vertically by grade level, so that today there are scores of Māori and Hawaiian full-immersion pre-K–12 schools as well as university based programs dedicated to the promotion of these languages. These efforts are widely recognized as language reclamation victories, leading to a growing Indigenous-language speaker base, significantly ameliorating enduring education disparities, and serving as models for Indigenous language rights. Today, Māori- and Hawaiian-style immersion programs can be found throughout the world.

Language reclamation when the speaker base is small(er)

For many Indigenous communities the speaker base is relatively small – sometimes just a few elderly speakers. Yet the terms 'small' or 'smaller' hide the fact that these are often whole communities embarked upon an effort to recreate vital contexts and spaces for reactivating Indigenous-language use (McCarty *et al.*, 2006). For many communities, the Master-Apprentice Program (MAP) has been an especially valuable reclamation and revitalization approach. Developed by the Advocates for Indigenous California Language Survival (AICLS) and University of California–Berkeley linguist Leanne Hinton, the MAP grew out of the needs of diverse Native California communities, which, by the late 20th century, faced a situation in which none of their languages was being used for daily communication (Hinton, 2001a). In these settings, elder speakers are the primary language carriers. The MAP pairs elders as language teachers in a close, long-term relationship with language learners – often one or more family members. The master and apprentice work together for 10 to 20 hours per week and for one to three years at a time, communicating in the target language in everyday situations such as gardening, cooking and taking walks. The teams' work is reinforced by multigenerational language immersion camps and, in a few cases, school-based programs.

The AICLS and the University of California–Berkeley also sponsor the biannual Breath of Life workshop for Native California communities with few speakers and the National Breath of Life Archival Institute for Indigenous Languages held at the Smithsonian Institution in Washington DC. Both initiatives support community-based language planners in using archival documentation for language revitalization.[3] According to Hinton (2017), over 100 California MAP teams have been trained and the program has been adopted and adapted by communities around the world. This in turn has been a force for building a global network of language revitalization support, reflected in organizations such as the American Indian Language Development Institute (AILDI; http://aildi.arizona.edu/), the Canadian Indigenous Language and Literacy Development Institute (CILLDI; http://www.cilldi.ualberta.ca/), the Stabilizing Indigenous Languages Symposium (SILS; http://jan.ucc.nau.edu/ ~ jar/History.html), the Endangered Language Alliance (http://elalliance.org/programs/revitalization/), the Child Language Research and Revitalization Working Group (http://www.edc.org/language-documentation-revitalization-and-reclamation) and the International Centre for Language Revitalisation (https://www.facebook.com/LanguageRevive/), to name a few.

In Tyendinaga Mohawk Territory in southeastern Ontario, the grass-roots non-profit organization, Tsi Tyonnheht Onkwawenna (TTO) Mohawk Language Circle, began in 2001 with six community members. TTO's mission is to keep the Mohawk way of life alive 'by promoting and revitalizing our Kanyen'kehaka [Mohawk] language and culture' (Maracle *et al.*, 2011: 84). The TTO aims to develop the language abilities of adult community members who may eventually become language teachers. The TTO also includes a Mohawk-language immersion preschool, *Totahne*, which serves the children of cohort members. While their parents attend TTO classes, the children also learn the language, creating new opportunities for language learning in families. This child–adult language-learning effort has produced 'speakers with varying degrees of fluency,' say the program's founders, with some adult learners becoming language instructors and the 'celebrated outcome of a "mother tongue" Mohawk-speaking toddler in the community' (Maracle *et al.*, 2011: 93).

The Saami (Sámi) are also a language community with a relatively small number of speakers who live in present-day Norway, Sweden, Finland and western Russia. Saami is a Finno-Ugric language with three major branches and nine still-spoken subgroups. According to Olthuis *et al.* (2013), the number of Saami speakers in 2013 was about 22,000. In Finland, a unique language reclamation approach is being used for Aanaar Saami, with about 350 speakers, almost half of whom are elders (Olthuis *et al.*, 2013). Full-immersion language nest preschools have been a key reclamation and revitalization strategy. But the focus on young children left what Olthuis *et al.* (2013) call a 'missing' generation: working adults between the ages of 20 to 49 who straddle the child generation learning Aanaar Saami as a second language and elders who learned Saami as a first language.

The Aanaar Saami Complementary Education (CASLE) project supports this generation of working adults in recovering the ancestral language through formal classes, cultural activities taught by local fisher-people, reindeer herders and cooking specialists, and MAP training in workplaces and elders' homes. The combination of preschool and adult revitalization-immersion has brought Aanaar Saami back into family homes. Thus, Olthuis *et al.* (2013: 1) assert, it 'is possible to revitalize a seriously endangered language!' (see also Olthuis & Gerstenberger, Chapter 7, this volume).

Australia traditionally ranked fifth in the world in terms of the diversity of its languages. Since colonization over 200 years ago, however, much of this diversity has been lost. Of the original 700–800 Indigenous language varieties, which have been grouped into 250–300 languages (Koch & Nordlinger, 2014), approximately 125 languages are still spoken today. However, of these, only about 13–14 are being learned by children as their first language, with all the implications for language loss that this entails (Marmion *et al.*, 2014). With increasing attention to the multiple benefits of engaging with their originary languages, revitalization has played an increasingly important role in both urban and more remote areas. Other revitalization activities include the work carried out by the Research Network for Linguistic Diversity, which provides an innovative grassroots training program to assist communities with documenting and revitalizing their languages (see also Kral & Ellis, Chapter 5, this volume).

Awakening 'sleeping' languages

What about situations in which there are no first-language speakers? Miami (myaamia) and Wampanoag (Wôpanâak) are cases of 'formerly sleeping languages' (Leonard, 2008) that have been successfully revived – recovered from long periods of dormancy to the point where they are being learned by community members and transmitted to children in family homes. Both are Algonquian languages originally spoken by peoples indigenous to the southern Great Lakes region in North America (myaamia) and the northeastern US coast (Wôpanâak). In both cases, the confiscation by White colonizers of traditional lands, forcible removal and population containment, foreign-introduced diseases, population decline and compulsory English-only schooling led to extreme language shift (Ó hIfearnáin, 2015). The last 'traditional' (first-language) speaker of myaamia passed away in the 1960s, and by the 1990s Wôpanâak had not been spoken in more than 150 years (Baldwin, 2003; little doe, 2000; little doe baird, 2013).

This is the sociohistorical context for two of the most impressive language reclamation efforts in the world. For the Miami, the 'Miami awakening,' myaamiaki eemamwiciki, began with the efforts of tribal citizens Julie Olds and Daryl Baldwin, the linguistic work of David Costa (1994), and strong support from the Miami Tribe of Oklahoma. A descendant of Miami leaders, Baldwin began learning the language out of personal interest. 'Simply put,' he relates, 'I wanted my children to have more of their heritage than I had growing up and I saw the language as the means to reconnect to my culture' (cited in McCarty, 2013b: 96). He and his wife Karen, who also learned the language, made Miami the language of their home (Baldwin *et al.*, 2013). In 1996, in collaboration with the Miami Tribe of Oklahoma, Baldwin and Olds began a community-based Miami language learning program. Miami tribal leadership established the Myaamia Project (now the Myaamia Center) at the tribe's namesake institution of higher education, Miami University (MU), in Oxford, Ohio (Baldwin & Olds, 2007). The Myaamia Center's mission is research to assist Miami language and culture reclamation and the education of community members and MU students in 'tribal efforts in language and culture revitalization' (www.myaamiacenter.prg/?page_id=81). Summing up these efforts, Baldwin notes that, 'We're very much a nation rebuilding and reawakening' (cited in McCarty, 2013b: 105).

Like myaamia, Wôpanâak has a large corpus of written documentation, and historically Native-language literacy was common among Wôpanâak speakers. Indeed, during the 18th century, 'Wampanoag literacy would rival that of the English' (www.wlrp.org/project-history.html). Wôpanâak language reclamation began in 1992, when jessie little doe baird, a citizen of the Mashpee Wampanoag Tribe of Cape Cod, determined 'that I was responsible for, and capable of, making a place for my language to be welcomed back into my community' (little doe baird, 2013: 21). Drawing on historical documents such as personal diaries, correspondence and a 1663 Bible translation, baird developed a Wôpanâak dictionary and curriculum, enabling the first language classes to be offered in 1997. Learning linguistics as she compiled language materials, little doe baird also looked to experts and documentation in other living Eastern Algonquian languages as resources.

From these efforts came the Wôpanâak Language Reclamation Project (WLRP), which currently offers classes for tribal and family members, immersion camps for all ages, and a language nest preschool, *Mukayuhsak Weekuw*, The Children's House (www.wlrp.org/). little doe baird says of the healing and ecological nature of these efforts: 'Reclaiming our language is one means of repairing the broken circle of cultural loss and pain. This is but one path which keeps us connected to our people, the earth and the philosophies and truths given to us by the Creator' (www.wlrp. org/project-home.html).

Language reclamation when the speaker base is large(r)

Elsewhere in the world Indigenous languages have many more speakers yet are nonetheless endangered. For example, Latin America is home to 40 to 50 million Indigenous people who speak some 700 languages (López & Sichra, 2008). Throughout this vast region, Indigenous language rights have come late and have confronted a cleavage between official policies recognizing those rights and local conditions, including limited education resources, poverty and racism. At the same time, recent decades have witnessed a growing Indigenous resurgence – a regrouping and reinvigoration of linguistic and cultural continuance, self-determination and rights (see, e.g. Gustafson *et al.*, 2015; López & García, 2016; Rockwell & Gomes, 2009). Today, the constitutions of most Latin American countries recognize the rights of Indigenous peoples to retain and sustain their distinctive languages and lifeways (Haboud *et al.*, 2016; Maxwell, 2016).

At the heart of these efforts are local programs of education for language revitalization (ELR) and bilingual/intercultural education (BIE) (López & García, 2016). While BIE tends to be school-based, ELR 'goes beyond school activities' such that 'homes, schools, and communities complement one another' (López & García, 2016: 121). One example of the strategic coupling of school- and community-based language reclamation is the long-standing Indigenous Bilingual Education Teacher Training Program of the Peruvian Amazon Basin (FORMABIAP), which prepares primary school teachers from 15 Indigenous groups. Kukamas are now convinced of the need to recuperate their language and culture. Maxwell (2016) and Messing and Nava Nava (2016) provide numerous examples of ELR and BIE for Nahuatl, Hñahñu and Isthmus Zapotec in Mexico; Mayan in Guatemala; Quechua, Shuar, Aymara and Guarani in the Andes; and Mapuche and Rapa Nui in Chile. (For additional examples, see Coronel-Molina & McCarty, 2016; de León, 2017; and Haboud & Limerick, 2017.)

As another example, David Hough and colleagues (2009) report on language reclamation in the Federal Democratic Republic of Nepal, where over 200 languages are spoken and half the nation's 23 million people are non-Nepali speakers. There, the Multilingual Education Project for All Non-Nepali Speaking Students of Primary Schools is a grass-roots effort in six Indigenous communities (Hough *et al.*, 2009). In this project, education practitioners and community members have collaborated to develop and implement a critical Indigenous pedagogy centered on local languages and knowledge systems, including herbal medicines and traditional healing practices, tribal oral histories and a traditional numerical system. Research to date indicates the project is having a positive impact on curricular reforms within local schools and teacher training programs, and it has become a model for larger language reclamation and education efforts (see also Phyak, Chapter 9, this volume).

Technology and language reclamation

Increasingly language reclamation is likely to take place in the virtual world. The presence of Indigenous languages in cyberspace is considerable, and both Indigenous and non-Indigenous agents have carved out virtual communities that are contributing to Indigenous language reclamation. Quechua scholar Serafín Coronel-Molina argues that language revitalizers should use their languages 'in their numerous national and local deliberations, academic forums and virtual communications' (2016: 309; see also Coronel-Molina, Chapter 4, this volume). The latter includes new technologies used to produce interactive textbooks, electronic dictionaries, stand-alone media such as CD-ROMs, multimedia, web portals, Facebook posts, interactive websites and discussion groups, podcasts, audio-video conferencing, text messaging, software localization and other web-based Indigenous-language resources (Holton, 2011). Hermes *et al.* (2016) provide compelling examples of such processes for Hawaiian, Cherokee, Ojibwe and Mohave in Native America (see also Hermes & King, Chapter 6, this volume). Native Hawaiian scholar-activist Candace Galla's (2016) research also reveals the important role of digital technology in language reclamation for Indigenous peoples in the US, Aotearoa/ New Zealand, Greenland, South America, Russia, Latin America, Australasia and the Pacific. While technology access remains a problem in many parts of the world, evolving developments in satellite and wireless technologies are beginning to ameliorate these inequities and expand the possibilities for technology access even in remote communities.

Language vitality and well-being

Finally, there is growing evidence linking language reclamation with physical, social, emotional, spiritual and academic well-being. The

Arctic Languages Vitality Project is an initiative by six Arctic Indigenous organizations to assess, monitor and promote the vitality of the 50–60 Indigenous languages of the Circumpolar North. All but one – Greenlandic – are endangered (Grenoble & Olsen, Puju, 2014). According to linguists Lenore Grenoble and Lindsey Whaley, who are collaborating researchers on the project, this work advances a 'new conceptualization' of language revitalization as a 'health promotion strategy' (Grenoble & Whaley, 2017). These researchers and their associates are studying 'nodes of socially meaningful action' where Indigenous languages are used in order to parse out language strengths and tipping points across a range of activities such as eating breakfast, travel to town, visiting relatives and cooking. This work takes a fine-grained look at what constitutes a sociolinguistic domain; by distinguishing language use within dynamic social networks, the research is exposing the 'connected but not causative' relationship between Indigenous language use and individuals' psychological, social and physical well-being (Grenoble & Whaley, 2017).

The Healing through Language Project is an Endangered Language Fund partnership with Native American language revitalization programs to assess their health benefits. One partner is the Myaamia Center directed by Daryl Baldwin (discussed above). In myaamia, says Baldwin, health translates as 'living well, living properly' (healingthrulanguage, 2013). Baldwin and his colleagues at the Myaamia Center and Miami University are conducting research on the individual and communal health benefits of efforts to promote ancestral knowledge and 'cultural fluency' in a community-driven education environment (Whalen et al., 2016: 2). In a 2016 longitudinal study of Miami college students, these researchers demonstrate the connections between academic well-being and opportunities to learn Miami language and culture through college classes and summer camps. Baldwin places these outcomes in the context of colonization and 'generations of cultural shame' (healingthrulanguage, 2013; see also Lagunas, Chapter 10, this volume). Youth's knowledge of their language and culture strengthens peer and intergenerational bonds and has 'profound impacts' on their cultural competence, the researchers state. This in turn contributes to the youth's academic retention and success (Mosley-Howard et al., 2016).

The Child Language Research and Revitalization Working Group (CLRRWG) is a US-based National Science Foundation-funded initiative focusing on the impact of language documentation and reclamation on young children and their communities. As the Working Group notes in a 2017 White Paper, the act of documentation itself can trigger language reclamation efforts that support 'cultural knowledge and pride, spiritual coping, and healing practices' (CLRTRWG, 2017: 15). The Working Group also cites a growing literature that correlates knowledge of Indigenous languages and cultural practices with academic success and retention (p. 15).

With regard to academic well-being, Stephen May, Richard Hill and Sarah Tiakiwai (2004) examined the international literature on Indigenous-language immersion schooling. These researchers correlated the level of immersion in the Indigenous language with academic outcomes. Not surprisingly, they found that the higher the level (i.e. more instructional time in the target Indigenous language), the more effective the programs were in developing students' bilingualism and biliteracy. Level 1 programs in which 90–100% of instruction is in the Indigenous language were found to be the most effective in achieving these outcomes and in promoting students' cultural knowledge and pride. Further, these benefits to academic well-being are heightened with the use of pedagogies that include 'an active commitment to equality,' strong parent–community engagement and caring student–student and student–teacher relationships (May *et al.*, 2004: 133–134). An emerging literature on the role of Indigenous youth complements these findings (e.g. Wyman *et al.*, 2014). A key element of this research is its praxis potential, as nuanced understandings of youth language ideologies and practices suggest new strategies for involving youth directly in language planning.

In support of all this work, researchers from the Universities of British Columbia, Oxford and Victoria present evidence linking knowledge of an Aboriginal language to the health and well-being of Indigenous youth (Hallett *et al.*, 2007). Carefully controlling for other variables, these researchers found that among First Nations bands in British Columbia, Aboriginal language knowledge, as a 'marker of cultural persistence,' corresponded 'strongly and independently' with low to absent teen suicide rates (2007: 392–393). The researchers conclude that these findings 'demonstrate that indigenous language use … is a strong predictor of health and wellbeing in Canada's Aboriginal communities' (2007: 398; see also Chandler & Lalonde, 2009; van Beek, 2016; Wexler, 2006).

Summing Up the 'Four Rs'

Throughout the world there is clear evidence of the generative ways in which Indigenous peoples are challenging hegemonic metaphors of language death and extinction and reconfiguring power relations to wedge open new spaces for language reclamation in and out of schools. This includes family language policymaking (Hinton, 2013; Romero-Little *et al.*, 2011), as well as assertions of educational sovereignty that promote language reclamation via decolonial, culturally revitalizing and sustaining pedagogies (Lee & McCarty, 2017; López, 2017). These efforts connect the local with the global, bottom-up with top-down, refusing grim prognostications of Indigenous-language 'failure' (Meek, 2011). As noted by Hornberger and McCarty (2012: 6) in a presentation of contemporary language projects among Indigenous peoples in Mozambique, the Andes, Native North America and northern Thailand, this work 'calls for expanded discourses on globalization that embrace Indigenous knowl-edges,' forefronting grassroots language planning and policy as a force for linguistic and social justice. It is to these efforts that we look in this volume.

Introducing the Chapters

We divide the remainder of the book into three complementary sections: Language Policies and Politics, Language Pedagogies and Processes and Prospects and Possibilities for Indigenous Language Reclamation. In Part 1, the authors take up two key language policy cases, looking at the impacts of language policies in relation to Indigenous peoples in Canada and post-apartheid South Africa. We begin with Barbra Meek's analysis of the history and politics of Aboriginal ethnolinguistic identity in Canada's Yukon Territory, which is unique in its official recognition of eight Aboriginal languages as well as French and English. Meek places these policies within the historical context of policy changes since the first documented references to First Nations peoples by non-Natives in the 19th century, tracing how difference has been regimented along racial, ethnic and linguistic lines. Connecting these notions of difference to Indigenous 'status[es]' enshrined in the Indian Act of 1876, she examines the intertwined national-level discourses of multilingualism and multicul-turalism with Indigenous claims to land, language and self-determination. Drawing on her long-term collaborative and ethnographic work with the Kaska (Meek, 2010), she provides insight into the ways in which a re-imaging of ethnolinguistic categories in terms of citizenship versus racial/ethnic membership opens up new possibilities for reclaiming Aboriginal languages and life-ways.

Post-apartheid South Africa's language policy also recognizes language diversity through the officialization, beginning in 1994, of nine African languages along with English and Afrikaans. However, as Nkonko Kamwangamalu argues in Chapter 2, language policy in itself does not guarantee that linguistic hierarchies will be transformed, particularly in education. Drawing on critical theory and language economics as well as empirical studies of Indigenous language revitalization from around the world, Kamwangamalu details the limited extent to which African lan-guages have been included in school curricula. English remains the greatest beneficiary of the post-apartheid language policy, resulting in subtractive rather than additive bilingualism. Transforming these inequities, Kamwangamalu states, requires 'a genuine, revised legislation supporting the demand for skills in the official Indigenous African languages for access to employment in the country's formal labor market and requiring indus-tries to provide services in these languages to the African people' (see also Kamwangamalu, 2016). Further, genuine change requires greater govern-ment investment in language education at all levels. Such policy changes and political action, he suggests, will not only aid the post-apartheid policy in achieving its language revitalizing and sustaining goals, but will support speakers and potential users of Indigenous African languages in accepting them as privileged media of instruction in the schools.

In Part 2, we turn to the processes and practicalities of teaching and learning Indigenous languages. Five case studies are presented of reclamation projects that are bringing Indigenous languages forward through curricular transformations and new developments in communication and language technology. In Indigenous communities in Latin America, Ojibwe language classes in the USA and among Ngaanyatjarra youth in Western Australia, virtual spaces are creating new functional sociolinguistic domains. In Finland's Aanaar Saami community, language technology is expanding the oral and written potential of Aanaar Saami learning and teaching. In Aotearoa/New Zealand, Māori tribal schools are bringing forward distinct Indigenous dialects to strengthen Māori identity.

In Chapter 3, Cath Rau, Waimātao Murphy and Pem Bird detail the emergence of the kura ā iwi schools in Aotearoa/New Zealand, which provide a tribally based education system to prepare Māori youth for community membership and global citizenship as an expression of educational self-determination. Birthright and inheritance foreground the belief that taking responsibility for their own destiny becomes viable through reaffirmation of a sense of belonging and the revitalization of ancestral roots. In 2006, the eight founding schools organized as Ngā Kura ā Iwi o Aotearoa (NKAI), defining themselves as tribal schools committed to developing a local tribal identity anchored in the concept of 'culturalcy.' Culturalcy is manifest in the 'gifts' of their tribal forebears – ancestral marae (gathering place), canoe, mountains, waterways, knowledge, customs, language and dialect. By 2015, the NKAI had increased from eight to 24 affiliated schools, and in partnerships with their constituent communities the schools were localizing and delivering the national curriculum through Māori as the medium of instruction. The collective has shown significant positive academic gains. The importance of distinct Māori dialects as key identity markers critical to localizing curriculum stands as a significant challenge addressed in the chapter. Two NKAI tribal schools from the same tribal group but differing in dialect are profiled to illustrate how each is expressing culturalcy in locally specific ways – developing a tribal identity derived from revered ancestors through genealogy passed down from generation to generation through a distinct tribal dialect.

In Chapter 4, we learn how the digital world is attracting Indigenous Latin American communities as contemporary sites of social interaction and communication – virtual spaces in which Indigenous peoples can create a new functional social domain for their languages. As Serafín M. Coronel-Molina shows, Indigenous digital activists, technology-savvy individuals, second-language learners and youth are on the forefront of creating a virtual Indigenous-language community. Coronel-Molina presents the current array of cultural production and linguistic expressions in Indigenous languages as key examples, representing both community entry and community building arenas in this digital world. This further affirms that Indigenous languages remain resilient in meeting the functional needs of Indigenous social life and their co-existence with privileged 'world' languages. The potential benefits of an Indigenous virtual linguistic community include the development of culturally sustaining and revitalizing pedagogies, melding traditional knowledge and modern technology, awakening linguistic and cultural pride and transforming negative ideologies, all with the broader aim of stimulating language reclamation. While the benefits are numerous, Coronel-Molina also presents a caveat that media and technology can further diminish intergenerational transmission of traditional practices such as oral tradition and cultural memory. Careful consideration of technology must come from within – it must belong to the Indigenous people – with the benefits aligned with community needs and goals.

In the Ngaanyatjarra Lands in the remote desert region of Australia, children enter school speaking their mother tongue, Ngaanyatjarra and a second dialect but no English. The Ngaanyatjarra people's teaching and learning methodology takes place in the countryside with elders and family members, where Ngaanyatjarra stories and knowledge are transported through multimodal speech arts – particular speech styles, registers and cultural practices – of Ngaanyatjarra oral tradition. However, as Inge Kral and Elizabeth Ellis show in Chapter 5, the remoteness of the Ngaanyatjarra lands have not kept the outside world at bay; English-only schooling, technology and social media have influenced social interaction and language socialization patterns in significant ways. Predominate among these influences are decreasing opportunities for Western desert youth to acquire the full expressive potential of the oral traditions of their culture. Kral and Ellis's research on the sand storytelling practices of old and young presents confirming evidence of impending change. Ngaanyatjarra youth are also negotiating new identities 'in response to the effects of globalized media on youth language and cultural practices.' As such the authors argue that youth's hybrid linguistic repertoires and contemporary language varieties are forms of meaningful language use. Thus, they suggest, youth language practices can inform everyday community-based language policy development that affirms contemporary Ngaanyatjarra youth identity and language choices which are likely to influence how they socialize their own children in the future.

In Chapter 6, Mary Hermes and Kendall King present the findings of a year-long Ojibwe language research project, *Developing Fluency*, in which they piloted a new model of language teaching for adult second language learners – communicative task-based learning in an interactive online space. As the project title suggests, developing fluency in a language rarely heard in everyday conversation because of a lack of first-language Ojibwe speakers necessitates a new way of acquiring the language. Moreover, the conventional grammar-based approach to language teaching and learning proved largely ineffective in advancing second language learners toward Ojibwe proficiency, even in the context of a strong language revitalization movement. Development of the task-based learning materials focused on addressing the need for targeted practice of particular verb forms within informal interactive structures (1–2 weekly meetings), while documentation of the learning process centered on conversational interaction between two learners and the engagement of each in the task. From the analysis of 22 weeks of conversational interactions in informal structures and environments within digital spaces, Hermes and King conclude that conversational interactions in which the negotiation of meaning is actively pursued between learners promote the potential for restoring the social use of Ojibwe.

In the final chapter in this section, Marja-Liisa Olthius and Ciprian-Virgil Gerstenberger examine the use of digital technology in language reclamation efforts amidst the challenges of meeting community needs that include sharing digital resources and language technology formats among Saami-language communities in Finland. The authors highlight the increase in the use of digital technology, and more specifically, language technology – a specialized domain of digital technology. Language technology has responded to the expansion of oral to written processes in language revitalization projects. Nevertheless, as university linguistic researchers answer to community needs in developing digital resources, they must also consider inquiring into the usefulness of the resources beyond development when utility is dependent on community use of those digital resources. In example of this, Olthius and Gerstenberger present a Machine Translation (MT) project, the outcome of a particularly successful collaboration between two university Saami Language Technology groups and the North Saami and Aanaar Saami communities, addressing the need to expand language usage into the written domain. While the outcome of the MT project has been a fully developed infrastructure especially suited for Saami languages, and the sharing of this digital resource has attracted international interest, the Aanaar Saami, as a successful case of community language revitalization (see Olthuis *et al.*, 2013), has shown little interest in utilizing this digital resource. The authors' inquiry into this phenomenon points to differing interests in the utility of the written processes of language revitalization.

Section III explores different approaches for sustaining the vitality of three languages: Hopi in the USA, Limbu in Nepal and Nahuatl (also called Mexicano) in Mexico. Each chapter approaches the topic from a different perspective. In Chapter 8, Sheilah Nicholas looks at the revitalization prospects for Hopi, a language spoken by peoples indigenous to what is now the southwestern USA. Prem Phyak takes a critical pedagogical approach to his collaborative work with Limbu youth in Nepal. Rosalva Mojica Lagunas considers the role of intergenerational family and community language transmission in the revitalization of Nahuatl, a language with millions of speakers yet nonetheless endangered. Each of these cases offers comparative insight into the prospects and possibilities for languages with varying speaker bases and sociolinguistic ecologies.

The close relationship between language and culture is well attested, and Sheilah Nicholas begins this section with an exploration of the potential consequences of this relationship for Hopilavayi, the Hopi language. This raises serious questions about sustaining Hopi cultural heritage, which continues to be strong but is threatened, Nicholas explains, since language is a crucial component of 'becoming Hopi.' This ethnographic study, set compellingly within the sociocultural and sociolinguistic ecology of the contemporary Hopi community in the southwestern US, focuses on three Hopi young people (one female, two male) with varying degrees of exposure to and proficiency in Hopilavayi. In this context, Nicholas draws on the youth's family histories to explore how this ecology has changed over time, and how the three young people are sustaining their cultural ties and engaging the Hopi philosophy and way of life. These adaptations, she shows, are expressions of 'language as cultural practice.'

As shown in the chapters in Part 1, official language policies are very often hegemonic. '[L]anguage policies are an important mechanism for the unequal distribution of economic resources and political power,' states James Tollefson (2013: 27). Working in Nepal, Prem Phyak illuminates these processes, explaining that Nepali and English are the two languages that are viewed as having value in terms of obtaining work within and outside Nepal. In many ways this chapter exemplifies the argument made by Kamwangamalu in Chapter 2 about the importance of ensuring a prominent place for Indigenous languages. Centering his analysis on the language-in-education policy engagements of Limbu Indigenous youth, Phyak examines the youths' critical awareness of linguistic discrimination as they analyze and contest prevalent ideologies that marginalize their communities, life-ways, knowledge and language. Through critical observation, interactions with teachers and parents, and dialogic engagement in Indigenous movements, these young people challenge linguistic inequalities rooted in nationalism and neoliberalism. In doing so, Phyak asserts, they reimagine 'language policy justice,' seeking and enacting 'meaningful participation in language policymaking processes.'

In the book's final chapter, Rosalva Lagunas brings the prospects and possibilities for language reclamation full circle, analyzing the language ideologies and practices of elders and youth in a Nahuatl community in Guererro, Mexico. Despite having a relatively large number of speakers – over 1 million in Mexico–Nahuatl (also called Mexicano) is rapidly losing ground to Spanish among the younger generation. Lagunas undertook an ethnographic exploration of the factors contributing to language loss, as well as those that might foster its continuance in future generations. She finds that the most significant factor is the presence of a Nahuatl speaking grandparent living in the home. Drawing from her larger ethnographic study, she focuses on elders as the 'key holders' in language reclamation, and thus the 'need for relationship building between youth and elders for language revitalization to occur.' While young people tend to prefer Spanish to Nahuatl, they express confidence that they too will speak Nahuatl when they get older. At the same time, youth express *la pena* – linguistic embarrassment or shame – a factor inhibiting intergenerational language transmission. While expected to teach some Nahuatl, the schools in reality do not have the resources to support it. Lagunas argues that to initiate language reclamation in the community, elders – the linguistic and cultural 'keyholders' – must be included in school settings as language teachers. 'They are the core of language maintenance,' she emphasizes, and youth, parents and elders need to 'continue this journey together to honor our past generations and our future ones.'

Taken together, the 10 chapters add new, empirically based insights into both the tensions and 'emergent vitalities' (Perley, 2013) of Indigenous language reclamation in diverse sociolinguistic ecologies around the world. Throughout the volume we privilege Indigenous and decolonial scholarship and ethnographic/qualitative accounts of community-driven language work. Many chapter authors report on language reclamation efforts in their own communities. All of the authors have long histories of experience in language planning and policy from the 'ground up' (Leonard & De Korne, 2017). Collectively we embrace a research ethic of relationality, respect, reciprocity and responsibility to the Indigenous communities with whom we work (Brayboy *et al.*, 2012). We offer these accounts in the spirit of expanding language reclamation research and praxis, inviting readers into this vibrant movement and 'a world of Indigenous languages.'

Notes

(1)   The use of lower-case for the initial letter in *myaamia* (the Miami language) reflects the way the language is normally written (W. Leonard personal communication: February 1, 2018).

(2)   At the time of this writing English was the most widely spoken, de facto 'official' language in Aotearoa/New Zealand, spoken by over 96% of the population (Statistics New Zealand/Tatauranga Aotearoa, 2013). However, English does not have de jure official standing in New Zealand.

(3)   In 2018 the University of California, Berkeley also had pending a PhD Designated Emphasis in Indigenous Language Revitalization, based in the Linguistics Department (P. Baquedano-López personal communication: February 18, 2018).

References

Amery, R. (2016) *Warraparna Kaurna! Reclaiming an Australian Language*. Adelaide: University of Adelaide Press.

Austin, P.K. and Sallabank, J. (2011) Introduction. In P.K. Austin and J. Sallabank (eds) *The Cambridge Handbook of Endangered Languages* (pp. 1–24). Cambridge: Cambridge University Press.

Baldwin, D. (2003) Miami language reclamation: From ground zero. Lecture presented by the Center for Writing and the Interdisciplinary Minor in Literacy and Rhetorical Studies, Speaker Series 24. Minneapolis: University of Minnesota. Retrieved 20 February 2018 from myaamiacenter.org/MCResources/Baldwin_biblio/Baldwin_ground_zero.pdf

Baldwin, D. and Olds, J. (2007) Miami Indian language and cultural research at Miami University. In D.M. Cobb and L. Fowler (eds) *Beyond Red Power: American Indian Politics and Activism Since 1990* (pp. 280–290). Santa Fe, NM: School for Advanced Research Press.

Baldwin, D., Baldwin, K., Baldwin, J. and Baldwin, J. (2013) myaamiaataweenki oowaaha: Miami spoken here. In L. Hinton (ed.) *Bringing Our Languages Home: Language Revitalization for Families* (pp. 3–18). Berkeley, CA: Heyday Press.

Brayboy, B.M.J., Gough, H., Leonard, B., Roehl, R. and Solyom, J. (2012) Reclaiming scholarship: Critical Indigenous research methodologies. In S. Lapan, M. Quartaroli and F. Riemer (eds) *Qualitative Research: An Introduction to Methods and Designs* (pp. 423–450). San Francisco, CA: Jossey-Bass.

Castagno, A.E. and Brayboy, B.M.J. (2008) Culturally responsive schooling for Indigenous youth: A review of the literature. *Review of Educational Research* 78 (4), 941–993.

Chandler, M.J. and Lalonde, C.E. (2009) Cultural continuity as a moderator of suicide risk among Canada's First Nations. In L.J. Kirmayer and G.G. Valaskakis (eds) *Healing Traditions: The Mental Health of Aboriginal Peoples in Canada* (pp. 221–248). Vancouver: UBC Press.

Child Language Research and Revitalization Working Group (CLRRWG) (2017) *Language Documentation, Revitalization and Reclamation: Supporting Young Learners and Their Communities*. Waltham, MA: Education Development Center.

Coronel-Molina, S.M. (2016) New domains for Indigenous language acquisition and use in Latin America and the Caribbean. In S.M. Coronel-Molina and T.L. McCarty (eds) *Indigenous Language Revitalization in the Americas* (pp. 292–311). New York: Routledge.

Coronel-Molina, S.M. and McCarty, T.L. (eds) (2016) *Indigenous Language Revitalization in the Americas*. New York: Routledge.

Dauenhauer, N.M and Dauenhauer, R. (1998). Technical, emotional, and ideological issues in reversing language shift: Examples from Southeast Alaska. In L.A. Grenoble and L.J. Whaley (eds) *Endangered Languages: Language Loss and Community Response* (pp. 57–98). Cambridge: Cambridge University Press.

De Korne, H. and Leonard, W. Y. (2017) Reclaiming languages: Contesting and decolonising 'language endangerment' from the ground up. In W.Y. Leonard and H. De Korne (eds) *Language Documentation and Description* 14, 5–14. London: EL Publishing.

de León, R. (2017) Indigenous language policy and education in Mexico. In T.L. McCarty and S. May (eds) *Language Policy and Political Issues in Education* (3rd edn) (pp. 415–433). Cham, Switzerland: Springer International.

Duchêne, A. and Heller, M. (eds) (2007) *Discourses of Endangerment: Ideology and Interest in the Defence of Languages*. London: Continuum.

Fishman, J.A. (1991) *Reversing Language Shift: Theoretical and Empirical Foundations of Assistance to Threatened Languages*. Clevedon: Multilingual Matters.

Fishman, J.A. (ed.) (2001) *Can Threatened Languages Be Saved? Reversing Language Shift, Revisited: A 21st Century Perspective*. Clevedon: Multilingual Matters.

Galla, C. (2016) Indigenous language revitalization, promotion, and education: Function of digital technology. *Computer Assisted Language Learning*, doi: 10.1080/09588221.2016.1166137

Grenoble, L. and Olsen, Puju, C. (2014) Language and well-being in the Arctic: Building Indigenous language vitality and sustainability. *Arctic Yearbook 2014*, 1–12.

Grenoble, L. and Whaley, L. (2017, April 20) A new conceptualization of language revitalization. Presentation at the First International Conference on Revitalization of Indigenous and Minoritized Languages, Barcelona, Spain.

Gustafson, B., Julca Guerrero, F. and Jiménez, A. (2016) Policy and politics of language revitalization in Latin America and the Caribbean. In S.M. Coronel-Molina and T.L. McCarty (eds) *Indigenous Language Revitalization in the Americas* (pp. 35–53). New York: Routledge.

Haboud, M. and Limerick, N. (2017) Language policy and education in the Andes. In T.L. McCarty and S. May (eds) *Language Policy and Political Issues in Education* (3rd edn) (pp. 435–447). Cham, Switzerland: Springer International.

Hale, K. (1997) Reasons to be optimistic about local language maintenance and restoration. Keynote Address, Linguistic Association of the Southwest (LASSO) Conference, Los Angeles, CA.

Healingthrulanguage. (2013) D. Baldwin discusses Myaamia language and well-being. Retrieved 19 February 2018 from https://www.youtube.com/watch?v=rytcqVIdTdA

Hermes, M., Bang, M. and Marin, A. (2012) Designing Indigenous language revitalization. *Harvard Educational Review* 82 (3), 381–402.

Hermes, M., Cash Cash, P. Donaghy, K., Erb, J. and Penfield, S. (2016) New domains for Indigenous language acquisition and use in the USA and Canada. In S.M. Coronel-Molina and T.L. McCarty (eds) *Indigenous Language Revitalization in the Americas* (pp. 269–291). New York: Routledge.

Hinton, L. (2001a) The Master-Apprentice Language Learning Program. In L. Hinton and K. Hale (eds) *The Green Book of Language Revitalization in Practice* (pp. 217–226). San Diego, CA: Academic Press.

Hinton, L. (2001b) Sleeping languages: Can they be awakened? In L. Hinton and K. Hale (eds) *The Green Book of Language Revitalization in Practice* (pp. 413–417). San Diego, CA: Academic Press.

Hinton, L. (2011) Revitalization of endangered languages. In P.K. Austin and J. Sallabank (eds) *The Cambridge Handbook of Endangered Languages* (pp. 291–311). Cambridge: Cambridge University Press.

Hinton, L. (ed.) (2013) *Bringing our Languages Home – Language Revitalization for Families*. Berkeley, CA: Heyday Books.

Hinton, L. (2017) Language endangerment and revitalization. In T.L. McCarty and S. May (eds) *Language Policy and Political Issues in Education* (3rd edn) (pp. 257–272). Cham, Switzerland: Springer International.

Hohepa, M.K. (2006) Biliterate practices at home: Supporting Indigenous language regeneration. *Journal of Language, Identity, and Education* 5 (4), 293–301.

Holton, G. (2011) The role of information technology in supporting minority and endangered languages. In P.K. Austin and J. Sallabank (eds) *The Cambridge Handbook of Endangered Languages* (pp. 371–399). Cambridge: Cambridge University Press.

Hornberger, N.H. and McCarty, T.L. (2012) Globalization from the bottom up: Indigenous language planning and policy across time, space, and place. *International Multilingual Research Journal* 6 (1), 1–7.

Hough, D.A., Magar, R.B.T. and Yonjan-Tamang, A. (2009) Privileging Indigenous knowledges: Empowering multilingual education in Nepal. In T. Skutnabb-Kangas, R. Phillipson, A.K. Mohanty and M. Panda (eds) *Social Justice through Multilingual Education* (pp. 159–176). Bristol: Multilingual Matters.

International Labour Organization (ILO) (1996–2018) Origins and history. Retrieved 20 February from http://www.ilo.org/global/about-the-ilo/history/lang—en/index.htm

Indigenous Language Institute (2004) *Awakening Our Languages: An Introduction*. Santa Fe, NM: Indigenous Language Institute.

Kamwangamalu, N.M. (2016) *Language Policy and Economics: The Language Question in Africa*. New York: Palgrave Macmillan.

Koch, H. and Nordlinger, R. (2014) The languages of Australia in linguistic research: Context and issues. In H. Koch and R. Nordlinger (eds) *The Languages and Linguistics of Australia: A Comprehensive Guide* (pp. 3–21). Berlin: Walter de Gruyter.

Kroskrity, P.V. (2012) Sustaining stories: Narratives as cultural resources in Native American projects of cultural sovereignty, identity maintenance, and language revitalization. In P.V. Kroskrity (ed.) *Telling Stories in the Face of Danger: Language Renewal in Native American Communities* (pp. 3–20). Norman: University of Oklahoma Press.

Lee, T.S. and McCarty, T.L. (2017) Upholding Indigenous education sovereignty through critical culturally sustaining/revitalizing pedagogy. In D. Paris and H.S. Alim (eds) *Culturally Sustaining Pedagogies: Teaching and Learning for Justice in a Changing World* (pp. 61–82). New York: Teachers College Press.

Leonard, W.Y. (2008) When is an 'extinct' language not extinct? Miami, a formerly sleeping language. In K.A. King, N. Schilling-Estes, L. Fogle, J.J. Lou and B. Soukup (eds) *Sustaining Linguistic Diversity: Endangered and Minority Languages and Language Varieties* (pp. 23–33). Washington, DC: Georgetown University Press.

Leonard, W.Y. (2011) Challenging 'extinction' through modern Miami language practices. *American Indian Culture and Research Journal* 35 (2), 135–160.

Leonard, W.Y. (2012) Framing language reclamation programmes for everybody's empowerment. *Gender and Language* 6 (2), 339–367.

Leonard, W.Y. (2017) Producing language reclamation by decolonising 'language.' In W.Y. Leonard and H. De Korne (eds) *Language Documentation and Description* 14, 15–36. London: EL Publishing.

Leonard, W.Y. and De Korne, H. (eds) (2017) *Language Documentation and Description* 14. London: EL Publishing.

Linn, M. and Oberly, S. (2016) Local and global dimensions of language revitalization in the USA and Canada. In S.M. Coronel-Molina and T.L. McCarty (eds) *Indigenous Language Revitalization in the Americas* (pp. 137–157). New York: Routledge.

little doe, j. (2000) The 're-awakening' of the Wôpanâak language. *Native Language Network* Winter, 3.

little doe baird, j. (2013) Wampanoag: How did this happen to my language? In L. Hinton (ed.) *Bringing Our Languages Home: Language Revitalization for Families* (pp. 19–30). Berkeley, CA: Heyday Press.

Littlebear, R. (2013) Foreword. In T.L. McCarty *Language Planning and Policy in Native America – History, Theory, Praxis* (pp. xiii–xvi). Bristol: Multilingual Matters.

Lomawaima, K.T. and McCarty, T.L. *'To Remain an Indian': Lessons in Democracy from a Century of Native American Education*. New York: Teachers College Press.

López, L.E. (2017). Decolonization and bilingual/intercultural education. In T.L. McCarty and S. May (eds) *Language Policy and Political Issues in Education* (3rd edn) (pp. 297–313). Cham, Switzerland: Springer International.

López, L.E. and García, F. (2016) The home–school–community interface in language revitalization in Latin America and the Caribbean. In S.M. Coronel-Molina and T.L. McCarty (eds) *Indigenous Language Revitalization in the Americas* (pp. 116–135). New York: Routledge.

López, L.E. and Sichra, I. (2008) Intercultural bilingual education among Indigenous peoples in Latin America. In J. Cummins and N.H. Hornberger (eds) *Encyclopedia of Language and Education Vol. 5: Bilingual Education* (pp. 295–309). New York: Springer.

Magga, O.H. (2015) Indigenous peoples' rights in Norway and the international Indigenous movement. In R. Dunbar-Ortiz, D.S. Dorough, G. Alfredsson, L. Swepston and P. Wille (eds) *Indigenous Peoples' Rights in International Law: Emergence and Application* (pp. 296–303). Kautokeino, Norway and Copenhagen, Denmark: Gáldu and IWGIA.

Maracle, I., Hill, K., Maracle, T. and Brown, K. (2011) Rebuilding our language foundation through the next generation. In M.E. Romero-Little, S.J. Ortiz, T.L. McCarty and R. Chen (eds) *Indigenous Languages Across the Generations – Strengthening Families and Communities* (pp. 83–94). Tempe: Arizona State University Center for Indian Education.

Marmion, D., Obta, K. and Troy, J. (2014) *Community, Identity, Wellbeing: The Report of the Second National Indigenous Languages Survey.* Canberra: Australian Institute of Aboriginal and Torres Strait Islander Studies.

Maxwell, J. (2016) Revitalization programs and impacts in Latin America and the Caribbean. In S.M. Coronel-Molina and T.L. McCarty (eds) *Indigenous Language Revitalization in the Americas* (pp. 247–265). New York: Routledge.

May, S. (2005) Introduction. Bilingual/immersion education in Aotearoa/New Zealand: Setting the context. *International Journal of Bilingual Education and Bilingualism* 8 (5), 365–376.

May, S. (2012) *Language and Minority Rights: Ethnicity, Nationalism and the Politics of Language* (2nd edn). New York: Routledge.

May, S., Hill, R. and Tiakiwai, S. (2004) *Bilingual/Immersion Education: Indicators of Good Practice.* Wellington, NZ: Ministry of Education.

McCarty, T.L. (2013a) Education policy, citizenship and linguistic sovereignty in Native America. In V. Ramanathan (ed.) *Language Policies and (Dis)Citizenship: Rights, Access, Pedagogies* (pp. 116–142). Bristol: Multilingual Matters.

McCarty, T.L. (2013b) *Language Planning and Policy in Native America – History, Theory, Praxis.* Bristol: Multilingual Matters.

McCarty, T.L., Zepeda, O. with Begay, V.H., Charging Eagle, S., Moore, S.C., Warhol, L. and Williams, T.M.K (eds) (2006) *One Voice, Many Voices – Recreating Indigenous Language Communities.* Tempe and Tucson, AZ: Center for Indian Education Arizona State University and American Indian Language Development Institute.

Meek, B. (2010) *We Are Our Language: An Ethnography of Language Revitalization in a Northern Athabaskan Community.* Tucson: University of Arizona Press.

Meek, B. (2011) Failing American Indian languages. *American Indian Culture and Research Journal* 35 (2), 43–60.

Messing, J. and Nava Nava, R. (2016) Language acquisition, shift, and revitalization processes in Latin America and the Caribbean. In S. Coronel-Molina and T.L. McCarty (eds) *Indigenous Language Revitalization in the Americas* (pp. 76–96). New York: Routledge.

Moore, R. (2017) Discourses of endangerment from mother tongues to machine readability. In O. García, N. Flores and M. Spotti (eds) *The Oxford Handbook of Language and Society* (pp. 221–242). New York, NY: Oxford University Press.

Moore, R., Pietikäinen, S. and Blommaert, J. (2010) Counting the losses: Numbers as the language of endangerment. *Sociolinguistic Studies* 4 (1), 1–26.

Mosley-Howard, G.S., Baldwin, D., Ironstrack, G., Rousmaniere, K. and Burke, B. (2016) Niila Myaamia (I am Miami): Identity and retention of Miami Tribe college students. *Journal of College Student Retention: Research, Theory and Practice* 17 (4), 437–461.

Ó hIfearnáin, T. (2015) Sociolinguistic vitality of Manx after extreme language shift: Authenticity without traditional native speakers. *International Journal of the Sociology of Language* 231, 45–62.

Olthuis, M-L., Kivelä, S. and Skutnabb-Kangas, T. (2013) *Revitalising Indigenous Languages: How To Recreate a Lost Generation.* Bristol: Multilingual Matters.

Perley, B.C. (2011) *Defying Maliseet Language Death: Emergent Vitalities of Language, Culture, and Identity in Eastern Canada.* Lincoln and London: University of Nebraska Press.

Perley, B.C. (2013) Remembering ancestral voices: Emergent vitalities and the future of Indigenous languages. In E. Mihas, B. Perley, G. Rei-Doval and K. Wheatley (eds) *Responses to Language Endangerment in Honor of Mickey Noonan* (pp. 243–270). Amsterdam/Philadelphia: John Benjamins.

Rockwell, E. and Gomes, A.M.R. (2009) Introduction to the special issue: Rethinking Indigenous education from a Latin American perspective. *Anthropology and Education Quarterly* 40 (2), 97–109.

Romero-Little, M.E., Ortiz, S.J., McCarty, T.L. and Chen, R. (eds) (2011) *Indigenous Languages Across the Generations – Strengthening Indigenous Language Communities.* Tempe: Arizona State University Center for Indian Education.

Ruiz, R. (1984) Orientations in language planning. *NABE Journal* 8, 15–34.

Ruiz, R. (1991) The empowerment of language-minority students. In C. Sleeter (ed.) *Empowerment through Multicultural Education* (pp. 217–227). Albany NY: State University of New York Press.

Skutnabb-Kangas, T. (2000) *Linguistic Genocide in Education—Or Worldwide Diversity and Human Rights?* Mahwah, NJ: Lawrence Erlbaum.

Skutnabb-Kangas, T. and Dunbar, R. (2010) Indigenous children's education as linguistic genocide and a crime against humanity? A global view. *Gáldu Cála Journal of Indigenous Peoples Rights* 2, entire.

Statistics New Zealand/Tatauranga Aotearoa (2013) 2013 Census totals by topic – Language-spoken tables. Retrieved 20 February 2018 from https://www.archive.stats.govt.nz/browse_for_stats/people_and_communities/Language.aspx

Task Force on Aboriginal Languages and Cultures (2005) *Towards a New Beginning: A Foundational Report for a Strategy to Revitalize First Nation, Inuit and Métis Languages and Cultures.* Ottawa, ON: Aboriginal Languages Directorate, Aboriginal Affairs Branch, Department of Canadian Heritage.

Tollefson, J.W. (2013) Language policy in a time of crisis and transformation. In J.W. Tollefson (ed.) *Language Policies in Education: Critical Issues* (pp. 11–34). New York: Routledge.

Tsui, A.B.M. and Tollefson, J.W. (2004) The centrality of medium-of-instruction policy in sociopolitical processes. In J.W. Tollefson and A.B.M. Tsui (eds) *Medium of Instruction Policies: Which Agenda? Whose Agenda?* (pp. 1–18). Mahwah, NJ: Lawrence Erlbaum.

Tuck, E. and Yang, K.W. (2014) R words: Refusing research. In D. Paris and M.T. Winn (eds) *Humanizing Research: Decolonizing Qualitative Inquiry with Youth and Communities* (pp. 223–247). Los Angeles, CA: SAGE.

United Nations General Assembly (2007) *United Nations Declaration on the Rights of Indigenous Peoples.* Paris: United Nations. Retrieved 20 February 2018 from www.un.org/esa/socdev/unpfii/documents/DRIPS_en.pdf

van Beek, S. (2016) *Intersections: Indigenous Language, Health and Wellness. Review of Literature.* Vancouver, BC: First Peoples' Cultural Council.

wa Thiong'o, N. (2009) *Something Torn and New: An African Renaissance.* New York: BasicCivitas Books.

Warner, S.N. (1999) *Kuleana*: The right, responsibility, and authority of Indigenous peoples to speak and make decisions for themselves in language and cultural revitalization. *Anthropology and Education Quarterly* 30 (1), 68–93.

Webster, A.K. and Peterson, L.E. (guest eds) (2011) Indians in Unexpected Places. Special issue, *American Indian Culture and Research Journal*, 35, entire.

Wexler, L.M. (2006) Inupiat youth suicide and culture loss: Changing community conversations for prevention. *Social Science and Medicine* 63 (11), 2938–2948.

Whalen, D.H., Moss, M. and Baldwin, D. (2016) Healing through language: Positive physical health effects of Indigenous language use. *F1000Research* 5, 1–9. Retrieved 20 February 2018 from https://f1000research.com/articles/5-852/v1

Wilkins, D.E. and Lomawaima, K.T. (2001) *Uneven Ground: American Indian Sovereignty and Federal Law*. Norman, OK: University of Oklahoma Press.

Wilson, W.H. (2014) Hawaiian: A Native American language official for a state. In T.G. Wiley, J.K. Peyton, D. Christian, S.C.K. Moore and N. Liu (eds) *Handbook of Heritage, Community, and Native American Languages in the United States: Research, Policy, and Educational Practice* (pp. 19–26). New York and Washington, DC: Routledge and Center for Applied Linguistics.

Wolfe, P. (1999) *Settler Colonialism and the Transformation of Anthropology: The Politics and Poetics of an Ethnographic Event*. London and New York: Cassell.

Part 1

Policies and Politics in Indigenous Language Reclamation

1 Configuring Language(s) and Speakers: The History and Politics of an Aboriginal Ethnolinguistic Identity in the Yukon, Canada

Barbra A. Meek

Language politics and policies mediate and are mediated by conventional conceptions of difference, often ideologically pitting marginalized and/or Indigenous peoples and languages against economically and politically dominant ones (and reifying lesser known languages as subordinate). This chapter examines the history of regimenting difference between First Nations peoples and other Canadian nationals in relation to race, ethnicity and language, and subsequent attempts to reconfigure this subordinate-dominant scaling, focusing especially on changes in Aboriginal policy that have occurred in the Yukon Territory since the 1800s. I begin by detailing how difference is recognized in terms of race and language in the reflections and correspondences of Hudson Bay traders when describing people they encountered in the economically underdeveloped region now known as the Yukon Territory. I connect this concept of difference to the legal framework defining Indian status (i.e. the 'Indian Act' of 1876). I then compare early concepts of racial/ethnic difference with categories of ethnolinguistic difference emerging in the 1970s and 1980s alongside national discourses of multilingualism and multiculturalism and movements for Aboriginal self-determination. Epitomizing this national transformation in Canadian–Aboriginal relations, the Yukon Territory created its own language policies, equally recognizing English, French and eight Aboriginal languages spoken in the Territory. The 21st century ushered in one more change, a re-imagining of ethnolinguistic categories in terms of citizenship rather than racial/ethnic membership. This last iteration begins to transcend the legacy of difference plaguing most settler societies and to ensure a process of linguistic sustainability.

Introduction

The past few decades have seen a surge of interest and investment in Indigenous language issues and projects. A response to histories of oppression, of political and economic subjugation, advanced through various practices of domination, this surge has resulted in both a growth in the funding and implementing of language projects institutionally and 'on the ground' (within Aboriginal and other Indigenous language communities, as well as between institutions and communities), and the expansion of research on topics ranging from language endangerment and revitalization to language maintenance through second language acquisition and the role of language ideologies and social practices in affecting current (and historical) sociolinguistic patterns and variation.

The discursive landscape within which these theories and practices have emerged continues to maintain a subtle conceptual juxtaposition of late modernity in the distinction between the Indigenous peoples who are invested in the recognition and recovery (or re-creation) of particular linguistic varieties and some 'elite' others who control the institutional representations, subtly reinforcing a configuration of cosmopolitan privilege in opposition to rural Indigenous oppression (cf. Huayhua, 2010; see also Hill, 2002). In both cases, two kinds of fluency are imagined in relation to two kinds of social origins that converge in the mutually entangled project of 'saving' a 'language' – the emblematized 'fluent,' ideally monolingual, imaginatively pre-contact, non-Western Aboriginal language 'speaker' (Moore *et al.*, 2010: 12; see also Moore, 2012: 60, 73) and the institutionally authorized and 'fluent' scholar-researcher most likely trained in the Western arts of categorization and enumeration.

To highlight the urgency of the need for Indigenous language revitalization, such extreme discursive oppositions are useful. They are well suited for attracting the attention and support of local, national and global audiences. By doing so, these discursive oppositions mediate and perpetuate already-entrenched political-ideological positions and divisions. The realization of these oppositions in 'elite' rhetoric is one that many linguistic anthropologists have begun to interrogate, especially in relation to divisions of ethnolingusitic difference (e.g. Duchêne & Heller, 2007; Errington, 2003; Hill, 2002; Moore, 2006, 2012; Moore *et al.*, 2010; Muehlmann, 2012; Suslak, 2009, 2011; Whiteley, 2003; see also Silverstein, 1996). Not as closely explored are the racialized divisions underscoring and emerging from these elite, privileged rhetorics (for an exception, see Kroskrity, 2011; Muehlmann, 2007), or the ways in which people are complicating and challenging these divisions today (Kroskrity, 2009; Kroskrity & Reynolds, 2001; Meek, 2010, 2014). Moving in this latter direction, this chapter examines the history of regimenting difference between First Nations peoples and other Canadian nationals ethnolinguistically – that is, in relation to race, ethnicity and language in the Yukon Territory, Canada – through changes in the representational categories and nomenclature appearing in 'elite' territorial documents since the 1800s when the Yukon Territory became officially recognized by the Canadian government. By focusing on the particular case of Kaska language revitalization, the final sections consider how these metrics of difference intersect representational practices of language in an ongoing project called the Kaska 'talking' dictionary (https://kaskadictionary.wordpress.com/; https://soundcloud.com/kaskadictionary/).

The use of 'ethnolinguistic' as a label refers to the conceptualization of groups of peoples in terms of linguistic practice, either current or historical Indigenous language practices – often referred to as 'ancestral' or 'heritage' languages in government documents. Ethnolinguistic relationships are ideological ones which identify and link particular language varieties and practices to particular groups of people; these relationships categorize people according to perceived or imagined (socio-)linguistic and ethnic similarities (along with other dimensions of semiotically constituted sameness) (Hymes, 1964; Silverstein, 2003). In the Yukon today, for example, this alignment of peoples and languages appears most literally in the government-funded Aboriginal language maps and the motto 'We Are Our Language' (for a detailed analysis of these media, see Meek, 2010). In these images produced by the territorial government and its subsidiaries, languages, groups of Aboriginal peoples and territories are discretely linked and compartmentalized, situating Kaska-speaking groups in the southeast corner of the territory, Tlingit-speaking groups in the southwest corner, Gwich'in speakers in the northernmost area of the territory, and so forth. These alignments and categories of people, places and languages gained substantial political traction in the 1990s when the territorial and federal governments began negotiating land claims settlements with the 14 Yukon First Nations (see http://cyfn.ca/ for a history of and current land claims settlement agreements).

An example of an ethnolinguistic orientation converging with the process of land claims settlements appears in the political alignment and stance-taking of Liard River First Nation and Ross River Dena Council. Both First Nations identify as Kaska, an ethnolinguistic label that unites them, such that neither First Nation has reached a settlement agreement nor do they have representation or membership in the Council of Yukon First Nations at the time of this writing (though they are still counted among the 14 mentioned above). These ethnolinguistic categories have become significant political symbols for Yukon First Nations and for the nation-state. However, in the earliest stages of mapping and settlement, Aboriginal groups were identified in relation to geography and race rather than linguistic difference. Contemporary uses of ethnolinguistic labels maintain this socio-historical racialized aspect.

Before Language: Historical Categories of Difference in the Yukon

The earliest documented references to First Nations peoples living in the Yukon Territory by non-First Nations individuals (government employees) were ethnically or racially based rather than linguistically oriented. As Burnaby has pointed out in relation to Canadian policy-making generally, 'In the 19th century, Canadian legal rights for the "English" and "French" populations focussed on religion rather than language ... Legislation specifically on language was rare' (Burnaby, 2008: 331). Explicit, institutional discourses linking Aboriginal languages and populations were also rare. Within early Yukon documents such as reports, diaries and newspaper articles, the primary distinction was 'Indian' and its implicit opposite, '(White) European' (the embodiment of a Hudson's Bay Company employee). When distinctions were noted, the terms used did not highlight linguistic differences; they referred to landscape features and named geographic locations.

Some of the earliest examples come from Robert Campbell's writings of his exploration of the Yukon Territory. In 1838, in the service of the Hudson's Bay Company, Robert Campbell arrived in the northwestern-most parts of the Canadian territories, established a trading post at Dease Lake in what is now British Columbia, and then abandoned this post a year later to continue exploration of these territories. Under commission by the resident governor of Hudson's Bay Company, Sir George Simpson, Campbell headed north up the Liard River, which flows through the current town of Upper Liard in the Yukon Territory and Kaska settlement areas. At the time of Campbell's departure up the Liard River, he wrote:

> In pursuance of these instructions I left Fort Halkett in May, with a canoe and seven men, among them my trusty Indians, Lapie and Kitza, and the interpreter, Hoole. After ascending the stream some hundreds of miles, far into the mountains, we entered a beautiful lake, which I named Frances Lake, in honour of Lady Simpson. Leaving the canoe and part of the crew near the southwest extremity of this branch of the lake, I set out with three Indians and the interpreter. Shouldering our blankets and guns, we ascended the valley of a river, which we traced to its source in a lake ten miles long, which, with the river, I named Finlaison's lake and river. (Campbell, in Selwyn, 1889: 137)

Other than referring to some of the men in his party as 'Indians,' he expands very little on their linguistic or cultural heritage, noting only their trustworthiness. In a similar document, Dr Dawson describes the pillaging of Fort Selkirk in 1853 by people he refers to as the Coast Indians, and reports that:

> the Chilkats, being unable to carry away all their plunder in the preceding year, had taken merely the guns, powder and tobacco. They had cached the heavier goods, which were afterwards found ... by the local or Wood Indians. (Selwyn, 1889: 267)

These early descriptions of local residents reveal a dichotomous geographical distinction, a distinction between the 'Coast' Indians (the Chilkats) and the 'Wood' Indians (the interior groups). Based on historical documents and narratives circulating among contemporary First Nations, this distinction reflected the socio-political hierarchy present at the time between groups living in these areas. It was a distinction based on the fact that the coastal Indians controlled the trade routes between the coast and interior areas. In a narrative entitled 'Tāltāni yéh Tot'ine yéh Ełegedigeh (War between the Tahltan and Tlingit)' told by Alfred Caesar, a Yukon First Nations elder, the physical, material and metaphysical power of the Tlingit, the Tot'ine, over other Indians is well illustrated. The following translated excerpt exemplifies the Tlingits' dominance.

> Tahltans came to Tlingits with bows and arrows to fight. [They captured and killed a young Tlingit girl.] [While the Tahltans celebrated elsewhere,] one Tlingit man who was a really powerful medicine man said, 'What is happening here? The people are all disappearing. Etsí' Dedele has disappeared as well.' It [had] snowed; there was deep snow, and he told them, 'Go around, go a long ways around and look for their tracks.' They did that and found the tracks of four men walking on top of the snow with snowshoes, heading away. Then they returned and told the people what they had found. 'Let's fight them,' the Tlingit said. 'Let's do that to them,' they were saying. 'Let's get revenge.' They had knives, big knives to stab through people with, and they had guns. The Tahltan had no guns, but the Tlingit had lots of guns, rifles. (Caesar, 1999: 108–112)

This narrative suggests that First Nations already had categories for identifying particular groups of people in the area and surrounding territory that recognized both personal and communal histories (Moore, 2003). But other documents, such as Murdoch McPherson's letter (May, 1847) to his superior regarding his arrival in the 'Youcon' at Peels River identified three different groups of people: 'Gens-du-fou' Indians, 'none of whom had before been so far in this direction' (coastal Indians); Russians (also referred to as 'Whites'); and 'Rat' Indians. Another category of person identified was 'halfbreed,' a term that as of yet has no Kaska equivalent. In a collection of letters by Alexander Hunter Murray, also at Peels River from June 1847 to May 1850, the term 'Indian' appears most frequently along with 'Peels River Indians' to refer to local inhabitants. Two less commonly used terms distinguish the 'Rat Indians' and the 'Esquimaux' in later letters.

Linguistically, these writers describe the Aboriginal languages spoken in a variety of ways, ranging from eloquent – 'The principal chief, after being spoken to by several others, walked to the front and made a speech, the longest I ever listened to, except, perhaps a cameronian sermon, and some parts of equally far from the text,' – to barbaric, loud and unintelligible:

> These Indians spoke in very loud tones and all at the same time, being anxious to give and receive information … [T]hat they spoke an almost

> unintelligible language etc – these were a set of as peacable Indians as exist, and who always take or send their furs to Peels River, they spoke exactly as the Indians of Peels River do … (Robert Campbell's diary, 1852: 70)

Only one example equating the name of the group with a linguistic code was found:

> One band of the 'Gens-du-fou' have, of late years, had much intercourse with the Loucheux Indians, and many of them speak the language, when a strange party of them come to trade in the Loucheux country, they generally bring a person to interpret for them, both of those here spoke Loucheux fluently. (Alexander Hunter Murray, May 1850, journal entry)

In these early reports of contact and trade, terminological conventions referring to groups of Aboriginal peoples, beyond the frequent 'Indian,' were seldom extended to the Aboriginal language spoken and vice versa. Ethnolinguistic nomenclature was a later innovation.

As with most colonial enterprises and projects of assimilation, these earlier periods of Aboriginal recognition were attempts to manage indigenous populations in ways that would accommodate the agenda(s) of a growing nation. Bureaucratically, the official status and definition of 'Indians' in Canada first became codified in 1850 through Canada's 'Indian Act.' The legislatures of Upper and Lower Canada passed parallel acts 'for the protection of Indians from imposition and the property occupied or enjoyed by them from trespass or injury.' Broadly defined, the term 'Indian' referred to 'any person deemed to be Aboriginal by birth or blood; any person reputed to belong to a particular band or body of Indians; and any person who married an Indian or was adopted by Indians' (http://www.ainc-inac.gc.ca/qc/csi/hist1_e.pdf). This definition underwent several modifications over the next several decades, where most modifications involved the clarification of 'enfranchisement' or the loss (or 'relinquishment') of Indian status and band membership, beginning with the definition of enfranchisement in 1857 (see also Patrick, 2007: 39–43, and Patrick, 2005 on legislation and Indian status in Canada). Loss of status, or 'enfranchisement,' occurred in relation to personal achievements and situations such as private land ownership, marriage to a non-Native man, completion of a degree of education, nonlocal residence or types of persons: persons of 'illegitimate' birth, unmarried women, widows (and children thereof), and so forth. For women in particular, 'Indian' status was determined or revoked through their husbands' status of band membership (legislation in 1869 and 1876). Furthermore, in 1951 the government of Canada established a centralized Indian Register comprised of two lists: one of bands and the other of persons entitled to Indian status,[1] defining the soon-to-be official First Nations and their respective citizens.

In the Yukon Territory, First Nations peoples were recognized primarily in relation to settlement areas. With the implementation of federally mandated residential schooling that accompanied a national trend toward 'Anglo conformity' (Burnaby, 2008: 331), school-aged children from communities where Aboriginal language practices dominated were separated from their families, often for the entire academic year and even the entire calendar year. The schools, run by religious organizations in the Yukon at that time, were intended to develop Aboriginal students' English competence in part through the suppression of their Aboriginal mother tongues (Meek, 2010: 18–19; see also Burnaby, 1999, 2008; Coates, 1991; Hinton & Meek, 2016). For the Kaska First Nations, much of the Kaska-speaking community attended a residential school at Lower Post, B.C. that was in operation from 1949 to 1975 (Meek, 2010: 339). The emphasis on English language education in Aboriginal communities and the creation of a national language policy by the late 1960s mark a transition in Canadian policy toward recognizing and configuring groups in relation to linguistic practice and linguistic heritage. However, this transition from peoples to language(s) retained the underlying racialized profile of Indian-ness.

The Emergence of Ethnolinguistic Categories in the Yukon Territory

The explicit delineation of ethnolinguistic categories in the Yukon Territory emerged in relation to Canadian and Yukon Territorial policy changes in the 1970s and 1980s resulting from national movements to improve the conditions of Aboriginal peoples and to define Canada as a multicultural and multilingual nation. With the official recognition of French as a national language and policy changes in relation to multiculturalism, the linking and demarcating of peoples and languages became politically salient and codified throughout Canada. This ethnolinguistic practice was further reinforced by Canada's efforts to recognize discrete First Nations and to authorize their self-governance through the establishment of opportunities for self-determination, one of which was language revitalization.

Aboriginal language revitalization in Canada has its origins in two political policy transformations: (1) the policy shifts in the mid- and late-20th century that changed the legal definitions and status of Aboriginal peoples, and (2) several legislative acts, such as the Official Languages Act of Canada, that led to a change in the status of minority languages. The first recognized First Nations as having legitimate claims to their traditional lands beginning in the 1970s. The second allowed for the reintroduction of traditional religion, customs and language into educational curricula (Burnaby, 1999: 306–307). This linking of land, people and languages eventually became epitomized through a Yukon government map.[2]

In the Yukon, these policy shifts led to land claims and self-government agreements, which contain explicit provisions for Aboriginal languages as well as the establishment of Aboriginal language projects and programs. The first Aboriginal languages project was officially started in 1977. The Council of Yukon Indians, now known as the Council of Yukon First Nations (CYFN), sponsored the project. The Project itself became known as the Yukon Native Language Centre (YNLC) in 1985. Since its inception, the Centre has been involved in recruiting Native speakers for language documentation and for training as Native language teachers in the public schools (Moore, 2002: 317). This latter goal became possible with the adoption of the Yukon Education Act in 1990 that opened the door for Aboriginal languages in local classrooms.

Accompanying these changes, a government-sponsored program for Aboriginal language revitalization emerged in the 1980s. As Canada was finalizing its Official Languages Act, the Yukon government seized the opportunity to negotiate an exclusion to this national Act and adopted its own, the Yukon Languages Act (1988), creating an atmosphere in which French, English and any Aboriginal language could be used in legislature and elsewhere (Languages Act, 1988). For Yukon Aboriginal languages in particular, this Act stated that

> The Yukon recognizes the significance of aboriginal languages in the Yukon and wishes to take appropriate measures to preserve, develop and enhance those languages in the Yukon ... (under advancement of status and use) Nothing in this Act limits the authority of the Legislative Assembly to advance the equality of status of English, French, or a Yukon aboriginal language. (http://www.canlii.org/yk/laws/sta/133/20041124/whole.html; 6 April 2005)

Additionally, the Canada-Yukon Cooperation and Funding Agreement on the Preservation, Development and Enhancement of Aboriginal Languages, a five-year language agreement between the Yukon government and the federal government, was signed on 24 February 1989. With this agreement came five years of funding, the option for renewal at the end of this period (following an evaluation), and the establishment of Aboriginal Languages Services (ALS), a program within the Yukon Government designed to distribute the funding and provide administrative support. This new recognition of and support for Aboriginal linguistic heritage through policies of multiculturalism retained vestiges of the earlier racializing discourses that defined 'Indians' in relation to land occupation, kinship and blood. That is, the configuration of Aboriginal difference emerging in the 1970s added Aboriginal languages to the discursive image of Aboriginality.[3]

Epitomizing Aboriginal Languages and First Nations

The most explicit articulation of ethnolinguistic categories appeared in the logo now used to represent Aboriginal language efforts and communities in the Yukon Territory. This image resulted from the institutionalization of Aboriginal languages through meetings for language planning, the evaluation of programming and public language events, and the implementation of Aboriginal language education in public schools, one of the primary concerns being the significantly lower rates of achievement of Aboriginal students in contrast to non-Aboriginal students.

The earliest meetings and reports of the territorial government focused on the importance of Aboriginal language learning to the wellbeing of Aboriginal communities and their children. These bureaucratic deliberations culminated in what was called 'the Yukon Program Model' developed by Aboriginal Language Services (a branch of the territorial government) for revitalizing Aboriginal languages. The initial guiding philosophy for this model was the idea that '[t]he people own the language' (Gardner and Associates, 1993: 15). This model was not only a discourse about Aboriginal languages, it was also a statement about Aboriginal cultures as well. Furthermore, it recognized that

> issues of language are complex and affected by many socio-cultural factors, profoundly linked to identity, self-concept and world view, and inseparable from culture. Because language issues were seen to be intimately linked with cultural issues, there was a need to recognize these issues as sacred and to approach them with an attitude of caution and respect. (Gardner and Associates, 1993: 14)

The inclusion of culture in the understanding of language arose in part from academic resources (see Meek, 2009), but also found expression in the discourse of Yukon elders, both of which reinforced a conceptualization of language as synonymous with cultural difference and foregrounded the concept of identity.

As Meek (2009) discusses, the Yukon Aboriginal Languages Conference of 1991 brought together elders from all over Yukon and provided a forum for them and any other stakeholder – that is, Yukon citizen – to share their ideas and concerns about the state of the territory's Aboriginal languages. The predominant theme was the idea that language is identity. This 'language as identity' theme was expressed in various ways. The territorial government reflected this theme in its own discourse through statements such as, 'Language, culture and identity are inseparable' (ALS, 1991: 29). Among First Nations participants, the connection between language and identity became configured as an internal, inheritable and unbreakable bond between speakers and their heritage. Tlingit Elder Pete Sidney expressed this as follows:

> Another thing I dislike hearing about is that we lost, we lost our heritage, we lost our language. Let's examine that for a minute. What is language? Where does it come from? ...Language is a gift of the Creator for the purpose of communication and any gift of the Creator you as well as

myself know that it can never deteriorate ... . All we have to do is dust it off. (ALS, 1991: 11; Meek, 2009: 163).

While not all participants expressed this view, many of the elders subscribed to some variety of linguistic essentialism.[4] Other First Nations people elaborated on this 'language as identity' idea by describing language as the primary means for creating and maintaining relationships and for understanding one's ancestral history. While acknowledging the importance of a Canadian public education (and English competence), First Nations participants also deemed it necessary to recognize education beyond a legislated Canadian curriculum.

> 'Education is very good for kids now days, but we still have to learn our culture, our language. We have to know who we are, and we have to have a string tied through everyone of us, we're related somehow, so this is why we respect each other,' Elder Dora Wedge. (ALS, 1991: 13; Meek, 2009: 163)

Moving beyond individual issues of identity, statements made during the 1991 Conference also related identity and language to group solidarity and self-government.

> 'As we talk about this self-government, I think it is a part of it that we try to do today [at the language conference]. I'm glad to see that we are doing this whole Yukon get-together to make a strong stand for our rights and for our future. I believe our kids will work hard to try to get back to pick up some of our language again.' Roddy Blackjack Sr., Northern Tutchone Elder (ALS, 1991: 19; Meek, 2009: 163–164)

Comparable views were also in print elsewhere: 'Indian unity, what some people call self-government, must be held together by the native languages. If you call yourself Indian and you want Indian self-government then you should conduct your business in the Indian language' (First Nations parent, quoted from Tlen, 1986: 30). As Meek notes, 'All of these statements represent aboriginal language as essential to aboriginal identity and to the establishment of what binds people together: "our relatives," "our heritage" is founded upon "our language"' (2009: 165). Thus, this theme became epitomized in the slogan, 'We Are Our Language,'[5] which formally codified these ethnolinguistic relationships.

The ethnolinguistic categories that emerged alongside a shifting political terrain in Aboriginal-state relations subsumed earlier racialized notions of Aboriginality while at the same time intersecting with local First Nations practices of recognition. On the ground, members of extended kin networks could identify relatives and non-relatives through a speaker's Aboriginal language dialect (McClellan, 1975; Meek, 2007). The practice of using a linguistic variety to identify relatedness was easily transposed onto bureaucratic discourses of ethnolinguistic difference, scaling up the level of groupness identified from immediate families to extended networks of relatives and in-laws organized around the territory they currently occupied. From both an 'elite' perspective and an Aboriginal one, the categorization of Aboriginal difference ethnolinguistically seemed transparent, and even self-evident.

Embellishing Ethnolinguistic Categories

The ongoing inclusion of Aboriginal voices in government documents and institutional positions has continued to affect bureaucratic rhetoric in the Yukon Territory. In the early 2000s, this rhetoric began to recognize the linguistic diversity within the ethnolinguistic categories devised by the government for tracking language loss. While the earliest reports used the labels for the eight officially recognized Aboriginal languages, the final reports produced by Aboriginal Language Services complicated these categories by identifying subcategories such as dialects, types of abilities (teach, read, write, speak, understand), and degrees of competence (see Meek, 2016 for a more elaborate discussion of the representational history of Yukon First Nations languages by governments).

These government reports expanded the configuration of ethnolinguistic difference through the diversification of the linguistic field, both in terms of languages (Kaska and English) and users of these languages. The earliest reports and statements imagined a singular correspondence between languages and peoples, and identified elders as 'experts.' For example, all Kaska people were lumped under the label 'Kaska' and the reports and graphs delineated competency differences in relation to age and categories of speakers (speaker/non-speaker, Kaska/English). Later documents recognized the multitude of dialects ('8 languages with many dialects' [ALS, 2004a: 12]) and began including diagrams tabulating the number of speakers for each dialect (ALS, 2004a). These reports also began to acknowledge the range of linguistic competence and expertise available within communities, noting that 'language expertise resides in more than one place' (ALS, 2004b: 28) and in more than just speaking. Furthermore, these configurations incorporated different ways of being with language, from self-evaluations of competence in writing and competence in reading, to self-assessments of potential future competencies in writing, reading, teaching and speaking. The discourse shifted from an immediate atemporal representation to a temporal one that entails a future – one of a multitude of uses and technologies for the Yukon's Aboriginal languages.

The configuration of knowledge itself also emerged as variable across individuals, changeable within individuals, and diversely distributed across age, gender and areas (see Meek, 2016 for further discussion). While such discursive modifications suggest an ideological transcendence and a more inclusive environment, in practice tensions – and potential divisions – remained. People would still discriminate based on language choice and style of performance, chastising youth for speaking the wrong dialect or elders for telling traditional Aboriginal stories in English. That is, the recognition of diversity in many guises does not necessarily alleviate the ideological censuring of ethnolinguistic identification.

In this case, the politics surrounding ethnolinguistic identification in the Yukon intersected with the politics surrounding land. Aggravated by, if not crucial to, the process of Yukon First Nations land claims, the convergence of these processes of recognition institutionally allowed for and afforded their projection onto and through other boundary-making projects, both geographically and socially. The question is where and when might this happen, the opportunities for projecting this national ethnolinguistic equivalence onto other domains, and how might such opportunities be challenged and reconciled on the ground.

Re-imagining Ethnolinguistic Diversity

One domain in which such contestations often arise is in considerations of where individuals and groups themselves might have been original to a particular place at a particular time? In public academic spaces in Canada such as institutional websites or conferences, it is becoming more common to acknowledge and thank the original inhabitants, the local First Nations, for sharing the land (see, e.g. the Department of Anthropology website, University of British Columbia, https://anth.ubc.ca/). Certainly, historical linguists have spent significant effort deliberating over the origins of languages and the reconstruction of ancestral proto-languages. While such exercises may seem abstractly academic or purely inquisitive, encompassing such seemingly benign inquiries are the social politics and histories that entangle people's lives, opportunities and languages. Michael Silverstein (2003), in a discussion of ethnolinguistic recognition, elaborates the politics surrounding the mere labeling and linking of groups and languages (see also Moore *et al.*, 2010). He concludes with an appeal to '[w]e, the intellectuals or knowledge workers of our societies' that we 'must engage, directly or indirectly, with the intellectuals and elites of the currently recognized as well as "wannabe" groups. We must understand where they are positioned in the dynamics of scheduling their, and others', identities' (Silverstein, 2003: 554). Perhaps more importantly, we must acknowledge that '[t]here is … no neutrally dispassionate, disinterested linguistic or ethnographic collecting and describing, whatever the explicit intent of the [researcher/scholar/etc.]' (2003: 554).

This chapter has sought to elucidate some of the social history and current politics that have resulted in the ethnolinguistic categories of recognition that delineate First Nations and Aboriginal languages in the Yukon Territory, Canada today; that is, the goal has been to understand the non-neutral, passionate and interested investment in these categories of recognition that define current Aboriginal language projects and practices. The ethnolinguistic linking of First Nations with particular Aboriginal languages might not merely be an act of accommodation or a sign of acquiescence to Canadian governments, but a successful political tactic on the part of First Nations in order to present a united front, or several fronts, on a national scale.

Although the discursive foregrounding of (linguistic) homogeneity may prove useful at a national (or territorial) scale, group-internal discourses may emphasize heterogeneity and language variation. If that is the case, almost any language venture will make salient the politics of a community or group of people and the boundary-making dimensions of language practices. Aboriginal language revitalization and preservation efforts often render these politics transparent. Intersecting many of the Kaska language events that have resulted from such efforts is the recognition of language variation, conceptualized as dialects and defined along matrilineal kinship lines. Discursively manifested, this variation becomes available for division and contestation. In Kaska country, these differences have evoked subtle disagreement across a range of educational settings, from preschool classrooms to literacy workshops, from individual correction to institutional assessment (see Meek, 2010 for illustrations). The most recent endeavor embarked upon by the Kaska First Nations, the Yukon Department of Education and the University of British Columbia is a collaboration intended to address the Kaska community's demand for a lasting user-friendly archive of the Kaska language, the Kaska 'talking' dictionary project. It is a project intended to involve as many community members as possible in its development, assessment, and use and to incorporate the wealth of linguistic diversity present in the community. However, even with the stated goal of recognizing and documenting the linguistic diversity within the community, objections emerge in trepidation of some imagined, potential projection of the state's generic formulation.

For the Kaska 'talking' dictionary project, as with Kaska language education more generally, the dialects being recorded become an object of scrutiny. For example, while working with teachers in school programs, some parents and grandparents would remark on how their home dialect was not the one being taught in the schools and that their children and grandchildren were learning the wrong variety. Although these adults seemed to still understand the child learners, they were disgruntled by the fact their children were learning someone else's 'dialect,' a variety not original to their family (Meek, 2007: 27; see also Meek, 2010).

The Kaska 'talking' dictionary project has also begun to attract such critical attention, even though the goal is to present and represent as many linguistic varieties as possible from as many different speakers as possible, as with the pre-online versions such as the Kaska noun dictionary and Kaska narratives (Moore, 1997; Moore, 1999). In actual practice, certain varieties and speakers get privileged because of individual ability, personal commitment and interest, project priorities and scheduling constraints. Such patterns afford interpretations of boundary-making. In this case, a privileging of one dialect over another remains a hushed discourse in the community. Most recently, our work created tension within the community because we worked primarily with one speaker, Mrs Leda Jules, who is accomplished at elaborating verb paradigms for our documentary efforts and recording them efficiently for the online dictionary. She has been the band's language resource person for the past few decades and she is one of the most committed language activists in the community. As part of this project, she also created three narratives for children that she recorded for this online language resource. Because of her commitment and expertise, our initial efforts focused on her dialect. As a result, there was some concern that other dialects would be excluded from this resource. To manage such potential anxiety, we began to regularly 'check in' with other elders and families, provide updates of our progress, and most recently set up a Facebook page for feedback, sharing and language promotion.

Another confounding element is the concern with correctness and documenting the 'right' form. This concern seeps into our everyday elicitation work such that we are regularly asked to 'check with the elders' on the forms that have been elicited. An anxiety over documenting and recording the 'correct' form lurks behind each recording and each step toward revitalization. During earlier fieldwork in classrooms, it became apparent that Aboriginal language teachers would avoid writing Kaska not only because they were uncomfortable with that practice of representation but because they did not know the 'right' way to represent their language. Students, on the other hand, were excited by the prospect of establishing orthographic conventions for their heritage language (Meek, 2010: 86–91).

The online dictionary project triggers a similar anxiety about correctness, though one that is rooted more in aging and retention rather than institutional experiences. In this case the concern with correctness is also a consideration of one's peers, one's relatives' evaluations of the performance, and a recognition of the eventual public availability of these recordings, and perhaps even the publics they will constitute. Even now by subscribing to the Kaska Wordpress page and accompanying Facebook site, an individual can access the posted recordings. It is a potential opportunity for both criticism and reward, and with Facebook, a member can post commentary for all other members to read. To date, though, the feedback on Facebook has been supportive and encouraging. It has been only in the face-to-face events where whispered criticisms find an audience, and sometimes only the whisperer's ear.

Jane Hill once noted that you can't save a language while there are speakers left. Perhaps she's right; as long as there are other speakers, there will always be the opportunity for someone to identify a word, phrase or utterance as 'wrong.' It is a difficult conceptual space to escape. The hope is that the online dictionary will be a versatile enough forum that speakers and learners can contribute, navigate and use the tool in ways that suit their own personal goals and interests, and that their participation and investment in the conceptualization and development of the infrastructure of the resource will lead to a break-through in usability, a goal yet to be achieved by published grammars and dictionaries. Users will be able to contribute their own versions of words, phrases and narratives, to add their own translations and analyses, and to select their own dialects. 'Correctness' will then emerge from use and discussion rather than institutional prescription, and perhaps be replaced entirely by some more relevant conception of the relationship between language, form and practice for those who identify in some way with the Kaska language.

Conclusion

This chapter detailed the emergence and evolution of an Aboriginal ethnolinguistic identity in the Yukon Territory, Canada, showing how the involvement of Aboriginal people changed and continues to change this configuration of language and identity in ways familiar and new to the institutions that rely on such discourses of recognition. It began by detailing a configuration of Aboriginality separate from Aboriginal language during the initial stages of settlement in the territory. Letters written by the key administrator at that time in the late 1800s and early 1900s demonstrate this initial conceptualization of difference. Following this settlement period came attempts to assimilate Aboriginal people into the Canadian polity through policy and education. Linguistically, English served as the primary tool for establishing and performing a Canadian identity in unstated opposition to an Aboriginal identity and language. A shift in the Canadian nation's representational economy happened most acutely in the 1970s when Aboriginal rights were at the forefront of Canadian–Aboriginal politics, resulting in the explicit linking of language to Aboriginal identity. In many colonial and post-colonial settings such ethnolinguistic equations were used to configure the nation-state (cf. Errington, 2001; Irvine & Gal, 1993, 2001). In Canada, these equations were used by local and national governments to empower Aboriginal groups. The final section examined some of the particular ways in which First Nations in the Yukon Territory modified state-sanctioned configurations of difference in recognition of both external and internal sociolinguistic divisions and how these conceptual interventions continue to influence contemporary Aboriginal language efforts.

In particular, this chapter has argued that the generic 'Indian' image in Canada became complicated and ethnolinguistically valenced as individual First Nations embarked on land claims settlements that demanded their recognition in relation to particular property or tracts of land.

Aboriginal languages became critical markers of Aboriginality and by extension served to establish a relationship between a people and a piece of land. Interestingly, while the national Canadian perspective divided up territories as property in relation to First Nations and individuals (Nadasdy, 2012), it lumped sociolinguistic practices into one (Aboriginal) language in relation to these same entities (particular First Nations and individuals). The Kaska First Nations' perspectives ultimately did the opposite; they discursively lumped together properties and divided up languages and linguistic practices. Thus, examining a range of practices of recognition reveals how what might seem mere strategic accommodation may in fact be a profound political move.

Finally, as both Aboriginal languages and Aboriginal control shift in Canada, the discourse of difference emerging first through contact narratives and later through government bureaucracy has also shifted in relation to the growing participation and inclusion of Aboriginal voices in their own discursive configuration, shifting from generic Indians to ethnolinguistically distinct groups to First Nation citizens. In the Yukon Territory, the language-nation link became most fully realized in connection with the settlement of land claims. On the ground, however, local discourse emphasized linguistic diversity. The Kaska 'talking' dictionary project illustrates one of the ways in which this diversity gets expressed and in which First Nations are finding new strategies for expressing their independence and for self-determination. Yet, even in such projects of (linguistic) diversification, subtle homogenizing discourses of correctness creep into the conversation. To mediate these creep-y entanglements, at least in the 'talking' dictionary case, technological tools are being developed to facilitate use across a broad range of users and a greater network of participants is influencing how these tools evolve. Even though 'Kaska language' remains the overarching rubric that contains and connects a range of linguistic information, the individual user will control the ways in which she or he engages with the Kaska language through the online dictionary and the opportunity to choose how, where, when and what (dialect or language or form) that might be. Categories of ethnolinguistic identification will become connected to new patterns, and mediums, of use, possibly transforming how we might think about or what we might mean by 'a language' and a 'Kaska language user.'

Notes

(1) With the passage of Bill C-31 in 1985, many of the practices of 'enfranchisement' were revoked, and those who had lost status and membership under these practices regained it. In particular, this bill was guided by the following three principles: (1) that all discrimination be removed from the Indian Act; (2) that Indian status within the meaning of the Indian Act and band memberships rights be restored to persons who had lost them; and (3) that Indian bands have the right to control their own membership (http://www.ainc-inac.gc.ca/qc/csi/present1_e.pdf).

(2) Donna Patrick (2007) makes a similar observation with respect to the federal government's discourse about Aboriginal languages and peoples in a 2005 Aboriginal
Languages Task Force Report created by a committee of ten people appointed by the
Department of Canadian Heritage. In particular, she discusses how this report
explicitly links spirituality, land and language together, 'emphasizing how Aboriginal
groups' spirituality, cultural relationships and connection to the land … are all tied
to "sacred and traditional knowledge", and particularly oral traditions, transmitted
through Aboriginal languages … a crucial part of Aboriginal existence and for understanding the "historic continuity" of Aboriginal peoples with the land' (2007: 45).

(3) The 'Indian' image became dissected further by individual First Nations' territories
and their languages. Interestingly, while the national Canadian perspective divided
up territories as property in relation to First Nations and individuals (Nadasdy, 2012),
it lumped together sociolinguistic practices and individuals in relation to (a) language,
whereas First Nations' perspectives lumped together property and divided up languages and linguistic practices.

(4) It is important to note that it is much easier for someone, such as an elder who has
experienced language socialization in the heritage language, to naturalize the language acquisition process and assume that the language is already inside of him or
her.

(5) This phrase traces back to the planning stages of the conference where it was agreed
upon as the conference theme and its meaning emerged in conversation with other
stakeholders at the conference, especially First Nations elders (Gardner and
Associates, 1997: 21; see Meek, 2009 for discussion). It is not a mantra vocalized by
First Nations citizens locally or their band governments, but an agreed-upon motto
to serve official state discourse (see Meek, 2010, Chapter 5).

Acknowledgements

Thank you to the editors for their patience and encouragement, to the
reviewers who helped me craft a better chapter, and to Sonia Das and
Sherina Feliciano-Santos for their insightful optimism. I am also indebted
to several organizations and people for their support: Liard First Nation,
SSHRC, the Yukon Department of Education, the Yukon Archives, the
University of Michigan, and my Kaska-using colleagues everywhere.

References

Aboriginal Language Services (ALS) (1991) *Voices of the Talking Circle*. Whitehorse:
Yukon Executive Council Office.
Aboriginal Language Services (ALS) (2004a) *Evaluation Report: Hope for the Future: A
Call for Strategic Action: Five Year Report, 1998–2003*. Whitehorse: Yukon Executive
Council Office.
Aboriginal Language Services (ALS) (2004b) *Sharing the Gift of Language: Profile of
Yukon First Nation Languages*. Whitehorse: Yukon Executive Council Office.
Burnaby, B. (1999) Policy on Aboriginal languages in Canada: Notes on status planning.
In L.P. Valentine and R. Darnell (eds) *Theorizing the Americanist Tradition* (pp.
299–314). Toronto, ON: University of Toronto Press.
Burnaby, B. (2008) Language policy and education in Canada. In S. May and N.H.
Hornberger (eds) *Encyclopedia of Language and Education, Volume 1: Language
Policy and Political Issues in Education* (2nd edn, pp. 331–341). New York, NY:
Springer.

Caesar, A. (1999) Tāltāni yéh Tot'ine yéh Ełegedigeh (War between the Tahltan and Tlingit). In P. Moore (ed.) *Dene Gudeji: Kaska Narratives* (pp. 108–123). Whitehorse, YT: Kaska Tribal Council.

Campbell, R. (1852) *Diary. Yukon Archives, Department of Tourism and Culture.* Whitehorse: Yukon Government.

Coates, K.S. (1991) *Best Left as Indians: Native-White Relations in the Yukon Territory, 1840–1973.* Montreal, QC: McGill-Queen's University Press.

Duchêne, A. and Heller, M. (eds) (2007) *Discourses of Endangerment: Ideology and Interest in the Defence of Languages.* London: Continuum.

Errington, J. (2001) Colonial linguistics. *Annual Review of Anthropology* 30, 19–39.

Errington, J. (2003) Getting language rights: The rhetoric of language endangerment and loss. *American Anthropologist* 105 (4), 723–732.

Gardner and Associates (1993) *Walking the Talk: Implementation and Evaluations of the Canada-Yukon Funding Agreement on the Development and Enhancement of Aboriginal Languages, 1988/89–1992/93.* Whitehorse, YT: Queen's Printer.

Gardner and Associates (1997) *We Are Our Language: An Evaluation of the Implementation and Impact of the Canada-Yukon Cooperation and Funding Agreement on the Development and Enhancement of Aboriginal Languages 1993–1998.* Whitehorse, YT: Queen's Printer.

Hill, J.H. (2002) 'Expert rhetorics' in advocacy for endangered languages: Who is listening and what do they hear? *Journal of Linguistic Anthropology* 12 (2), 119–133.

Hinton, L. and Meek, B. (2016) Language acquisition, shift, and revitalization processes in the USA and Canada. In S.M. Coronel-Molina and T.L. McCarty (eds) *Indigenous Language Revitalization in the Americas* (pp. 57–75). New York, NY: Routledge.

Huayhua, M. (2010) *Runama Kani icla Alqucha?: Everyday Discrimination in the Southern Andes.* Ph.D. dissertation, University of Michigan, Ann Arbor.

Hymes, D. (1964) Directions in (ethno-)linguistic theory. *American Anthropologist* 66 (3, part 2), 6–56.

Irvine, J.T. and Gal, S. (2000) Language ideology and linguistic differentiation. In P.V. Kroskrity (ed.) *Regimes of Language: Ideologies, Politics and Identities* (pp. 35–83). Santa Fe, NM: School of American Research Press.

Kroskrity, P.V. and Reynolds, J.F. (2001) Using multimedia in language renewal: Observations from making the CD-ROM *Taiaduhaan.* In L. Hinton and K. Hale (eds) *The Green Book of Language Revitalization in Practice* (pp. 317–329). San Diego, CA: Academic Press.

Kroskrity, P.V. (2009) Embodying the reversal of language shift: Agency, incorporation, and language ideological change in the Western Mono community of central California. In P.V. Kroskrity and M. Field (eds) *Native American Language Ideologies: Beliefs, Practices, and Struggles in Indian Country* (pp. 190–210). Tucson: University of Arizona Press.

Kroskrity, P.V. (2011) Facing the rhetoric of language endangerment: Voicing the consequences of linguistic racism. *Journal of Linguistic Anthropology* 21 (2), 179–192.

McClellan, C. (1975) *My Old People Say: An Ethnographic Survey of Southern Yukon Territory.* Ottawa, ON: National Museums of Canada.

Meek, B. (2007) Respecting the language of elders: Ideological shift and linguistic discontinuity in a Northern Athapascan community. *Journal of Linguistic Anthropology* 17 (1), 23–43.

Meek, B. (2009) Language ideology and Aboriginal language revitalization in the Yukon, Canada. In P.V. Kroskrity and M. Field (eds) *Native American Language Ideologies: Beliefs, Practices, and Struggles in Indian Country* (pp. 151–171). Tucson: University of Arizona Press.

Meek, B. (2010) *We Are Our Language: An Ethnography of Language Revitalization in a Northern Athabaskan Community.* Tucson: University of Arizona Press.

Meek, B. (2014) 'She can do it in English too': Acts of intimacy and boundary-making in language revitalization. *Language and Communication* 38, 73–82.

Meek, B. (2016) Shrinking indigenous language in the Yukon. In E.S. Carr and M. Lempert (eds) *Scale: Discourse and Dimensions of Social Life* (pp. 70–88). Oakland: University of California Press.

Moore, P. (2003) Lessons on the land: The role of Kaska elders in a university language course. *Canadian Journal of Native Education* 27 (1), 127–139.

Moore, P. (ed.) (1997) *Guzagi K'úgé: Our Language Book: Nouns, Kaska, Mountain Slavey and Sekani*. Whitehorse, YT: Kaska Tribal Council.

Moore, P. (ed.) (1999) *Dene Gudeji: Kaska Narratives*. Whitehorse: Kaska Tribal Council.

Moore, R. (2006) Disappearing, Inc.: Glimpsing the sublime in the politics of access to endangered languages. *Language and Communication* 26, 296–315.

Moore, R. (2012) 'Taking up speech' in an endangered language: Bilingual discourse in a heritage language classroom. *Working Papers in Educational Linguistics* 27 (2), 57–78.

Moore, R., Pietikäinen, S. and Blommaert, J. (2010) Counting the losses: Numbers as the language of language endangerment. *Sociolinguistic Studies* 4 (1), 1–26.

Muehlmann, S. (2007) Defending diversity: Staking out a common global interest. In A. Duchêne and M. Heller (eds) *Discourses of Endangerment: Ideology and Interest in the Defence of Languages* (pp. 14–34). London: Continuum.

Muehlmann, S. (2012) Rhizomes and other uncountables: The malaise of enumeration in Mexico's Colorado River Delta. *American Ethnologist* 39 (2), 339–353.

Murray, A.H. (1847–1850) Personal letters. Yukon Archives.

Nadasdy, P. (2012) Boundaries among kin: Sovereignty, the modern treaty process, and the rise of ethno-territorial nationalism among Yukon First Nations. *Comparative Studies in Society and History* 54 (3), 499–532.

Patrick, D. (2005) Language rights in Indigenous communities: The case of the Inuit of Arctic Québec. *Journal of Sociolinguistics* 9 (3), 369–389.

Patrick, D. (2007) Indigenous language endangerment and the unfinished business of nation states. In A. Duchêne and M. Heller (eds) *Discourses of Endangerment: Ideology and Interest in the Defence of Languages* (pp. 35–56). London: Continuum.

Selwyn, A.R.C. (1889) *Geological and Natural History Survey of Canada, 1887–88, Annual Report, Vol. 3, Part 1*. Montreal, QC: William Foster Brown and Co.

Silverstein, M. (1996) Encountering language and languages of encounter in North American ethnohistory. *Journal of Linguistic Anthropology* 6 (2), 126–144.

Silverstein, M. (2003) The whens and wheres – as well as hows – of ethnolinguistic recognition. *Public Culture* 15 (3), 531–557.

Suslak, D. (2009) The sociolinguistic problem of generations. *Language and Communication* 29 (3), 199–209.

Suslak, D. (2011) Ayapan echoes: Linguistic persistence and loss in Tabasco, Mexico. *American Anthropologist* 133 (4), 569–581.

Tlen, D. (1986) *Speaking Out: Consultations and Survey of Yukon Native Languages Planning, Visibility, and Growth*. Whitehorse, YT: YNLC.

Whiteley, P. (2003) Do "language rights" serve indigenous interests? Some Hopi and other queries. *American Anthropologist* 105 (4), 712–722.

2 Language Policy in Post-Apartheid South Africa – An Evaluation

Nkonko M. Kamwangamalu

More than 25 years have passed since South Africa liberated itself from apartheid in 1994 and adopted a multilingual language policy. The policy gives official recognition to 11 languages, including English and Afrikaans, previously the only two official languages of the apartheid state, and nine African languages, all newcomers to the official languages landscape. It is opportune to evaluate the policy, a stage that Fishman refers to as 'the bête noire of all planning,' to determine whether it has achieved its main goal to revitalize the Indigenous African languages in particular by using them as the medium of instruction in the schools. The main claim of the chapter is that if South Africa's language-in-education practices are any indication, the country's multilingual language policy has failed. The chapter draws on two theoretical frameworks – language economics and critical theory, especially Bourdieu's idea of cultural capital, as well as on empirical studies of Indigenous language revitalization in polities around the world – to explain why the new language policy has failed but, more importantly, to suggest ways in which it can be aided to achieve its intended goal.

Introduction

South Africa has a long history of language struggle, which was brought about by Western powers that colonized the country for over 300 years. It was colonized first by the Dutch from 1652 to 1795; next by the British from 1795 to 1948; and once again by the Dutch, who by then called themselves Afrikaners, from 1948 until the country liberated itself from apartheid in 1994. For 342 years up until the demise of apartheid in 1994, South Africa was historically known as a bilingual state, with English and Afrikaans (1795–1948) and later Afrikaans and English (1948–1994), in that diglossic order, as the two official languages of the state (Kamwangamalu, 2000). Grosjean (1982: 12) refers to this situation as 'the personality principle' – a situation in which bilingualism is the official policy of the country but the majority of the population is multilingual.[1]

As a result of the end of apartheid in 1994, South Africa has recognized its linguistic diversity by giving official status to 11 languages including English and Afrikaans, and nine African languages from the country's nine provinces. The main goal of the policy is to revitalize previously marginalized languages, in this case South Africa's Indigenous languages, by promoting their use in high-status domains such as the educational system. The literature shows, however, that English, Afrikaans and the nine Indigenous languages are of unequal status, for only English and Afrikaans are associated with the functions that official languages are expected to perform in a polity (Eastman, 1990; Fishman, 1971). A true official language, says Fasold (1984), fulfills all or some of the functions listed in 1–5 below, to which Fishman (1971) would add those in (6) and (7). The official language is used:

(1) as the language of communication by government officials in carrying out their duties at the national level;
(2) for written communication between and internal to government agencies at the national level;
(3) for the keeping of government records at the national level;
(4) for the original formulation of laws and regulations that concern the nation as a whole;
(5) for forms such as tax forms;
(6) in the schools; and
(7) in the courts.

Kaplan *et al.* (2011) point out that when a language is granted official status, it is presumed that this enhances its prestige, extends its use into educational and non-educational domains, and privileges its speakers. Language practices in South Africa, however, indicate that only inherited colonial languages, in this case English and to a lesser extent Afrikaans, have prestige and perform most or all of the afore-listed functions. Put differently, official recognition has not equalized opportunities for the nine, then-newly minted official African languages and their speakers. Rather, the recognition has provided a cover for what Pennycook (1994) calls the planned reproduction of socioeconomic inequality. It follows that independent South Africa, like many African countries that secured political independence from Western powers long before South Africa, suffers from what Bamgbose (1991) refers to as *an inheritance situation*. This has to do with 'how the colonial experience continues to shape and define post-colonial problems and practices' (Bamgbose, 1991: 69).

There is a growing body of literature showing that South Africa's language policy has not achieved its central goal to revitalize African languages, for it has failed to promote their use in such high-status domains as the educational system (Alexander, 1997; Banda, 2010; G. De Klerk,

2002; Heugh, 2009; Tshotsho, 2013; Webb, 2004). On the contrary, despite South Africa's constitutional commitment to multilingualism, the cited literature indicates that the country has been drifting steadily towards unilingualism in English at the expense of the other official languages, an unwelcome development that the Language Plan Task Group (LANGTAG) (1996) warned against soon after the demise of apartheid in 1994.

What the literature has hardly explored, however, is how the new language policy could be aided to ensure that it achieves its intended goal (Heugh, 2009). In this chapter, I aim to do just that. More specifically, I not only offer a critical evaluation of the new language policy, I also draw on theoretical developments in language economics (Grin, 2017; Grin *et al.*, 2010) and critical theory (Bourdieu, 1991; Tollefson, 2013) to explore ways in which the new language policy could be implemented for the benefit of all rather than a select few, the elite. Critical theory can shed light on why South Africa's new language policy has benefited only the elite and their preferred language, English, while marginalizing many, the majority of the country's population – the African people – and their economically minoritized languages, the Indigenous African languages. Economics, notes Grin (2003), can help to look at different choices about language in terms of advantages and drawbacks.

Some might argue that since language planning is a long-term affair, it may be too soon to evaluate the policy. I argue that language policy must be evaluated periodically, especially if language practices do not match the intended goal of the policy, as the literature on language policy and practices in post-apartheid South Africa has documented. But first, in the next section, I briefly discuss the historical context in which South Africa's new language policy was developed. This is important because language policy is a context-bound activity; that is, it can only be understood in the socio-historical context in which it was developed (Cooper, 1989; Ricento, 2013; Tollefson, 2013). The subsequent section presents the new language policy itself. This will be followed by a discussion of the two theoretical frameworks mentioned earlier – critical theory and language economics – for they have the potential to not only explain why South Africa's new language policy has failed, but also to offer useful insights for policy implementation. The last section offers suggestions for policy revision and implementation, drawing on both language economics and critical theory as well as successful case studies of Indigenous language revitalization around the world.

The Historical Background to South Africa's Multilingual Language Policy

Language played a pivotal role in apartheid South Africa, for the apartheid government used language as a tool for discrimination against and oppression of the country's majority population, the African people. A case in point is the 1953 apartheid legislation known as The Bantu Education Act, which I have discussed elsewhere (Kamwangamalu, 2008). Briefly, the legislation, the effects of which are likely to negatively impact South Africa's language policies for generations to come, was aimed at reducing the influence of English in Black schools, enforcing the use of both English and Afrikaans on an equal basis as languages of learning and teaching in these schools, and extending mother tongue education (i.e. education through the medium of an African language) from grade 4 to grade 8. Black pupils' resistance to this legislation and the apartheid government's determination to enforce it led to the 1976 bloody Soweto uprisings, in which several pupils were killed.

As a result of the Bantu Education Act, in Black communities education through the medium of an Indigenous African language became synonymous with inferior education (Alexander, 1997; UNICEF, 2016). It was also perceived as a lure to self-destruction and as a trap by the apartheid government to prevent the oppressed majority from acquiring sufficient command of the high-status languages (English and Afrikaans), for it would enable them to compete with their White counterparts for well-paying jobs and prestigious career options. This stigma lingers on and has, in part, contributed to the negative attitudes that the African people have towards African languages as potential media of learning and teaching. It is against this background that, when apartheid ended in 1994, South Africa developed a new language policy, which I discuss in the next section.

The discussion of the new language policy draws attention to recent debates over the medium of instruction at South Africa's schools, including elementary (K-12), secondary, and tertiary institutions (Ndlangamandla, 2010; Nkosi, 2014; Rudwick & Parmegiani, 2013). The focus of the discussion here is on using the Indigenous languages, in addition to English and Afrikaans, throughout the entire educational system rather than at a particular educational level, whether K-12, secondary or tertiary education. I argue, in agreement with the afore-cited literature, that there is a mismatch between the new language policy and language practices in virtually all the high-status domains, including education. The mismatch, I argue further, is due to factors both internal and external to the policy. Internal factors include the escape clauses embedded within the policy, suggesting that the policy was not, at the outset, intended to change hearts and minds of the target population. External factors have to do with the *inheritance situation*, especially the legacy of the Bantu Education Act, and ensuing negative attitudes towards African languages as the medium of instruction in the schools. Other contributing factors include the stakeholders' vested interests; the lack of the political will to change the status quo; and the hegemony and instrumental value of English and Afrikaans vis-a-vis the official African languages in what

Bourdieu (1991) refers to as the linguistic marketplace – that is, the context in which the languages are used.

South Africa's New Language Policy: An Evaluation

Like language policy developments anywhere in the world, South Africa's new language policy is informed by language ideologies, which Tollefson (2011: 801) defines as a specific set of ideas or beliefs that individuals and groups advocate (e.g. communism, individualism, liberalism, socialism) (also, see McGroarty, 2010; Ricento, 2013). Shohamy (2006: xvii) views language ideologies as 'manipulative devices that central authorities use to inform language-in-education policies in particular purposely to serve their vested interests, "create language hierarchies, and marginalize and exclude groups…"' (see also Zhao, 2011: 917). Language ideologies, note Dyers and Abongdia (2010), are reflected in actual language practices – in the ways people talk, in what they say about language, their language choices, and their sociopolitical positioning with regards to different languages. Cobarrubias (1983) and Schmidt (1998) present language ideologies that capture the essence of South Africa's new language policy, the most relevant for our purpose being *pluralism, internationalization* and *vernacularization. Pluralism* entails the selection of several languages as official languages of the state. *Internationalization* refers to the choice of an exoglossic (i.e. external) language, usually a former colonial language such as English, as the official language of the state. In contrast, *vernacularization* refers to the selection of an Indigenous language as the official language of the state. South Africa's new language policy is a combination of all of these ideologies. It is pluralistic in the sense that it has given official recognition to 11 languages. Among the languages, one, English, is exoglossic; hence *internationalization*. Also, the policy involves *vernacularization* since it calls for African languages to be used in the high-status domains such as the educational system. The policy itself is stipulated as follows in South Africa's 1996 Constitution:

> (i) The official languages of the Republic (of South Africa) are Sepedi, Sesotho, Setswana, siSwati, Tshivenda, Xitsonga, Afrikaans, English, isiNdebele, isiXhosa and isiZulu. (The Constitution, 1996, Chapter 1, Section 6 (1))

The central goal of the new language policy has been to elevate the status of the nine official African languages against the backdrop of past discriminatory apartheid language policies such as the Bantu Education Act, as discussed in the previous section. In this respect, the Constitution states that:

> (ii) recognizing the historically diminished use and status of the indigenous languages of our people, the state must take practical and

positive measures to elevate the status and advance the use of these languages. (The Constitution, 1996, Chapter 1, section 6 (2))

One area where the government has sought to elevate the status of and thus revitalize the Indigenous languages is education. Concerning language use in this area, the post-apartheid Constitution stipulates that:

(iii) matters such as the medium in which a pupil's instruction takes place and the number of languages that are to be compulsory school subjects may not conflict with the language clause in the Constitution (Section 3) nor with Section 32, which provides that every person shall be entitled to instruction in the language of his or her choice *where this is reasonably practicable.* (The Constitution, 1996, Section 32(c), emphasis added)

Other language-related clauses in South Africa's Constitution include the following:

(iv) all official languages must enjoy parity of esteem and must be treated equitably. (The Constitution, 1996, Section 6 (2))

(v) the national government and provincial governments **may use** *any particular official languages* for the purposes of government, taking into account usage, practicality, expense, regional circumstances and the balance of the needs and preferences of the population as a whole or in the province concerned; but the national government and each provincial government **must** use at *least two official languages* (emphasis added).

Language planning scholars hailed the new language policy, with some describing it, perhaps too soon, as the most democratic on the continent (Chisanga, 2002: 101), ground-breaking and a milestone in the history of language policy and planning in the African continent. For example, Bamgbose (2003) writes that

viewed against the background of policies generally in Africa, … perhaps the most significant aspect of South Africa's language policy is respect for multilingualism … I am of the opinion that this policy stands to yield better dividends than monolingual policy embraced by many African countries. For one thing, the problem of exclusion of the masses will be considerably reduced, since nine African languages will be available to different segments of the population for participation in the national system. (2003: 51–52)

To verify the success of a language policy, one must determine whether the policy is reflected in language practices. It seems that South Africa's language-in-education practices do not match the listed constitutional language clauses. Note that a Black child is exposed to an education through the medium of an African language in only the first three years of primary education or K-12 level. During this period, English is taught as a subject but, thereafter, it takes over as the sole medium of instruction for the remainder of the educational system, including secondary and tertiary education. The abrupt switch from the medium of an African language to English as the medium of learning, the inadequate linguistic preparation of pupils in English prior to its use as the medium of learning, and pupils' lack of exposure to English in their everyday lives generally result in high failure rates and dropouts (Alexander, 1997; Webb, 2004). These outcomes have prompted calls for African languages to be used as the medium of learning throughout the entire educational system, as is the case for English and Afrikaans (Banda, 2010; Brock-Utne, 2009).

Despite these calls, African languages continue to be marginalized from the educational system in post-apartheid South Africa, much as they were in the apartheid era. But why is this so? I have already alluded to a number of factors, both internal and external, that interact in complex ways to impede policy implementation. One external factor, the Bantu Education Act, along with ensuing negative attitudes towards African languages, has already been discussed. Here, I would like to focus on internal obstacles to the policy, especially the escape clauses that are embedded within the policy itself. The escape clauses, which Bamgbose (2004: 68) describes as 'a clever device of making it possible for the implementation of the policy to be avoided,' can be noted in clauses (iii) and (v), above. With regard to clause (iii), it is realistically impossible in any multilingual society for everyone to receive an education through the language of their own choice. Being aware of this, policymakers perhaps intentionally embedded the escape clause, 'where this is reasonably practicable' in the language clause in the Constitution to impede policy implementation. Likewise, in clause (v), one notes such embedded clauses as '*may use any particular official languages*' and '*must use at least two official languages.*' The epistemic modal auxiliary 'may' and the deontic modal 'must' ensure that the status quo remains.

Until the end of apartheid in 1994, South Africa used only English and Afrikaans for the conduct of the business of the state. Since the post-apartheid Constitution does not specify which official languages should be used in which province or by the national government, both provincial and national governments have tacitly opted for the status quo; that is, they use English and Afrikaans as the languages of administration, much as was the case in the apartheid era. Consider, in the following subsection, language policy initiatives at South African schools, including K-12 and colleges and universities, which are intended as a response to the national language policy goal to revitalize the Indigenous African languages.

African language revitalization initiatives at K–12, and colleges and universities

As already noted, in South Africa the Indigenous African languages have traditionally been used both as the subject and medium of learning only in the first three years in K-12 education. In 2014, however, the government introduced a new policy mandating incremental learning of an African language in all schools through K-12. (For additional detail on K-12 language policy, see http://www.education.gov.za; http://www.thutong.doe.gov.za.) The policy does not, however, change the fact that subtractive bilingualism remains the norm in the South African educational system. Also, it is worth noting that the constitution of post-apartheid South Africa provides for the protection of such minority languages as the Khoisan languages. Some of these languages, such as Nama, Xu and Khwe, are now being taught in schools that have a high density of speakers of these languages. Further, the South African Broadcasting Corporation (SABC) has launched a radio station in the Northern Cape Province to revitalize the Khoisan languages (Kamwangamalu, 2008: 141–142). There is also the Khoekhoe and San Active Awareness Group (KSAAG), whose focus is on the preservation, promotion and development of the Khoikhoi language through various cultural initiatives, and the creation of opportunities to translate cultural resources into cultural capital to bring about local social development for the Khoisan people (http://ksaag.wordpress.com).

Language revitalization activities have also been undertaken at higher institutions. Recently, some South African colleges and universities have taken the initiative to revitalize African languages by using them as the medium of learning and teaching within their institutions (Rudwick & Permegiani, 2013). The University of KwaZulu-Natal, for instance, has included Zulu in its curriculum, requiring every student to learn the language. Zulu is also used as the medium of instruction for some subjects in the Department of isiZulu. Nkosi (2014: 249) reports that at this university, students in the School of Education 'are now able to conduct their research projects in the medium of isiZulu.' Along these lines, Turner and Wildsmith-Cromarty (2014: 303–304) report that Rhodes University has introduced first and second language isiXhosa courses, as well as Xhosa for a variety of disciplines, such as psychology, pharmacology, education, media studies and others. Similar policies have been put in place at South Africa's five historically White universities, as Turner and Wildsmith-Cromarty (2014) note in their survey of language policies and practices at those institutions.

Also noteworthy are Indigenous language revitalization activities for medical students at some of the country's institutions of learning. In this regard, Turner and Wildsmith-Cromarty (2014: 301) point out that the University of KwaZulu-Natal, for example, has introduced a language policy stipulating that no medical student can graduate without passing courses in isiZulu through a process of on-site clinical examination. The University of Cape Town has a similar language policy, requiring medical students to be proficient in isiXhosa and Afrikaans. The student is assessed by linguistic as well as clinical skills experts when a patient is being examined, to determine how efficiently the student is able to examine the patient in their mother tongue, be it Xhosa, English or Afrikaans. Along these lines, Alexander (2009: 16) notes that to increase enrollments in departments of African languages, the South African government has already begun offering attractive bursaries to students who intend teaching African languages or teaching in these languages.

South Africa's institutions of learning must be commended for their efforts to promote the development and use of African languages as the medium of learning. Despite these efforts, Turner and Wildsmith-Cromarty (2014) found that for all of those institutions, English remains the primary language of instruction and administration. Also, the institutions do not address the issue that is at the heart of the present study – the payoff of an education through the medium of an African language such as isiZulu or isiXhosa compared with that of an education through the medium of English or Afrikaans. I will address that issue in the last section of this chapter.

In sum, if South Africa's post-apartheid language practices are any indication (Kamwangamalu, 2000; Turner & Wildsmith-Cromarty, 2014), the country's new language policy informing language policy developments at K-12 and colleges and universities can be described as symbolic at best. This is because the policy has what Schiffman (1996) calls *a false front*; that is, it publicly and constitutionally promotes *pluralism*, but it conceals the reality that in practice only the former two official languages of the state, English and to a limited extent Afrikaans, benefit from the new language policy. This is captured in an article aptly titled, 'When 2 + 9 = 1: English and the Politics of Language Planning in a Multilingual Society – South Africa,' in which Kamwangamalu (2003) demonstrates that English remains the main language for the conduct of the business of the state. English has become so hegemonic that in terms of the social meanings – 'the set of values which a language itself encodes or symbolizes and which its use communicates' (Downes, 1984: 51) – the majority of parents in post-apartheid South Africa (including parents in some sections of the Afrikaans-speaking communities) want their children to be educated through the medium of English (V. de Klerk, 2000; Dyers, 2004).

It should be noted that the Pan South African Language Board (PANSALB) survey refuted the above claim, and the majority of parents who participated in the survey chose both the home language and English as their preferred medium of instruction through the entire educational system (PANSALB, 2002). It is noted further that since the government has not implemented additive bilingual policy, the parents choose the best resourced schools for their children's education, and English served as proxy. Yet, it has been nearly 20 years since the PANSALB study was conducted. Recent studies suggest strongly that African people hold negative attitudes towards African languages as mediums of instruction in the schools (e.g. Bekker, 2005: 237; Beukes, 2009: 43, 45; Kamwendo, 2006:

55; Masoke-Kadenge & Kadenge, 2013: 36; Ndlangamandla, 2010: 68; Nkosi, 2014: 248; Rudwick & Permegiani, 2013: 89; Tshotsho, 2013: 38–41; Turner & Wildsmith-Cromarty, 2014: 299). Reports in these and related studies (Kamwendo, 2006; Mutasa, 2006; Nodoba, 2010) show overwhelming preference for English – the language of power, prestige and high social status – over the Indigenous languages as instructional media. This is because, as Lazdina (2013: 398) remarks,

> [E]ven though most individuals in most ecolinguistic situations have many reasons for preferring one language over another in specific contexts, economic rationales are often a strong motivation for learning (or not learning) a regional or minority language than a societal ideology as advanced by language policy-makers or activists aiming to protect and promote a language. Many people want to understand how they can benefit from skills in a specific way.

In addition, the reports indicate that where learners have indicated a preference for an African language as an instructional medium, they have done so due to the loyalty and cultural affinity they have for these languages, a point that Rudwick (2004) has captured in a paper aptly titled 'Zulu – we need [it] for our culture: The Umlazi Township youth,' in which she explores attitudes towards Zulu as the medium of learning and teaching.

But how can South Africa extricate itself from this state of affairs and revitalize the Indigenous African languages? The question, as Mufwene and Vigouroux (2009: 20) put it, is 'whether the current ethnographic ranking of languages inherited from the colonial period, which has associated the non-European languages with less prestige, can be changed' to create space for the revitalization of African languages in the high-status domains such as the educational system. In the following section, I return to the two theoretical frameworks mentioned earlier, critical theory and language economics, to not only further explain why South Africa's new language policy has failed, but also to explore, subsequently and in response to Mufwene and Vigouroux's question, ways in which the policy can be aided to achieve its central goal to revitalize the Indigenous African languages in education.

Language Planning in South Africa: A Bourdieusian and Language Economics Perspective

To better understand why South Africa's post-apartheid language policy has not worked for all, I draw on Bourdieu's (1991) theory of practice, which addresses a wide range of issues concerned with language and language use. According to Bourdieu, individuals – Bourdieu calls them *agents* – have a set of dispositions or *habitus*, which incline them to act and react in certain ways. Bourdieu theorizes that all human actions take place within social fields, which are areas of struggle for institutional resources and forms of privilege and power. This has arguably been more so in South Africa than in any other African countries because of South Africa's complex colonial history. The country is known to have had a very long history of struggle, both political and linguistic, initially involving whites of British origin and whites of Dutch origin, and later the latter and the local majority African population. Following Bourdieu, the individuals who participate in language struggle have different aims – some (e.g. the elites/policymakers) will seek to preserve the status quo by legitimatizing some linguistic capital, in this case former colonial languages such as English and Afrikaans in South Africa; others (e.g. language activists and language professionals) to change it – and differing chances of winning or losing, depending upon where they are located in the structured space of their respective positions in society (Bourdieu, 1991: 14).

Bourdieu's theory of practice allows us to understand why the majority of South Africans value and prefer an education through the medium of an ex-colonial language such as English over an education through the medium of an African language. They view English as a commodity that commands an exchange value; perceive it as more advantageous than African languages in the benefits that it can bring to the user or, in Bourdieu's terms, they see linguistic capital inherent in this (ex-colonial) language (Tan & Rubdy, 2008). Put differently, South African parents associate ex-colonial languages such as English with a high socioeconomic value because an education through the medium of an ex-colonial language opens up doors of employment opportunities both at home and abroad. In contrast, an education through the medium of an African language does not offer comparable benefits even in the local linguistic marketplace. This state of affairs, which has been the norm both in South Africa and across the African continent as a whole since the colonial era to the present, is likely to endure unless the receivers of language planning (e.g. the masses) and policymakers work in tandem to change it. By not contesting the status quo, the receivers of language planning unwittingly collude in their own subjugation by the elites and collaborate, as Bourdieu (1991: 7) puts it, 'in the destruction of their instrument of expression' – the Indigenous languages.

The complementary theoretical framework, *language economics*, can also shed further light on why post-apartheid South Africa's multilingual language policy has not achieved its goal to promote African languages as the medium of instruction in the schools. *Language economics*, also known as the *economics of language*, focuses on theoretical and empirical analyses of the ways in which linguistic and economic variables influence one another (Grin, 2001; Vaillancourt, 1996). Understanding the interplay between economic and linguistic variables, say Grin *et al.* (2010: 140), 'is relevant to language policy, since this understanding sheds light on why firms require foreign language skills ...' or, in the context of the present study, why there is so much demand for these skills on South Africa's labor market, but virtually none for African languages. Some of the issues raised in *language economics* that are relevant to our evaluation of South Africa's multilingual language policy include the relevance of language as a defining element of economic processes such as production, distribution and consumption; and the relevance of language as a commodity in the acquisition of which individual actors may have a good reason to invest.

Within the framework of *language economics*, linguistic products such as language, language varieties, utterances, and accents are seen not only as goods or commodities to which the market assigns a value, but as signs of wealth or capital, which receive their value only in relation to a market, characterized by a particular law of price formation (Bourdieu, 1991). This means that the market, which Bourdieu defines as the social context in which linguistic products are used, fixes the price for a linguistic product or capital, the nature, and therefore the objective value of which the practical anticipation of this price helped to determine. The market value of linguistic capital such as a language or language variety is determined in relation to other linguistic products in the planetary economy (Coulmas, 1992). In South Africa, language practices in the educational system overwhelmingly indicate that English has by far more market value than its sister official languages, including Afrikaans and the nine African languages. This, I argue, is the unintended outcome of the policy itself, as is evident from the escape, language-related clauses embedded within the country's constitution.

South Africa's New Language Policy: A Way Forward

To find the way forward for post-apartheid South Africa's arguably staled language policy, I return to Bourdieu's approach to language, which has much in common with language economics. Recall that for Bourdieu – and this is also the view in language economics – linguistic products are a form of capital, which can be used to access other forms of capital – economic, cultural, political, and so on. African languages are not associated with any of these, despite the fact that, according to South Africa's Constitution, they are officially equal to English and Afrikaans. In other words, like the rest of the African continent, the discourse of language planning and policy in South Africa has never linked African languages with economic returns. What is needed, then, is for policymakers to establish this missing link between African languages and the economy so that speakers and potential users of these languages can view them as a commodity in which they can invest. Also, as I have noted elsewhere (Kamwangamalu, 2016: 172–173), the debate over Indigenous language revitalization in Africa, including South Africa, has tended to stress the costs rather than the benefits of revitalizing the Indigenous languages. It is usually argued that the costs of using African languages as instructional media will be too prohibitive: teachers must be trained to teach through the medium of the target language; didactic materials must be written; there are too many languages to accommodate them all as instructional media. In response, Brock-Utne (2005: 179) remarks that, 'when economists try to figure out how much it will cost to publish textbooks in African languages, they also have to figure out how much it costs to have African children sit year after year in school, often repeating a class, without learning anything.' In agreement, Vaillancourt and Grin (2000) note, very much to the point, that it costs more to train teachers to use a language in which they are not proficient – in this case a former colonial language – than to train teachers to teach through the language(s) they know and speak well – in this case an African vernacular. What this means is that Indigenous language revitalization need not be understood only in terms of the economic incentives that will make these languages attractive as instructional media to their speakers, but also in terms of the costs and benefits associated with educating South African children in their own languages compared with an education through a former colonial language. In other words, the costs-related argument usually overlooks the cognitive advantages that children have if they are schooled through the medium of their native languages. As UNICEF (2016: 2) notes aptly, 'learning in the child's own language results in better achievement than does learning in a language the child has not mastered.' (See also UNESCO, 2010, 2013.)

To change South Africa's inherited *habitus* – the fact that language 'consumers' are used to viewing African languages as unsuitable media of instruction in the schools – the languages must be assigned an economic value in South Africa's formal linguistic marketplace. This entails meeting at least the following condition: a certified knowledge of African languages must become, for speakers and non-speakers of the Indigenous languages, one of the requirements for access to employment in the public sector in particular. Indeed, in African schools, a certificate in an African language (in addition to a pass in English) is one of the requirements for graduation from K-12, but speakers of English or Afrikaans as mother tongue are not required to have certified knowledge of an African language. Also, the labor market does not require certified knowledge of an African language for access to employment. The government must work in tandem with the private and public sectors to enforce such a requirement. This requirement has served Dutch, and later English and Afrikaans, quite well in the history of South Africa's language planning and policy. Here, I will comment on how Afrikaans, which was viewed negatively as 'a kitchen language' (i.e. inferior, not suited for public use) when Whites of British origin were in power in South Africa (1795–1948), came to be associated with power, privileges, and upward social mobility (Malherbe, 1977). (See also Kathryn Graber's [2012] study of Buryat, showing its shifts from being a 'kitchen language' to a language of the nation.)

As I have pointed out elsewhere (Kamwangamalu, 2016), the oppressive nature of apartheid language-in-education policies to promote use of

Afrikaans in the high-status domains (education, media, government and administration) against the Indigenous languages is well documented (Alexander, 1992; Banda, 2010; Heugh, 2009; Stroud, 2001). I am not by any means advocating such policies, nor am I comparing the policies of an oppressive system – the apartheid system – with the policies of a demo-cratic society – post-apartheid South Africa. Instead, what I have sought to do is highlight the relationship between Afrikaans and formal economy, as reported in Malherbe (1977), for this has hardly been mentioned in the discussions of South Africa's post-apartheid language policy. Malherbe acknowledges that Afrikaans benefited both from the language loyalty of its speakers and the political and material support it received from the state. However, other factors, such as incentives and monetary awards, tend to be overlooked in the discourse about the success of Afrikaans. In this regard, Malherbe points out that Afrikaans was promoted through incentives and rewards for top achievers in the language. He notes that in order to encourage pupils to become bilingual in English and Afrikaans, the governments of Transvaal and Natal awarded monetary grants – then known as *bilingual bonuses or merit grants* – as inducements. Attached to these grants was the condition that such pupils, on completion of high school, had to go to a training college in order to become teachers. Put dif-ferently, Afrikaans speakers accepted Afrikaans as a viable medium of edu-cation because they knew what an Afrikaans-medium education would do for them in terms of upward social mobility.

Today, despite its diminished status and clout as a result of the end of apartheid and constitutional power shift in April 1994, Afrikaans contin-ues to compete with English in all the high-status domains of language use in post-apartheid South Africa: It is used in parliament, in primary, sec-ondary and tertiary education, in business, commerce and industry, and public signage. That incentives motivate students to learn a language is also reported in Nkosi's (2014) investigation into attitudes toward isiZulu as the medium of learning in the B.Ed program in the School of Education at the University of KwaZulu-Natal. She found that the students who agreed to enroll in this program did so because they received full tuition remission in recompense.

It follows that the African people, including speakers of English, Afrikaans and African languages, would be receptive to an education through the medium of an African language if that education would pro-vide for their needs and facilitate access to resources and employment (Kamwangamalu, 2004). As Eastman (1990) points out, people (and in this case the majority of South Africa's population) would not want to be educated through the medium of an Indigenous language if that language has no cachet in the broader social, political, and economic context. Also, the literature indicates that language policies tend to succeed if they are associated with economic outcomes (Grin, 2010, 2017). Grin (1996), for example, refers to a paper by Allan Sproull regarding the success of the

Gaelic language in Scotland. It is explained that the vernacularization of Gaelic succeeded because of what Sproull calls *Gaelic economy*, which he defines as all those activities (and jobs) whose principal purpose is the provision of Gaelic-related goods and services (Sproull & Ashcroft, 1993). Dominguez (1998) observes that the fact that access/promotion to certain jobs requires a language qualification creates a very visible economic component. This, says Grin (1996: 16), explains 'why people learn certain languages and why, if they have the choice of using more than one, they prefer to use one or the other.' Along these lines, in her article on the language situation in Nepal, Giri (2010) notes that speakers of Sino-Tibetan languages in that country are attracted to Nepali rather than to their own Indigenous languages as the medium of instruction. She says that, in Nepal, Nepali and English are status symbol and tools in the hands of the ruling elites, who use them to create linguistic hegemony within the polity. As a result, speakers of Sino-Tibetan languages choose Nepali as their second language because their own Indigenous languages do not have the same value as Nepali in the linguistic marketplace.

Conclusion

Success in language planning, says Ager (2005: 1039), is about 'succeeding in influencing language behavior, whether this is behavior in using language, identified with the phrase language-as-instrument, or behavior toward language, often described as language-as-object.' A piece of legislation, no matter how well crafted, cannot in itself succeed in changing African people's attitudes towards their Indigenous languages against the background of apartheid linguistic oppression, especially the Bantu Education Act. What is needed is a genuine, revised legislation supporting the demand for skills in the official Indigenous African languages for access to employment in the country's formal labor market, and requiring industries to provide services in these languages to the African people. These requirements will not only aid the new, post-apartheid policy in meeting its central goal to revitalize the Indigenous African languages, they will also serve as a catalyst for speakers and potential users of the Indigenous African languages to accept them as suitable media of instruction in the schools. Like any language planning exercise, the proposed revised legislation will come at a price. Money must be spent on curriculum materials development, teacher training, and research, as well as on making the consumers aware of the link between academic knowledge of the Indigenous African languages and economic payoffs.

In previous work (Kamwangamalu, 1997, 2015), I have called for research into African language revitalization to go beyond critiquing the wrongs of colonialism, inherited colonial policies and post-colonial language policies, for the criticism alone does not change the power relation in South Africa between English and Afrikaans and the Indigenous African languages. The suggestions presented in this chapter, drawing on insights from language economics and critical theory, are a modest response to that call.

Note

(1) Related to the 'personality principle' is the 'territoriality principle,' which constrains the choice of a language to be used in a given territory within a polity (Grosjean, 1982).

References

Alexander, N. (1992) Language planning from below. In R.K. Herbert (ed.) *Language and Society in Africa: The Theory and Practice of Sociolinguistics* (pp. 143–149). Johannesburg: Witwatersrand University Press.

Alexander, N. (1997) Language policy and planning in the new South Africa. *African Sociological Review* 1 (1), 82–98.

Alexander. N. (2009) Evolving African approaches to the management of linguistic diversity: The ACALAN project. *Language Matters* 40 (2), 3–18.

Ager, E.D. (2005) Prestige and image planning. In E. Hinkel (ed.) *Handbook of Research in Second Language Teaching and Learning* (pp. 1035–1054). Mahwah, NJ: Lawrence Erlbaum.

Bamgbose, A. (1991) *Language and the Nation: The Language Question in Sub-Saharan Africa.* Edinburgh: University of Edinburgh Press.

Bamgbose, A. (2003) A recurring decimal: English in language policy and planning. *World Englishes* 22, 419–431.

Bamgbose, A. (2004) Language planning and language policies: Issues and prospects. In P.G.J. van Sterkenburg (ed.) *Linguistics Today: Facing a Greater Challenge* (pp. 61–88). Amsterdam: John Benjamins.

Banda, F. (2010) Defying monolingual education: Alternative bilingual discourse practices in selected colored schools in Cape Town. *Journal of Multilingual and Multicultural Development* 31 (3), 221–235.

Bekker, I. (2005) Language attitudes and ethnolinguistic identity in South Africa: A critical review. In K.T. McAlister, K. Rolstad and J. MacSwan (eds) *ISB4: Proceedings of the 4th International Symposium on Bilingualism* (pp. 233–239). Somerville, MA: Cascadilla Press.

Beukes, A.-M. (2009) Language policy incongruity and African languages in post-apartheid South Africa. *Language Matters* 40 (1), 35–55.

Bourdieu, P. (1991) *Language and Symbolic Power.* Cambridge: Polity Press.

Brock-Utne, B. (2005) Language-in-education policies and practices in Africa with a special focus on Tanzania and South Africa – Insights from research in progress. In A.M.Y. Lin and P. Martin (eds) *Decolonization, Globalization – Language-in-Education Policy and Practice* (pp. 173–193). Clevedon: Multilingual Matters.

Brock-Utne, B. (2009) The adoption of the Western paradigm of bilingual teaching – Why does it not fit? In K.K. Prah and B. Brock-Utne (eds) *Multilingualism: An African Advantage* (pp. 18–51). Cape Town: CASAS.

Chisanga, T. (2002) Language policy in the new South Africa: A critical overview. In K. Legere and S. Fitchat (eds) *Talking Freedom: Language and Democratisation in the SADC Region* (pp. 95–108). Windhoek: Gamsberg Macmillan.

Cobarrubias, J. (1983) Ethical issues in status planning. In J. Cobarrubias and J.A. Fishman (eds) *Progress in Language Planning* (pp. 41–85). The Hague: Mouton.

Cooper, R.L. (1989) *Language Planning and Social Change*. Cambridge: Cambridge University Press.

Coulmas, F. (1992) *Language and the Economy*. Oxford: Blackwell.

De Klerk, G. (2002) Mother-tongue education in South Africa: The weight of history. *International Journal of the Sociology of Language* 154, 29–46.

De Klerk, V. (2000) To be Xhosa or not to be Xhosa … that is the question. *Journal of Multilingual and Multicultural Development* 21 (3), 198–215.

Dominguez, F. (1998) Toward a language-marketing model. *International Journal of the Sociology of Language* 134, 1–13.

Downes, W. (1984) *Language and Society*. London: Fontana Paperbacks.

Dyers, C. (2004) Attitudes and identity among some South African school children. *Per Linguam* 20 (1), 22–35.

Dyers, C. and Abongdia, J.-F. (2010) An exploration of the relationship between language attitudes and ideologies in a study of Francophone students of English in Cameroon. *Journal of Multilingual and Multicultural Development* 31 (2), 119–134.

Eastman, C. (1990) Language planning in post-apartheid South Africa. *TESOL Quarterly* 24 (1), 9–22.

Fasold, R. (1984) *The Sociolinguistics of Society*. Oxford: Basil Blackwell.

Fishman, J.A. (1971) The sociology of language. In J.A. Fishman (ed.) *Advances in the Sociology of Language Vol. 1* (pp. 217–404). The Hague: Mouton.

Giri, R.A. (2010) Cultural anarchism: The consequences of privileging languages in Nepal. *Journal of Multilingual and Multicultural Development* 31 (1), 87–100.

Graber, K. (2012). Public information: The shifting roles of minority-language news media in the Buryat Territories of Russia. *Language and Communication* 32 (2), 124-136.

Grin, F. (1996) The economics of language: Survey, assessment, and prospects. *International Journal of the Sociology of Language* 121, 17–44.

Grin, F. (2001) English as economic value: Facts and fallacies. *World Englishes* 20 (1), 65–78.

Grin, F. (2003) Language planning and economics. *Current Issues in Language Planning* 4 (1), 1–66.

Grin, F. (2017) The economics of language education. In T.L. McCarty and S. May (eds) *Language Policy and Political Issues in Education* (3rd edn, pp. 111–122). Cham, Switzerland: Springer International.

Grin, F., Sfreddo, C. and Vaillancourt, F. (2010) *The Economics of the Multilingual Workplace*. London: Routledge.

Grosjean, F. (1982) *Life with Two Languages*. Cambridge, MA: Harvard University Press.

Heugh, K. (2009) Into the cauldron: An interplay of Indigenous and globalized knowledge with strong and weak notions of literacy and language education in Ethiopia and South Africa. *Language Matters* 40 (2), 52–75.

Kamwangamalu, N.M. (1997) Multilingualism and education policy in post-apartheid South Africa. *Language Problems and Language Planning* 21 (3), 234-253.

Kamwangamalu, N.M. (2000) A new language policy, old language practices: Status planning for African languages in a multilingual South Africa. *South African Journal of African Languages* 20 (1), 50–60.

Kamwangamalu, N. M. (2003) When 2 + 9 = 1: English and the politics of language planning in a multilingual society: South Africa. In C. Mair (ed.) *The Politics of English as a World Language* (pp. 235–246). New York, NY: Rodopi B.V.

Kamwangamalu, N.M. (2004) Language policy/language economics interface and mother tongue education in post-apartheid South Africa. *Language Problems and Language Planning* 28 (2), 131–146.

Kamwangamalu, N.M. (2008) Can schools save Indigenous languages? Commentary from an African and international perspective. In N.H. Hornberger (ed.) *Can Schools Save Indigenous Languages? Policy and Practice on Four Continents* (pp. 136–151). New York, NY: Palgrave MacMillan.

Kamwangamalu, N.M. (2015) The sociolinguistic and language education landscapes of African Commonwealth countries. In A. Yiakoumetti (ed.) *Multilingualism and Language in Education – Sociolinguistic and Pedagogical Perspectives from Commonwealth Countries* (pp. 1–18). Cambridge: Cambridge University Press.

Kamwangamalu, N.M. (2016) *Language Policy and Economics: The Language Question in Africa.* London: Palgrave Macmillan.

Kamwendo, G.H. (2006) No easy walk to linguistic freedom: A critique of language planning during South Africa's first decade of democracy. *Nordic Journal of African Studies* 15 (1), 53–70.

Kaplan, R.B., Baldauf, R.B. and Kamwangamalu, N.M. (2011) Why educational language plans sometimes fail. *Current Issues in Language Planning* 12 (2), 105–124.

LANGTAG (1996) *Towards a National Language Plan for South Africa.* Pretoria: Government Printer.

Lazdina, S. (2013) A transition from spontaneity to planning? Economic value and educational policies in the process of revitalizing the regional language of Latgalian (Latvia). *Current Issues in Language Planning* 14 (3-4), 382–402.

Malherbe, E.G. (1977) *Education in South Africa II: 1923–75.* Cape Town: Juta and Co.

Masoke-Kadenge, E. and Kadenge, M. (2013) 'Declaration without implementation': An investigation into the progress made and challenges faced in implementing the Wits language policy. *Language Matters* 44 (3), 33–50.

McGroarty, M. (2010a) The political matrix of linguistic ideologies. In B. Spolsky and F.M. Hult (eds) *The Handbook of Educational Linguistics* (pp. 98–112). Malden, MA: Wiley-Blackwell.

Mchombo, S. (2014) Language, learning, and education for all in Africa. In Z. Babaci-Wilhite (ed.) *Giving Space to African Voices: Rights to Local Languages and Local Curriculum* (pp. 21–47). Boston, MA: Sense Publishers.

Mufwene, S. and Vigouroux, C.B. (2008) Colonization, globalization and language vitality in Africa: An introduction. In C.B. Vigouroux and S. Mufwene (eds) *Globalization and Language Vitality: Perspectives from Africa* (pp. 1–31). New York, NY: Continuum.

Mutasa, D.E. (2006) *African Languages in the 21st Century: The Main Challenges.* Pretoria: Simba Guru.

Ndlangamandla, S.C. (2010) (Unofficial) multilingualism in desegregated schools: Learners' use of and views towards African languages. *Southern African Linguistics and Applied Language Studies* 28 (1), 61–73.

Nkosi, Z.P. (2014) Postgraduate students' experiences and attitudes toward isiZulu as a medium of instruction at the University of KwaZulu-Natal. *Current Issues in Language Planning* 15 (3), 245–264.

Nodoba, G.T. (2010) Language preferences and behaviors of selected students and staff in the Faculty of Humanities at the University of Cape Town, in the context of the university's implementation of its 2003 language policy and plan: A qualitative study. Master's thesis. University of Cape Town.

PANSALB (2002) *Annual Report, 2001/2002.* Pretoria: Pan South African Language Board.

Pennycook, A. (1994) *The Cultural Politics of English as an International Language.* London: Longman.

Ricento, T. (2013) Language policy, ideology, and attitudes in English-dominant countries. In R. Bayley, R. Cameron and C. Lucas (eds) *The Oxford Handbook of Sociolinguistics* (pp. 524–544). Oxford, UK: Oxford University Press.

Rudwick, S. (2004) Zulu – We need [it] for our culture: The Umlazi Township youth. *South African Linguistics and Applied Language Studies* 22 (3/4), 159–172.

Rudwick, S. and Parmegiani, A. (2013) Divided loyalties: Zulu vis-à-vis English at the University of KwaZulu-Natal. *Language Matters* 44 (3), 89–107.

Schiffman, H.F. (1996) *Linguistic Culture and Language Policy.* London: Routledge.

Schmidt, R.J. (1998) The politics of language in Canada and the United States: Explaining the differences. In T. Ricento and B. Burnaby (eds) *Language and Politics in the United States and Canada* (pp. 37–70). Mahwah, NJ: Lawrence Erlbaum.

Shohamy, E. (2006) *Language Policy: Hidden Agendas and New Approaches.* London: Routledge.

Sproull, A. and Ashcroft, B. (1993) *The Economics of Gaelic Language Development.* Glasgow: Glasgow Caledonian University.

Stroud, C. (2001) African mother-tongue programs and the politics of language: Linguistic citizenship versus linguistic human rights. *Journal of Multilingual and Multicultural Development* 22 (4), 339–355.

Tan, P. and Rubdy, R. (eds) (2008) *Language as a Commodity: Global Structures, Local Marketplaces.* London: Continuum.

The Constitution of the Republic of South Africa (1996) Pretoria: Government Printer.

Tollefson, J.W. (2011) Ideology in second language education. In E. Hinkel (ed.) *Handbook of Research in Second Language Teaching and Learning* (pp. 801–816). New York and London; Routledge.

Tollefson, J.W. (2013) Language policy in a time of crisis and transformation. In J.W. Tollefson (ed.) *Language Policies in Education – Critical Issues* (2nd edn, pp. 11–34). New York, NY: Routledge.

Tshotsho, Baba P. (2013) Mother tongue debate and language policy in South Africa. *International Journal of Humanities and Social Science* 3 (13), 1–44.

Turner, N. and Wildsmith-Cromarty, R. (2014) Challenges to the implementation of bilingual/multilingual policies at tertiary institutions in South Africa (1995–2012). *Language Matters* 45 (3), 295–312.

UNESCO (2010) *Education for All Global Monitoring Report: Reaching the Marginalized. Regional Fact Sheet – Sub-Saharan Africa.* Paris: UNESCO.

UNESCO (2013) *Adult and Youth Literacy: National, Regional and Global Trends, 1985–2015.* UIS. June 2013.

UNICEF (2016) The impact of language policy and practice on children's learning: Evidence from Eastern and Southern Africa. Retrieved 13 December 2017 from http://nces.ed.gov/surveys/pirls/countries.asp

Vaillancourt, F. (1996) Language and socioeconomic status in Quebec: Measurement, findings, determinants, and policy costs. *International Journal of the Sociology of Language* 121, 69–92.

Vaillancourt, F. and Grin, F. (2000) *The Choice of a Language in Instruction: The Economic Aspects. Distance Learning Course on Language Instruction in Basic Education.* Washington, DC: World Bank Institute.

Webb, V. (2004) African languages as media of instruction: Stating the case. *Language Problems and Language Planning* 28 (2), 147–173.

Zhao, S. (2011) Actors in language planning. In E. Hinkel (ed.) *Handbook of Research in Second Language Teaching and Learning Vol. 2* (pp. 905–923). New York, NY: Routledge.

Part 2

Pedagogies and Processes in Indigenous Language Reclamation

3 The Impact of 'Culturalcy' in Ngā Kura ā Iwi Tribal Schools in Aotearoa/NZ: *Mō Tātou, Mā Tātou, E Ai Ki a Tātou* – For Us, By Us, Our Way

Cath Rau, Waimātao Murphy and Pem Bird

This chapter describes implementation processes and outcomes of Te Marautanga o Aotearoa (TMoA), the national curriculum for learners in Māori medium settings. Schools that implement TMoA develop a localized curriculum (marau ā kura) and graduate profile (whakaputanga ākonga) that together express the values, principles and behaviors desired by a school's community for its children. Schools that affiliate to Ngā Kura ā Iwi o Aotearoa are particularly committed to meeting tribal aspirations via these two mechanisms. Two tribal schools affiliated with this organization are profiled here to illustrate how 'culturalcy' contributes to the academic, linguistic and cultural success of learners in such settings.

Introduction

Ngā Kura ā Iwi o Aotearoa (NKAI) comprises an independent professional community of schools in Aotearoa/New Zealand committed to advancing and realizing the aspirations of Māori tribal groups and entities in education. Membership in this organization is voluntary. There are currently 24 affiliated tribal schools serving approximately 2900 students and their communities. Student numbers in schools range from 18 in the smallest school to 350 in the largest.

It is incumbent upon these schools to provide learning contexts that not only equip graduates with the skills, motivation, confidence and academic qualifications to pursue the careers and vocations of their choosing but to do so in ways that nurture, value and celebrate their (tribal) identity, culture and language, supporting them to be valued members of their tribal groups, society in general and global citizens.

NKAI refers to this as 'culturalcy,' arguing that this better guarantees success for Māori students. The academic track record of senior students in tribal schools is adding credence to this claim, challenging the legacy of underachievement that has long been the experience of Māori students where English language is the predominant and often sole language of instruction (i.e. English medium schooling).

This chapter describes initiatives and opportunities that have coalesced for Māori medium settings and how NKAI as an organization is leveraging these, forging new pathways that privilege a tribally based education in the compulsory schooling sector. Two kura ā iwi schools are profiled, providing insights into how culturalcy is expressed and translated into practice.

Ngā Kura ā Iwi o Aotearoa: Genesis, Organization, Principles, Values and Practices

Genesis

A gathering to discuss the formation of a collective of schools to create a unique learning opportunity for students grounded in the cultural inheritance of tribal forebears was convened in 2006 by Pem Bird, the principal of Te Kura Kaupapa Motuhake o Tawhiuau, a school in the small rural township of Murupara. Representatives from eight schools from the Bay of Plenty, Waikato, Tainui and Raukawa areas attended. After receiving the endorsement of their respective tribal communities, a further series of gatherings took place, during which the kura ā iwi name was adopted. A constitution was developed encapsulating the hopes, dreams and aspirations of this small number of tribal educators and the collective was formalized in 2009 as an Incorporated Society with a starting membership of 11 schools. Pem Bird was voted as the inaugural chairperson.

Te Ariki Tumu Te Heu Heu, the paramount chief of the Ngāti Tuwharetoa tribe and the recognized leader of one of the two remaining 'royal houses' of Māoridom, formally endorsed NKAI at the Annual General Meeting in 2010. This provided a major boost for the organization. NKAI does not have a formal recruitment policy, preferring instead for schools and their tribal communities to initiate contact and pursue affiliation. In 2015, the membership grew to 24 schools.

Organizational structure

The philosophy, curriculum and practices of NKAI derive from and belong to tribal groups (*iwi*), and Māori is the primary language of instruction in NKAI schools. Te Kāhui Reo Taketake is the tribal arm of the organization and comprises respected tribal elders and representatives. Recognized as guardians and custodians of their respective tribal knowledge and dialect(s), they act as cultural advisors and work with their schools to ensure their tribal identity is the basis of educational provision.

Ngā Ringa Raupā is the professional arm of NKAI, and is made up of representatives from affiliated schools, including students. Support from Ngā Ringa Raupā is particularly focused on the governance and management of Ngā Kura ā Iwi as an organization and the well-being and success of schools in the collective. Te Kahui Reo Taketake, Ngā Ringa Raupā and the operational arm of the organization led by Te Kaiwhakahaere (executive officers) are collectively named Te Maru o Ngā Kura ā Iwi o Aotearoa.

Principles and values

As expressed in its constitution, NKAI seeks to privilege tribal knowledge, customs, and language in teaching and learning programs, and promote the tribal ancestral world nationally and internationally. Additional clauses provide the blueprint for how the membership behaves and interacts to achieve its aims and objectives, including collaborating and caring for one another, ensuring that customary practices guide ways of working, commenting on educational matters and facilitating the interests of NKAI and the tribal groups served.

Practices

In order to progress its aims and objectives, NKAI has a comprehensive program of development that is supported by funding from the New Zealand Ministry of Education. Major activities include the delivery of a professional development program designed to assist NKAI schools to be highly responsive to the tribal groups they serve as well as strengthen the capability of school governors, managers and teachers. The membership is also actively exploring new approaches to personalizing instructional programs for students and designing online solutions to address issues such as access to teachers of specialized senior secondary school subjects. Migrating to iCloud services will also greatly advance opportunities for all participants in the NKAI movement to interact and network for a variety of purposes.

A NKAI research project is currently seeking to identify innovative practices consistent with the NKAI ethos in order to retain newly trained teachers. Alarming national attrition data indicate that 70% of Māori medium teachers vacate their teaching positions in Māori medium classrooms, usually to take up other positions within the education sector within five years of entering the Māori medium workforce (Ministry of Education, 2010).

A memorandum of understanding with the Ministry of Education sets out the nature of the relationship and guides interactions between its national and regional offices and NKAI to ensure that the interests of NKAI are best served. NKAI is also working with other government agencies such as the Education Review Office (ERO), which is responsible for evaluating and reporting on the education and care of students in schools and early childhood services. Reviews are carried out approximately every three years. NKAI and ERO have co-constructed a framework that is being piloted for conducting reviews and evaluating the performance of NKAI membership schools. A common denominator of these initiatives and activities is that NKAI sets the direction and is proactive in finding its own solutions to the issues and challenges the membership identifies and faces.

In her address at an NKAI gathering in July 2015, the Minister of Education – the first Māori in history to hold this office – used the phrase 'future focused, ancestrally driven' to describe the agenda of Ngā Kura ā Iwi. This description was received with enthusiasm by the membership, aptly and succinctly representing the underlying philosophy and practices of NKAI.

NKAI Key Terms

The key terms and phrases that surround Figure 3.1 form the discourse in NKAI. They have been included here because they provide insights into NKAI ways of thinking and being that help define the nature of relationships between schools and communities, and influence and shape decisions about what constitutes valuable and valued learning and teaching in affiliated schools.

The State of the Māori Language and Tribal Dialects

The educational initiatives that emerged in the 1970s and 1980s, including *kōhanga reo* (early childhood Māori 'language nest' preschools) and *kura kaupapa Māori* (Māori-language schools) have contributed significantly to the revitalization of the Māori language (Ka'ai, 2004; Moorfield & Johnston, 2004; O'Regan, 2012). Despite these and other efforts, census data report a decline in the number and percentage of Māori speakers of the Māori language from 25.2% in 2001 to 21.3% in 2013 (Ministry of Social Development, 2016),[1] while statistics generated by the Ministry of Education (n.d.) show a trend of reducing participation in Māori medium education.

In a 2010 report, the Waitangi Tribunal, a permanent inquiry commission on Māori claims related to breaches of the 1840 Treaty of Waitangi,[2] criticizes the Crown for its failure to uphold law and policy to protect and preserve the Māori language and safeguard tribal dialects. The promotion

Iwi	Iwi – literally bones – refers to a group of people, including tribes who are descended from an eponymous ancestor and associated with a distinct territory; hence, Kura ā Iwi – tribal schools.
Mana whenua	This term acknowledges the jurisdiction that a particular group or groups (often iwi sub-groups) have over specific land or territory, usually achieved through occupation over generations. This occupation is often enshrined in that tribe's history and legends. NKAI schools acknowledge and privilege mana whenua.
E kore au e ngaro, he kākano i ruia mai i	'My *iwi* identity will not fade.' 'It is derived from my revered *Rangiatea* ancestors through genealogy passed down generation to generation and lives on in myself and my descendants.' This well-known proverb appears in the NKAI logo (Figure 3.1) and reinforces the importance of belonging and knowing who you are.

Figure 3.1 Ngā Kura ā Iwi o Aotearoa logo

Tukuihotanga	The gifts – knowledge, language and dialects, and customs passed down from forebears – i.e. culturalcy. The term culturalcy was coined by Pem Bird, founding member and, at the time of this writing, co-chair of NKAI, to counterbalance the (over)emphasis placed on literacy and numeracy in the Māori medium equivalent of national standards, Ngā Whanaketanga Rumaki Māori (Ministry of Education, 2010), introduced into the primary school sector in 2011.
Uri	Uri means descendants and is the preferred NKAI term for a student or learner. It infers a duty of care and responsibility that transcends traditional, western centric understandings and expressions of the teacher–student relationship.
Mana motuhake	Embraces and celebrates the diversity and uniqueness of NKAI school communities and their right to self-determination (mana motuhake).
Te Tihi o Angitu	Refers to the focus of NKAI as symbolized in the NKAI logo (Figure 3.1) – achieving the pinnacle of excellence for uri and all NKAI stakeholders.
Mō Tātou, Mā Tātou, E Ai Ki a Tātou	This translates as 'for us, by us, our way.' This expression of self-determination is used to emphasize the resolve of NKAI to take responsibility for its own destiny based on a profound belief in its inherent capability to do so.

of dialect became a casualty in a process that required tribal groups to come together to form a united national front and to concentrate on the survival of the Māori language in response to the alarming statistics about its health that emerged in the 1970s.

Māori tribal dialects are associated with expansive geographic areas that include regional variations, and within those regions, tribal variations. In general, dialects are not so distinct as to be incomprehensible to speakers of other tribal dialects. The major differences lie in the pronunciation of words, vocabulary choices and idiomatic expressions (Harlow, 2005). However, despite these subtle differences, O'Regan (2006) emphasizes the importance of the different dialects of Māori as key identity markers.

The fragility of Māori tribal dialects was illustrated by the Waitangi Tribunal (2010) in the following statement:

> In any language with faltering health – or, in this case a faltering revival – its own variations must be its most vulnerable elements. This is the inevitable state of tribal dialects today, with some elements already all but gone and others clearly in peril. Unless dialects begin to be spoken more by younger Māori, their prospects beyond the next 20 years are obviously bleak. (p. 41)

The efforts of Ngā Kura ā Iwi to promote dialect

NKAI is consciously and deliberately focused on working closely with tribal groups to secure, protect and promote dialect. NKAI has developed a tool (*Mana Reo*) to enable tribal schools in the membership to evaluate their practice and efforts towards preserving and promoting tribal dialect and the Māori language. The following statements in the tool capture what *te tihi o angitū* – the pinnacle of excellence – epitomizes in this respect, and outlines the shared responsibility of school, school communities and tribal groups in achieving this.

- **Students** build high levels of proficiency in the Māori language as they progress through the school; they strongly value and advocate for the Māori language and are often heard speaking Māori spontaneously with each other.
- **Tribal groups** feel highly valued as language owners and partners. They readily share their expertise to build school capability in the Māori language and the local dialect. They highly value their partnership with the school and see it as a critically important vehicle for maintaining and growing the language. Iwi can clearly see that the school is raising the profile of the Māori language and its local dialect and impacting positively on its use in the wider community.
- **School leadership** has created a high sense of clarity around what the school and its mana whenua seek to achieve for the language

proficiency of students, and effectively mobilizes the full range of talents, expertise and resources from the wider school community to realize the vision. There is a clear shared understanding of the individual and collective roles and responsibilities of families, sub-tribes and tribes, and the school to grow the local dialect and the Māori language. Each of the different kinds of contribution are valued.

• **Teachers, school leaders, students, families and tribal groups** all have a sound understanding of effective language acquisition theory and practice, such that they can all effectively support learning in and through the Māori language. They clearly value, enthusiastically promote and take great pride in everyone's use of the Māori language and dialect. As a result, students see their bilingualism as highly advantageous. Their demeanor, attitude and behavior reflect high levels of self-worth, self-esteem and personal pride.

• **The curriculum and the provision of instruction** in Māori (and other languages) are configured in such a way as to maximize high levels of student language proficiency and academic success as Māori. This means making the best possible use of resources and capabilities the school can access for the benefit of students. The school is collaborating with tribal groups to create its own resources to help support and sustain the growth of the Māori language and local dialects. Critical thinking about historical and contemporary issues is taught from and embedded in a distinctively Māori and local iwi political and cultural perspective, and this is used to guarantee that the Māori language and Māori perspectives are given power and influence in society. Dialect permeates all communications, written and oral, from and within the kura. It is a clear strategic priority to nurture and grow *te mita o te iwi* (the rhythm, intonation, pronunciation and sound of the language and the rules governing language use) and *me ngā tikanga* (customary practices) – as evidenced in the dedication of time, effort and resources.

NKAI co-chairperson Pem Bird expressed the importance of his tribal language and the personal responsibility he feels for its survival:

> My wellbeing, my wellness, my health lives in my reo [language]! Conversely the wellness, wellbeing and health of my reo lives in me! We are inseparable! If my reo dies, I die! I cease to have an identity! I cease to have a culture! My uniqueness is no more! I will have become an extinct species! But it is I however, who holds the fate of my reo and thus my own fate in my very own hands. It is I and I alone who is responsible as to whether my reo has a future. No one else has the mana to make me want to learn my reo! And it is I who has to be held to account for the fate of my reo. (personal communication with Cath Rau, 2015)

The Efforts of Ngā Kura ā Iwi to Strengthen Tribal Identity

According to Statistics New Zealand (2013), most Māori adults – 80% – are able to identify their tribal affiliations. Seventy-one percent know their ancestral tribal gathering place (*marae*). Knowledge of other identity markers (such as ancestral canoe, ancestor, mountains, and waterways) ranged from 52% to 58%. Of the 371,000 Māori adults who knew their ancestral marae, 77% thought of it as the place where 'they belonged' (their *tūrangawaewae*). Even after decades of assimilation and the effects of urbanization where young Māori adults left their traditional homes to chase employment opportunities, they have maintained a strong sense of tribal identity.

One of the complexities resulting from the mobility of the Māori population is that teachers in Māori medium schools may not be speakers of the local dialect. Likewise there are increasing numbers of students in Māori medium schools (and their families) who are geographically, linguistically, spiritually and emotionally distanced and disconnected from their ancestral tribal roots. In the latter case, NKAI sees this as an opportunity to ensure that these students acquire a tribal identity in relation to their geographical location, arguing that this is better than not having one at all. This can lead to those students actively seeking out their genealogical tribal identity while the schools also endeavor to make those tribal links more explicit. NKAI schools have also been actively 'growing' their own workforce, targeting and encouraging students to gain teaching qualifications and return to take up teaching positions in NKAI schools.

Ngā Kura ā Iwi and Māori Education

Māori medium schooling

The vast majority of Māori students in Aotearoa/New Zealand are enrolled in English medium classrooms. Māori medium includes students who are taught the curriculum in the Māori language for at least 51% of the time (Māori language immersion levels 1–2; see May *et al.*, 2004 for a discussion of immersion levels). Table 3.1 indicates the number of enrollments in level 1 immersion programs has been gradually increasing over time, whereas the numbers of enrollments in level 2 programs has tended to fluctuate over the same period.

As of the first of July 2014, there were a total of 118,503 Māori students in year 1 to 8 classrooms. Of those students, 17,713 (15%) were enrolled in Māori medium programs in 282 schools. Students in Māori medium schooling represent a mere 2.3% of the total school population (Ministry of Education, n.d.)

Twenty-four schools, all located on the North Island, are currently members of NKAI and serve approximately 2900 students. These schools

Table 3.1 Number of students in Māori medium by Māori language immersion level (2009–2014)

Māori language immersion level (% instruction in Māori)	2009	2010	2011	2012	2013	2014	Change 2013–2014
Level 1: 81–100%	11,634	11,738	11,818	11,816	12,028	12,704	679
Level 2: 51–80%	5161	4587	4729	4976	5315	5009	−306
Māori medium total	16,795	16,325	16,547	16,792	17,343	17,713	370

Source: New Zealand Ministry of Education (n.d.).

Table 3.2 Constituency in NKAI schools, 2015

Number	Level/Type	Years	Student years of age
11	Primary	1–8	5–12 years
11	Composite	1–13	5–18 years
1	Intermediate/ Secondary	7–13	12–18
1	Secondary	9–13	14–18

account for 16% of the student population in Māori medium education. Table 3.2 shows the NKAI constituency in 2015.

Twenty-three NKAI schools deliver level 1 immersion in Māori programs in which the Māori language is used instructionally for 81–100% of the time. At the time of this writing, the remaining school was working towards delivering a level 1 immersion program.

How well are Ngā Kura ā Iwi schools doing academically on national measures?

Ngā Whanaketanga Rumaki Māori (the Māori medium equivalent of National Standards)[3] describe the oral language, reading, writing and mathematics skills and knowledge that year 1 to at least year 8 students need to learn in all other learning areas across the Māori medium curriculum (Te Marautanga o Aotearoa). Ngā Whanaketanga Rumaki Māori results were first published in 2012. As Table 3.3 shows, in 2014, achievement levels of NKAI students were similar to the achievement levels of all students in Māori medium programs.

The goal of the current government is for 85% of students to be achieving or exceeding national expectations by 2017 in these specified learning strands. Based on these results there is still much work to be done across the Māori medium sector including strengthening teacher capability to make accurate judgements of achievement levels.

Table 3.3 Comparison of student achievement in NKAI schools with student achievement in all Māori medium schools from Whanaketanga Rumaki Māori data in 2014

Learning strand	Percentage of students in NKAI schools achieving national expectations	Percentage of all students Māori medium achieving national expectations
Reading	65%	67.2%
Oral language	60%	59%
Writing	58%	57.7%
Mathematics	59%	58%

Source: New Zealand Ministry of Education (personal communication).

The National Certificate of Educational Achievement (NCEA) provides an opportunity to analyze the achievement of students aged 14 to 17. NCEA 2 is considered the minimum requirement for success, opening a range of training and vocational choices post-secondary school. The results since 2011 indicate high success for students in Māori medium (non-NKAI schools) and the best results since 2011 are being achieved by students in NKAI albeit that this is less than 20% of the total population of Māori medium enrollments (Table 3.4). While the achievement for Māori students in English medium schools has been improving, it is still well below the achievement of students in Māori medium and NKAI schools.

Table 3.4 Percentage of students leaving school with NCEA level 2 or above (2010–2014)

Student population	2009	2010	2011	2012	2013	2014
Students in Ngā Kura a Iwi schools	64.6%	71.4%	78.6%	79.4%	85.4%	85.2%
Māori medium students (non-NKAI schools)	57.4%	65.0%	75.0%	72.2%	77.4%	76.5%
Māori students in English medium schools	45.6%	49.5%	52.5%	55.4%	55.8%	58.6%
All Students	67.5%	70.2%	72.4%	74.7%	74.7%	77.1%

Source: Ministry of Education, 2015 (personal communication with Cath Rau).

Opportunities the National Curriculum Affords Tribal Schools

The revised national curriculum for Māori medium settings which came into effect in 2008–2009 – *Te Marautanga o Aotearoa* – includes a directive to schools to design and implement a localized curriculum or *marau ā kura*. This gives NKAI schools license to deliberately and freely co-construct with mana whenua (i.e. the group or groups with occupational rights over the tribal territory where the school is located) teaching and learning contexts that privilege the knowledge, language, practices and culture of mana whenua. This is premised on the belief that a deeper understanding of one's own localized identity improves the chances of relating to the identity and reality of others, thus expanding individuals' sense of self and relative place in the world.

Decades of colonization have meant that historically the experiences of non-Māori and 'others' have been deemed to be of greater value, while the experiences and realities of Māori have been treated as inconsequential and inferior. As discussed earlier, NKAI unabashedly seeks to develop a local tribal identity. For many Māori students who have strong genealogical links to the area, this is their birthright and inheritance. For Māori students from other tribal areas, this can reaffirm their sense of belonging or strengthen their resolve to discover their ancestral roots.

NKAI has developed an evaluative tool in the form of a rubric to enable schools in the membership to evaluate their practice and relationship with mana whenua (tribal entities with recognized authority over land). The tool captures what te tihi o angitū – the pinnacle of excellence – epitomizes in this respect by providing descriptions of high to low levels of capability for defined criteria. These criteria require consideration of the extent to which tribal identity and aspirations are infused into the localized curriculum, how well mana whenua as co-educators are valued and involved in the co-construction and delivery of the curriculum, how well school leaders, teachers, students and tribal members are actively 'growing' tribal knowledge, the extent to which school staff are actively participating in local tribal events, and the role of school governance in setting strategic direction to align with tribal aspirations.

Te Marautanga o Aotearoa further instructs schools to develop a graduate profile in consultation with its community (Ministry of Education, 2008). This provides schools in NKAI's membership with the opportunity to identify, agree upon and nurture with families, mana whenua and other tribal entities, the values, beliefs, attitudes and attributes considered desirable for students who will eventually emerge from the compulsory school sector and take their place in society as valued, well-grounded and contributing citizens.

Kua Ea, NKAI's strategic plan, seeks to ensure that students are culturally and intellectually autonomous and enjoy good health and wellbeing. Each tribal school in NKAI is charged with the responsibility of working towards and achieving these high-level outcomes with the flexibility to shape how this is expressed and manifested at the local level. To illustrate this, two schools from the Waikato/Tainui tribal region – Te Kura Kaupapa Māori o Bernard Fergusson, a school that serves year 1–8 students, and Ngā Taiātea Wharekura, a secondary school for years 9–13 students – are profiled in the next section.

Two Kura ā Iwi Schools

Ko Tainui te waka
Ko Taupiri te maunga
Ko Waikato te awa
Ko Te Wherowhero te tangata.

Tainui is the ancestral canoe
Taupiri is the mountain
Waikato is the river
Te Wherowhero is the revered ancestor.

Māori invariably identify and reference themselves (among other things) to an ancestral canoe, significant geographical landmarks and an eponymous ancestor. Multiple tribal memberships result in multiple references being claimed. Both tribal schools profiled in this section are located within the tribal boundaries of Waikato/Tainui. Waikato, the tribe, has the distinction of being the only tribe in Aotearoa/New Zealand that takes its name from its ancestral river. Waikato/Tainui is also acknowledged as the guardian and caretaker of Kīngitanga – a political institution founded in 1858 with the aim of uniting Māori under a single sovereign (Dictionary of New Zealand Biography, 1996).

The tribal strategic plan, Whakatupuranga Waikato-Tainui 2050 (Waikato Tainui, n.d.), provides the blueprint for the cultural, social and economic advancement of descendants of Tainui – the ancestral canoe that traveled from Hawaiiki, the homeland, to Aotearoa/New Zealand – and Waikato, the tribal collective. Three critical elements in Whakatupuranga Waikato-Tainui 2050 have been identified as fundamental in equipping Waikato-Tainui generations with the capacity to shape their own future. These include:

(1) a pride and commitment to uphold their tribal identity and integrity;
(2) a diligence to succeed in education and beyond; and
(3) a self-determination for socio-economic independence.

The first element recognizes the importance of Waikato/Tainui tribal history, tribal-specific knowledge and knowledge systems, dialect and customary practices. The focus of the second element of the tribal strategic plan is to create a culture of success that generates opportunities and choices, so that tribal members enjoy success in all their endeavors. The contribution of the individual is valued in that individuals contribute to collective capability from which the whole

---

Tāwhiao, second King of the royal house of Waikato/Tainui (born 1822 – died 1894), stated 'Maaku anoo e hanga tooku nei whare ...' let us be in control of our own destiny in order to face and overcome the challenges of the future.

collective can potentially benefit. Determination to develop and grow tribal assets characterizes the focus of the third element of the strategy. Fundamental to this is having tribal personnel with the requisite skills and capability.

Te Kura Kaupapa Māori o Bernard Fergusson

The first author of this chapter is a former teacher at this school; her husband has been the chairperson of the governing body, the Board of Trustees, for five terms (15 years), and their three children are all graduates of the school. Te Kura Kaupapa Māori o Bernard Fergusson is located in a semi-rural town called Ngāruawahia, which is approximately 100 kilometers or a 1¼ hour's drive south of Auckland and a 20–minute drive north of the city of Hamilton. The school is located in close proximity to Tūrangawaewae Marae. This significant tribal meeting place, landmark and complex was established during the 1920s and 1930s and is attributed to the efforts of (Princess) Kirihaehae Te Puea Herangi, of the royal Waikato/Tainui household (King, 1977). The place is considered to be the center of the Kīngitanga movement. Today Tūrangawaewae (which means a place to stand, a place of belonging) hosts many tribal and national events. Many of the descendants of Te Puea and the families who traveled with her in the early 1920s from their settlement further north to establish Tūrangawaewae (including the family of the current Board of Trustees chairperson) attend the school.

A well-known saying of Princess Te Puea – *Mahia te mahi hei painga mō te* iwi (work for the betterment of the people) – is the guiding philosophy of the school and forms the basis for upholding and perpetuating the following values:

Manaakitia te iwi	Know how to care for and provide hospitality for and to the people.
Whāngaitia te tangata	Feed (nurture) people irrespective of where they are from.
Kia mau ki te aroha me te	If all else fails, hold fast to the values of love, peace and goodwill.

The original name of Ngāruawahia was Wāhia Ngā Rua (Latta, 1980), which literally means 'open the foodpits.' The mountain range that marks one of the town's boundaries is called Hakarimata (the 'feast of uncooked food'). Both names are associated with a great celebration that took place in the 17th century on the banks of the Waikato River, which bisects the town. In Māoridom, great honor and prestige are attributed to being able to care for and provide for the comfort of visitors. Waikato/Tainui and Tūrangawaewae in particular pride themselves on their reputation to be able to cater for events on a grand scale and in great style.

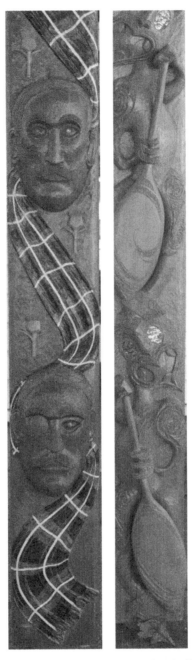

Figure 3.2 Carvings that adorn the entrance to the school office of Te Kura Kaupapa Māori o Bernard Fergusson School

The school is named after a former Governor General of Aotearoa/ New Zealand, who was a great friend of the Māori Queen Dame Te Atairangikāahu, niece to Princess Te Puea (in Figure 3.2, refer to the carving on the left which, with the carving on the right, adorns the entrance to the school office). A native of Scotland, Bernard Fergusson was known to be a speaker of Māori which signaled that the school which originally delivered the curriculum exclusively in English was destined to become a school that delivered instruction in both Māori and English. At the behest of parents and grandparents, Bernard Fergusson School transitioned to Bernard Fergusson Bilingual School in 1986 and to Te Kura Kaupapa Māori o Bernard Fergusson in 1993.

The parents and families of the school and elders of the local sub-tribe have expressed a strong desire that the school provides support for events at tribal gathering places, imbues the key principles of Kīngitanga throughout the curriculum, and engages with tribal elders across a variety of settings. Consequently, graduating criteria for students at Te Kura Kaupapa Māori o Bernard Fergusson include:

- working for the collective good;
- understanding that excellent work will always be acknowledged and receiving a treat as a consequence is not an end in itself;
- knowing how to express a deep care for others, including visitors and tribal elders;
- knowing how to express a deep care for their peers and people in their community.

The school's curriculum statement acknowledges the Waikato River as a treasure and living embodiment of tribal identity, and it is used as a metaphor for lifelong learning. The river also forms the framework for organizing, planning and delivering local content.

When journeying on the river from Tūrangawaewae marae (Figure 3.3) in Ngāruawahia, one arrives at Taupiri Mountain, another significant Waikato/Tainui tribal identity marker. The mountain is a burial ground for the Waikato/Tainui royal family as well as tribal members, and as such represents traditional knowledge. Mangatawhiri, which features in the story of the river, was once a stronghold of colonial British troops and represents the place where the Western world and the Māori world collided. This symbolizes the need to equip students with the knowledge, skills and strategies to function in the Western world. This also provides the rationale for the introduction of explicit instruction in the English language at year 6. Historical events and significant geographical features along the journey form topics of study. Te Paina, the original stronghold of Princess Te Puea, symbolizes the preparation of students at the school for careers and vocations that conribute to tribal growth and development.

Figure 3.3 Tūrangawaewae Marae, Ngāruawahia to Te Paina Pā, Mangatawhiri Google Maps (2016). Retrieved from: https://www.google.co.nz/maps/@-37.5121768,175.1876762,11z

In 2013, the school consulted with local elders to replace generic references to school buildings with names that were more locally and tribally specific and meaningful. These naturally create authentic topics for students to learn about and contribute to their sense of belonging in the community. They include the following.

- **Tainamau/Dynamo** (Administration Office). Dynamo was the original name of a shed sited on Tūrangawaewae marae that housed a generator used to power the lights. It also housed the printing press *Te Hokioi*. The name reflects what happens in the administration office.
- **Kimikimi** (Hall). The original Kimikimi was a house at Tūrangawaewae marae where guests slept. It was demolished in 1973 and reopened on 9 February 1974 as a multifunctional building. This

reflects how the building named Kimikimi at the school is also utilized.

- **Te Ohonga Ake** (the teaching block for senior school students). This is taken from another of Te Puea's sayings – '*I te ohonga ake i aku moemoea, ko te puawaitanga ko te whakaaro*' (When I awoke from my dream, my aspirations were realized'). It references the senior students' transition from the first stage of their compulsory schooling years to their second stage at secondary school.
- **Manawaroa** (the teaching block for middle school students). The original Manawaroa building on Tūrangawaewae marae was used to take the overflow of people of royal standing from Tūrongo house. It was operated by key personnel to ensure that the visitors were well cared for.
- **Akara** (the teaching block for junior middle school students). Arkle or Akara was the local manager of a general department store, Farmers Trading Company, who befriended Te Puea and provided new iron to cover a humble abode used to serve the people at Tūrangawaewae marae. Humility and servitude are values that are instilled in middle school students through adhering to Te Puea's saying, *Mahia te mahi hei pāinga mō te iwi* (Work for the betterment of our people).
- **Manawanui** (the teaching block for junior school students). '*Haere mai ki te kura kia manawanui!*' ('Welcome to kura, be steadfast in your faith!'). This building represents Te Puea's place of residence at Mangatāwhiri until she established Te Paina at Mercer and was known as Manawanui.
- **Raukawa Fergusson** (the room where English language instruction takes place). This name was gifted by Geordie Fergusson, son of Sir Bernard Fergusson, to commemorate the link between the Fergusson Scottish Clan and the tribal group Ngāti Raukawa. It is also the middle name of Geordie's son Alexander.
- **Te Puna Aroha o Te Puea** (library and resource room). As a repository of knowledge and information old and new, this is a fitting memorial to Te Puea's legacy.
- **Te Paina** (Adventure Playground). '*Te paina o tēnei wāhi*' ('a good place to be'). This is an obvious reference to the settlement established by Te Puea at a place north of Ngaruawahia called Mercer.

Ngā Taiātea Wharekura

The second school we profile, Ngā Taiātea Wharekura, is a popular choice for students from Te Kura Kaupapa Māori o Bernard Fergusson beginning their secondary school education (Figure 3.4). The husband of the second author of this chapter has served as chairperson of the school's Board of Trustees. He is also mana whenua – a member of the sub-tribe (Ngāti Māhanga) that has territorial claim by occupancy over the land where the school is located. Two of their three children are graduates of the school while the third child is currently enrolled as a student.

Figure 3.4 Ngā Taiātea Wharekura School logo

In 1996, families associated with local Māori medium schools and units within English medium schools from around the Waikato region joined together to establish a Kaupapa Māori secondary school catering to year 9 to 13 students. After years of lobbying, the then Labour Government agreed to the establishment of the first Māori medium secondary school in Hamilton City in 2002. The school, Ngā Taiātea Wharekura, officially opened in 2004. Unlike Te Kura Kaupapa Māori o Bernard Fergusson where there is more homogeneity in tribal affiliation, Ngā Taiātea Wharekura provides for students from a wide range of tribal groups. This presents both challenges and opportunities for the school.

References to these other tribal groups appear in signage around the school and buildings are named after ancestral canoes. Ngāti Mahanga subtribe, as the mana whenua, is acknowledged in school documentation; staff and students participate in significant events at the Ngāti Māhanga traditional gathering place (marae), and Ngāti Māhanga are called upon to carry out important ceremonies and rituals. A position on the Board of Trustees is reserved by right for a member of Ngāti Māhanga, who define their own appointment processes, unlike the remaining members who are voted into the position by parents.

The vision of the school is *e puta ki taiāte,* 'empowered by the past and present to lead in the future.' It is acknowledged that collective effort is required to realize this: *Ka taea e tātou,* 'Together we can succeed.' A triple hull ocean-faring vessel (Figure 3.5) is used as a metaphor to conceptually represent the relationship between the school's organizational structure and strategies designed to achieve the school's vision.

The graduate profile describes the desired values and attributes to be developed in students and explicitly acknowledges the role and responsibility of the key stakeholders (families/parents, students and school staff) in ensuring a successful outcome. Students are expected to:

- have a strong command and commitment to the Māori language and customs (*oranga tukuihotanga*);
- have the attitude, knowledge, skills, qualifications and plan to lead into their next step in life (*oranga hinengaro*);

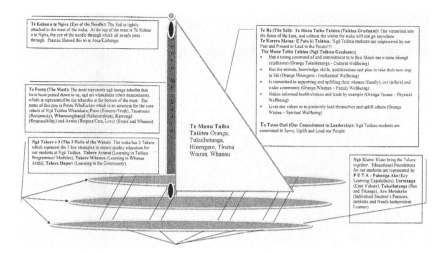

Figure 3.5 Ngā Taiātea Wharekura organizational structure using an ocean-faring vessel as a metaphor

- be committed to supporting and uplifting their family, tribal group(s) and the wider community (*oranga whānau*);
- make informed health choices and lead by example (*oranga tinana*);
- live values in ways that positively uplift themselves and others (*oranga wairua*).

By way of illustration, for oranga tukuihotanga, parents and families strive to:

- further develop their own Māori language proficiency;
- support the school's focus on honoring the tribal identity of Waikato (the local tribe) and Tainui (the ancestral canoe);
- strengthen their child's knowledge and appreciation of who they are – their individual and collective identity.

School staff undertake to:

- speak as much in the Māori language as possible at school;
- develop their own proficiency in the Māori language;
- actively support key tribal events;
- nurture and support the tribal identity of each student;
- express and celebrate Ngā Taiātea, mana whenua and tribal identity through song and performance.

Students commit to:

- developing their own Māori language proficiency;
- participating in key tribal events;
- expressing and celebrating identity through song and performance;

- being the best examples and representatives of their respective tribes and subtribes;
- being able to recite, understand and execute the prophetic sayings of revered Waikato/Tainui tribal leaders.

Students are expected to complete tasks and activities that demonstrate oranga tukuihotanga (culturalcy); oranga hinengaro (academic prowess); oranga whānau (contribution to collective wellbeing) and oranga wairua (spiritual strength) during the academic year. Only those senior students (years 11 to 12) who achieve the criteria for each oranga are awarded a certificate of acknowledgment at the end of year prize-giving ceremony. These awards are prestigious and highly valued by the students. Where many secondary schools are exclusively focused on academic results as affirmation of their efficacy and success, this is a school that has a more expansive view of what constitutes success and is clearly pushing the boundaries of what is actually possible.

Another feature of the school is the emphasis on nurturing the uniqueness of each student. This manifests in the development of personal learning plans developed with students and their parents and families at the beginning of each year. This includes accounting for the aspirations, dreams and passions of the student in subject choices and mapping out potential career and vocational pathways. Passion projects require years 9–11 students to undertake an activity of high personal value that will also benefit someone other than themselves, while internships for years 12–13 students expose them to real-life experience in their chosen field of interest. In the words of the school:

> … we want our students to have a firm commitment to the advancement of their family, their iwi and our people. These commitments include our commitment to our reo [language] and tikanga [customs], the welfare of our people, and the advancement of initiatives that empower our people … (http://www.taiatea.school.nz/)

Both Te Kura Kaupapa Māori o Bernard Fergusson and Ngā Taiātea Wharekura schools demonstrate their commitment to achieving tribal goals as expressed in the Waikato/Tainui strategic document, Whakatupuranga 2050. Unsurprisingly, these are wholly consistent with the strategic goals of Ngā Kura ā Iwi o Aotearoa.

Conclusion

Ngā Kura ā Iwi o Aotearoa – the organization and its affiliate schools – are committed to upholding and revitalizing tribal identity. This is achieved in strong partnership with the tribal communities they serve. While the national curriculum document, Te Marautanga o Aoteroa, sets the direction for teaching and learning in Māori medium classrooms, there is ample flexibility for schools to design and deliver a localized curriculum in partnership with their constituent communities. The affiliate schools profiled in this chapter provide insights into how two school communities from the same tribal group are expressing their culturalcy in locally specific ways.

Ngā Kura ā Iwi subscribes to the notion that culturalcy is the domain around which all learning coheres, and that success in literacy and numeracy and all learning areas of the national curriculum is better guaranteed when this is the case. The NCEA results of year 9–13 students in Ngā Kura ā Iwi o Aotearoa since 2010 bear testament to this.

The final words lie with Ngā Kura ā Iwi who have defined culturalcy for themselves in this way:

> Culturalcy … includes embedding identity markers such as language/dialects, our way of life, our view of the world, creating our own unique epistemology (curriculum, pedagogy, values), and a governance model and policy framework to support that. To have the freedom to live with authority as Ngāti, Ngai[4] – kinship in our own tribal context. To be key decision makers on all aspects of the education of our uri. (Ngā Kura ā Iwi information brochure, n.d.)

Notes

(1) To qualify as a speaker of Māori for the census, Māori needed to self report they were at least able to hold a conversation about everyday things in the Māori language.
(2) The Treaty of Waitangi signed in 1840 is the founding document of Aotearoa/New Zealand. It was signed by representatives of the Crown and tribes and sub-tribes and outlines the respective rights of Māori and the obligations of the Crown in the formation of a nation.
(3) Achievement levels for Ngā Whanaketanga Rumaki Māori and National Standards are determined by teachers with the expectation that multiple sources of evidence generated from the classroom instructional program form the basis for those judgments as opposed to national testing.
(4) Ngāti or Ngāi are prefixes for a tribal group; hence Ngāti Manawa, Ngai Tai, and so on.

References

Dictionary of New Zealand Biography (1996) Te Kīngitanga: The People of the Māori King Movement. Auckland, NZ: Auckland University Press.
Harlow, R. (2005) Māori: Introduction. In A. Bell, R. Harlow and D. Starks (eds) Languages of New Zealand (pp. 59–66). Wellington: Victoria University Press.
Ka'ai, T. (2004) Te mana o te reo me ngā tikanga: Power and politics of the language. In T.M. Ka'ai, J.C. Moorfield, M.P.J. Reilly and S. Mosley (eds) Ki te Whaiao: An Introduction to Māori Culture and Society (pp. 201–213). Auckland: Pearson Education.
King, M. (1977) Te Puea: A Biography. Auckland: Hodder and Stoughton.
Latta, A.M. (1980) Meeting of the Waters: The Story of Ngāruawahia. Hong Kong: Ngaruawahia Lions Club.
May, S., Hill, R. and Tiakiwai, S. (2004) Bilingual/Immersion Education: Indicators of Good Practice. Final Report to the Ministry of Education. Wellington: Ministry of Education, New Zealand.

Ministry of Education (2008) *Te Marautanga o Aotearoa*. Wellington: Ministry of Education.

Ministry of Education (2010) *Te Marautanga o Aotearoa: Whanaketanga Te Reo Matatini: He Aratohu Mā Te Pouako*. Wellington: Te Pou Taki Kōrero Whāiti.

Ministry of Education (n.d.) *Māori Language in Education*. Retrieved from Education Counts: https://www.educationcounts.govt.nz/statistics/maori-education/maori-in-schooling/6040.

Ministry of Social Development (2016) *The Social Report – Te Pūrongo Oranga Tangata*. Wellington, NZ: Ministry of Social Development. Retrieved from http://socialreport.msd.govt.nz/cultural-identity/maori-language-speakers.html

Māori Medium Workforce Advisory Group (2010) *Māori Medium Workforce Advisory Group Report*. Wellington: Ministry of Education.

Moorfield, J. and Johnston, E.L. (2004) Te reo Māori: Origins and development of the Māori language. In T.M. Ka'ai, J.C. Moorfield, M.P.J. Reilly and S. Mosley (eds) *Ki Te Whaiao: An Introduction to Māori Culture and Society* (pp. 201–213). Auckland: Pearson Education.

O'Regan, H. (2006) State of the reo nation: Māori language learning. In M. Mulhullond, *State of the Māori Nation: Twenty-first Century Issues in Aotearoa* (pp. 157–168). Auckland: Reed Publishing NZ.

O'Regan, H. (2012) The fate of the customary language: Te reo Māori 1900 to the present. In D. Keenan (ed.) *Huia Histories of Māori: Ngā Tāhuhu Kōrero* (pp. 298–323). Wellington: Huia Publishers.

Statistics New Zealand. Tatauranga Aotearoa. *Te Kupenga* (2013) Retrieved from: http://www.stats.govt.nz/browse_for_stats/people_and_communities/maori/TeKupenga_HOTP13/Commentary.aspx#use

Waikato Tainui (n.d) *Waikato- Tainui Whakatupuranga 2050*. Retrieved from http://www.waikatotainui.com/wpcontent/uploads/2013/12/WhakatupurangaWT2050.pdf

Waitangi Tribunal (2010) *Pre-publication Report 262*. Wellington: Author.

4 Media and Technology: Revitalizing Latin American Indigenous Languages in Cyberspace

Serafín M. Coronel-Molina

This chapter examines Indigenous language practices using digital media and technology to promote Indigenous language revitalization. It follows the growing online presence of Latin American Indigenous languages as communities that make use of digital and multimodal literacies to further the cause of cultivating and propagating these languages. Formal education is important to revitalize or document Indigenous languages, but of equal – or perhaps even greater – importance is for people to see the presence of their language on a daily basis in media and technology. Utilizing these modes of communication can strengthen the status of Indigenous languages and contribute to both awakening pride and modifying negative attitudes on the part of both users and nonusers of these languages. Increasing linguistic pride will, to some degree, help stimulate language maintenance and revitalization. This research examines selected virtual archival data on Quechua, Aymara, Guarani, Mayan languages, Náhuatl, Ashaninka and Mapudungun (Mapuche), including mass media such as the internet, films, documentaries, television and radio programs, and all forms of print media, in paper and digital formats. Data were also collected on social media such as Facebook, Twitter, YouTube, blogs, online forums and wikis.

Introduction

The world is a multilingual, pluricultural and multiethnic social milieu. Currently, there are about 7000–7500 known spoken languages. It is estimated that every two weeks one language disappears as the last first-language speaker dies. This means that linguistic and cultural diversity are in constant decline across time and space. According to sources from the mid-1990s (AILLA, n.d.), of the estimated 1750 Indigenous languages in use in Latin America before the European invasion, only 550–700 are still in use today. This is despite the approximately 40 million Indigenous people, or about 10% of the total population, who live there. 'In some countries, the majority of the population is indigenous. In Bolivia, for example, more than half of the total population is indigenous' (Human Resources Development and Operations Policy, 1993).

Indigenous languages in Latin America have coexisted with other powerful languages in diglossic or multiglossic situations for centuries.[1] This asymmetric relationship of power and prestige, and the negative attitudes and isolationist ideologies on the part of most speakers of dominant languages at the societal level, have negatively impacted the recognition and valorization of Indigenous languages. Despite these competing ideologies and negative attitudes, the constant demands of the linguistic market and cultural capital, and the pressures of multiple sociohistorical, religious, educational, migratory, psychological, economic, sociolinguistic and geopolitical factors, some Latin American Indigenous languages still remain relatively vital, although most of them are endangered.

The use of media and technology is becoming increasingly common relative to Indigenous languages of Latin America. Nowadays scientists, language planners, researchers, Indigenous and non-Indigenous language activists, educators, students and people from all walks of life are embracing media and technology to carry out research and promote their diverse projects. It is important to point out that such information is available in multiple languages. The predominant languages are the powerful ones: English, Spanish, German, Chinese, French, Portuguese and Italian (see Crystal, 2001). Because of this new *cyberglossic* or *cybermultiglossic* phenomenon, UNESCO considers it a high priority to continue development of the internet in order to elaborate the content of websites not only *in* Indigenous languages, but also *about* their respective cultures (see Montviloff, 2002). As long as this does not take place, it will be a great challenge for Indigenous languages to appropriate media and technology in order to reduce the digital divide that exists between the 'haves' and the 'have nots.' Lieberman (2002: 83), in particular, emphasizes this situation:

> Our increasingly interdependent world faces many challenges. One of the most critical of these is how to reach equality in health, education, and economic levels, without sacrificing the human diversity that makes our planet so interesting and likely holds the key to our species' continued survival. An important step is to help [...] indigenous populations to take ownership of ICTs [information and communication technologies] and cross the digital divide without distancing themselves from their culture and language.

There are researchers who are convinced that not only is it possible, but also necessary for Indigenous people to maintain their languages and traditions to preserve their identities, making good use of the technological tools and opportunities the modern world offers (Hinton & Hale, 2001; Montviloff, 2002). According to Lieberman (n.d.):

> To get ahead in the modern world without losing their heritage, indigenous communities need to develop a biculturalism that enables them to move between two cultures and to combine certain elements of each harmoniously ... . In a digital world, it means Internet chats in indigenous languages, indigenous web pages, multimedia CD-ROMs for learning indigenous languages, and cultural information published by indigenous groups for a global audience. These are proven examples of how traditional knowledge and modern technology can be blended.

Without a doubt, Indigenous people are aware of the importance of media and technology to revitalize their languages in contemporary times. In recent years, the use of these technological tools has increased tremendously. In terms of participatory projects that imply interaction between people, Buszard-Welcher (2001: 342) recognizes this necessity, and proposes another intriguing interactive project: the creation of a virtual linguistic community consisting of

> a constructed immersion setting where members of the speech community meet, interact, and communicate in the native language. [...] The Internet is not one-way, nor is it passive. People receive information, but they create and send it too. The Web is a very social place that encourages participation and community building.

> While real face-to-face interaction will always be the primary domain of language learning, many *real* speech communities would nevertheless benefit by having an added virtual community. [...] What a benefit a *virtual* community would be if [...] participants could meet each other online, learning new languages and reinforcing their language use. (emphasis in original)

Buszard-Welcher is correct when she says that face-to-face interaction is the most appropriate means of communication, but the idea of building virtual communities also has merit. The great benefit of media and technology is their quick connectivity that enables long-distance communication and networking (see Wagner & Hopey, 1999). These new ways of virtual communication can contribute to the efforts of language revitalization.

In their struggle to survive, in recent years, some Latin American Indigenous languages have gained new domains of functionality thanks to media and technology, top-down and bottom-up efforts, and initiatives carried out by numerous language planning agencies such as governmental and nongovernmental organizations, Indigenous leaders, and individuals from different backgrounds at the local, regional, national, international and transnational levels. Through media and technology, language planners and activists have started empowering Indigenous languages to bridge the digital divide. These language planners are trying to bridge the gaps between the local and the global. This means that the presence of Indigenous languages is becoming more prevalent not only in rural and urban domains, but also in virtual global spheres.

In this chapter, I trace the path of some innovative ways Indigenous languages are being maintained and revitalized in Latin America; I will also demystify the beliefs that view these languages as only ancient and local languages, demonstrating through key examples that they are also global languages, ready to face the challenges of contemporary times. In short, Indigenous languages are not static, but just as dynamic as any powerful language in the world. Hence, trying to museumize, romanticize and essentialize them is a counterproductive endeavor.

Indigenous languages of Latin America are receiving considerable attention at present within fields with an interest in linguistics and socio-linguistics, including anthropology, history, sociology and language peda-gogy. In particular, many investigators, language planners and owners and users of these languages are interested in revitalizing and document-ing them through media and technology. Latin American Indigenous lan-guages are relatively vital in some areas but slowly dying out in many others, as speakers come to believe that the only way to better their lives is to abandon their mother tongue in favor of dominant languages. Such language shift is well documented in many diglossic and multiglossic soci-eties, and is strongly correlated with the relative status of the languages involved. 'Language status' refers to the functional domains filled by a language or variety within a society – e.g. which language is an official language used in many domains, and which is used only in more limited contexts.

Digital media and technology, in addition to print media, have greatly expanded access to linguistic and cultural information produced in Indigenous languages locally and globally. In the 21st century, literacies in both traditional and emerging genres are present in mass media and social media as performances in written and oral forms, and more recently in multimedia formats. These developments support language policy and planning (LPP), and language revitalization (LR) and documentation of Latin American Indigenous languages, and they are accessible to some community members.

In any LPP and LR goals, it is essential to take into consideration how the local informs the global and vice versa. This means that we need to pay attention to both rural and urban contexts because of migration and diaspora movements. Many speakers of Indigenous languages are now located in metropolitan areas. For example, there are more speakers of Indigenous languages in Lima, the capital of Peru, than in the Andean region. The same is true in the United States, where new waves of immi-grants are composed of speakers of many Indigenous languages from Latin America. This situation is creating new challenges for the US edu-cational system, and it also creates challenges – and opportunities – for revitalization and maintenance of these languages.

Cultural production and linguistic expression in Indigenous languages are taking different forms according to the multiplicity of contexts in virtual spaces. Indigenous languages are being preserved, promoted, studied and revitalized in cyberspace by virtual agents from the top down and the bottom up, and from local and global perspectives. Media and technology are contributing to the creation of new hybrid, heteroglossic cultural and linguistic forms through complex interplays between virtual and real communities in contemporary times. Virtual spaces are multilingual, pluricultural, multiethnic, translingual, transcultural and translocal where cyberdiglossia and cybermultiglossia (the asymmetric relationships of languages in cyberspace) are present. In order to alleviate this asymmetrical situation, the Indigenous languages are being documented and revitalized in virtual spaces by diverse agents.

Functional Domains of Language Use

The functional domains of language use at the societal level – a principal concern of status planning – are the different social contexts in which a language is used on a daily basis. This means that the more societal domains in which a language is used, the higher its status. There are numerous paradigms that identify common domains of language use, including specific analysis of Indigenous languages in Latin America. The two primary models for evaluating the status of these languages are Stewart's (1968) and UNESCO's (Gadelii, 1999). For the case of Latin America and the Caribbean, see Coronel-Molina (2013, 2016), and for Peru specifically, see Coronel-Molina (1999, 2015). The specific functional domains of languages used at the societal level include official use, government use, legal/court/judiciary uses, provincial use, regional use, wider communication, international use, business use, capital use, administrative use, education, literature and translation, religion, and academic and social domains.

Indigenous languages do not maintain a visible presence in very many functional domains of use. However, with the help of social media and technology, these languages are gaining ground in some already inhabited spheres, and making new inroads into others. At the same time that this new growth contributes to increasing the status of both languages, it also makes contributions to the areas of both corpus planning and acquisition planning.

The use of the internet is perhaps the most significant example of the media and technology. Although the information found on the internet is available in numerous languages, those that predominate, in general, are the more widely spoken world languages. Hence, it should be a high priority to develop content for websites not only *in* minority languages, but also *about* their respective cultures. When this begins to happen, it will be a true step forward for Indigenous languages in reducing the digital divide that currently exists.

In recent years, a great number of groups and individuals interested in the development and teaching of Indigenous languages have taken on this challenge, exerting considerable effort on behalf of those languages. There are innumerable initiatives around the world that seek to avoid the extinction of Indigenous languages, or at least to reverse the phenomenon of language shift. The internet houses an enormous number of websites created by Indigenous organizations, governmental and nongovernmental organizations, religious, political, philanthropic and academic entities, publishing houses, as well as researchers, activists and simply individuals with a strong interest in Indigenous languages. These websites contain abundant links to available resources in and about Indigenous languages.

Many times, the most successful projects are those that involve a wide range of participants, especially members of the communities the projects seek to serve. Given this, institutions try to involve Indigenous communities in programs developed specifically to benefit them. For example, there are some projects in different parts of the world that involve the creation of digital videos about Indigenous cultures. These videos often are made by community members themselves, which it is hoped will serve not only to help revitalize the languages and cultures of their respective nations, but also to reaffirm their ethnic identity.

Likewise, media and technology can play an essential role in pedagogy and the creation of a wide range of teaching materials. In the Latin American region, media and technology can make great contributions to the innovation of mother tongue teaching and learning. For instance, documenting all the nuances, functions and paralinguistic features of Latin American Indigenous languages can be of tremendous benefit for their maintenance and revitalization.

Although multimedia technology is a challenge for educators and learners, its use is fundamental. That is why it is necessary to support educators and learners in using these technologies, both for the development of teaching materials and for language teaching and learning, bearing in mind the sociolinguistic context and its idiosyncrasies. Making these initiatives a reality will depend on the accessibility of technological equipment and resources, which can vary according to sociocultural contexts. It is necessary to utilize media and technology in the production of interactive textbooks in Indigenous languages for students who participate in Bilingual Intercultural Education programs in Latin America. The production of textbooks in Indigenous languages will not only help to increase the status and corpus of these languages, but also will contribute to their revitalization.

Such pedagogical materials would be useful not only within the classroom context, but also for long-distance education. Traditionally, long-distance education was carried out through radio and television programming. Now, however, there are many long-distance education programs in almost all parts of the world. Technology has revolutionized education, which can now be carried out through multimedia education modules transmitted via computer. You can even record a class or create virtual courses in one place and transmit them via television or the internet to just about any other destination in the world. These programs can take advantage of self-teaching materials and can count on the assistance of a virtual tutor.

In any effort of language revitalization, the central role played by media and technology cannot be ignored. Obviously, a formal education through the school system is important, but of equal – or perhaps greater – importance is for people to see that their language is present on a daily basis in media and technology, such as radio, television, newspapers, magazines, informational bulletins, videos, films and so on. After all, it is appropriate to use these means of communication to strengthen the status and corpus of Latin American Indigenous languages and to contribute to the awakening of pride and the modification of some negative attitudes and ideologies on the part of both users and nonusers of these languages. Increasing linguistic pride will to some degree help stimulate language revitalization even more.

Mass Media

Radio is one of the mass media that has opened its doors to Indigenous languages of Latin America. Currently, a good number of urban, regional, national and international radio stations broadcast at least some programming in Indigenous languages in all parts of Latin America. These stations and associations fulfill different objectives and are involved in the transmission of programs of a religious, educational and cultural nature. Thus, the presence of Indigenous languages in the mass media today is not a novelty. Nevertheless, the persistence of diglossia, manifested in various ways in relation to these languages in the media, cannot be denied. This diglossia becomes more obvious when one realizes that radio programs in Indigenous languages are limited to very restricted, and generally not very desirable, time slots.

As opposed to the case of radio programming, there is a huge barrier facing Indigenous languages in the written press, such as newspapers and magazines. Even so, this does not mean that they have no periodical presence at all. This innovative effort contributes in some small measure to the initiatives to revitalize Indigenous languages. What is lacking is the publication of more newspapers in Indigenous languages. It is absolutely necessary to include in such periodicals the same content that appears in any regular newspaper. Obviously, publishing an Indigenous-language newspaper would not be a simple undertaking, since it would be necessary to constitute a panel of experts in the language, as well as the need for the appropriate equipment and technology. All of this also involves financial resources and planning at all levels. But through careful planning and the active collaboration of language planners and Native reporters and writers, it should be possible to fulfill this objective. Publishing such periodicals online would reduce – or even eliminate – the costs of paper and printing, and would also permit the publication to reach a wide international audience instantaneously, conveniently and cheaply.

As with the press, the presence of Indigenous languages on television is virtually nonexistent, with some sporadic exceptions such as documentaries, plays, reports, and folkloric festivities in which small segments in these languages might appear. On the other hand, some communication technologies that are popular in the modern world and that can support the interaction of a virtual community include virtual forums, chat rooms and electronic bulletin boards, email and listservs. Many Native-language speakers are appropriating these technologies to communicate in their own languages and share any information of common interest.

With regard to the codification of Latin American Indigenous languages – that is, the production of dictionaries, grammars, and glossaries – new technologies, particularly the internet, play a fundamental role in attempts at language revitalization, so much so that a great number of publications in different Indigenous languages already exist. It is crucial to continue to enhance the production of a wide range of both print and digitally recorded material of the spoken language. These basic resources should be digitized and made available on the internet, perhaps in a virtual library created specifically for this purpose. It is absolutely necessary to continue with the production of written and oral texts at all levels, taking advantage of the opportunities that media and technology offer. Table 4.1 contains selected examples of the presence of some Latin American Indigenous languages in mass media such as magazines, newspapers, radio and television programs, films, documentaries and the internet.

Social Media

Kaplan and Haenlein (2010: 61) define '[s]ocial media as a group of Internet-based applications that build on the ideological and technological foundations of Web 2.0, which allows the creation and exchange of user-generated content.' Social media have become ubiquitous; very few people who have used the internet at one time or another in the last ten years or so have not heard of, or more likely used, online or mobile interfaces including Facebook, Google+, Twitter, YouTube, blogs, online forums, chat rooms, wikis and podcasts. The great advantages to social media are that individual users can interact with many people at once, and they can share all manner of user-generated content, including videos,

Table 4.1 Latin American Indigenous languages in mass media

Magazines and Newspapers

In Quechua
Atuqpa Chupan   http://atuqpachupan.blogspot.com/
Noqanchis   http://www.guamanpoma.org/blog/?p=2749
Pututu   https://hawansuyo.files.wordpress.com/2015/11/pututu-54.pdf
CENDA, Bolivia   http://www.cenda.org/

In Aymara
Jayma – Periódico Digital Aymara   http://periodicojayma.webnode.es/

In Guarani
ARA periódico Guaraní   http://www.araguarani.com/
Guaraní Ñanduti Rogue   http://www.staff.uni-mainz.de/lustig/guarani/

In Mayan Languages
La Jornada – K'untsil
    http://periodistas-es.com/mexico-la-jornada-primer-diario-en-lengua-maya-56631

In Mapudungun
Chile/Wallmapu Nütxamkan de Medios en Temuco
    http://www.yepan.cl/chilewallmapu-nutxamkan-de-medios-en-temuco/

Radio Programs

In Quechua/Quichua
Alero Quichua Santiagueño   http://www.aleroquichua.org.ar/sitio/index.php
Red Kichwa Satelital   http://rks.aler.org/
Asociación Pukllasunchis: radio con niños y niñas de Cusco
    http://www.pukllasunchis.org/radio/programas.php
Red ACLO–Bolivia   http://aclo.org.bo/bolivia/

In Aymara
Aymara Pachamama: la Voz del Sur Andino   http://www.pachamamaradio.org/otros/aymara
San Gabriel Radio and Newspaper   http://www.radiosangabriel.org.bo/?lang=aym
Radio and the Voice of the Aymara People by Karl Swinehart
    http://soundstudiesblog.com/2014/04/10/radio-de-accion-radio-and-the-voice-of-the-
    aymara-people/

In Guarani
Ecos del Paraguay
    http://www.ecosdelparaguay.com/2009/12/comenzo-el-ciclo-de-programas-radiales.html

In Mayan Languages
Maya T'ann   http://turix.yoochel.org/category/mayataan/

In Náhuatl
Xezon la voz de la sierra de Zongolica
    http://www.cdi.gob.mx/ecosgobmx/xezon.php
Podcast cultural/radial de la Universidad de UNAM
    http://descargacultura.unam.mx/app1?sharedItem=15075

In Ashaninka
Servindi   http://servindi.org/categoria/producciones/audios/resumen-ashaninka

In Mapudungun
Radio Program – Wixage Anai   http://wixageanai.blogspot.com/
Mapuche: First Radio Station in Argentina   http://unpo.org/article/15578

(*continued*)

Table 4.1 (*Continued*)

Television Programs

In Quechua
Ñuqanchik   http://www.tvperu.gob.pe/programas/nuqanchik
Kichwashun TV   https://www.youtube.com/results?search_query=Kichwashun
Quechua TV   https://peruquechuamedia.wordpress.com/2012/12/09/quechua-tv/
Saqrakuna 1   https://www.youtube.com/watch?v=w5wD3QN5rps
Saqrakuna 2   https://www.youtube.com/watch?v=_q3qpqe9VgM
Saqrakuna 3   https://www.youtube.com/watch?v=f2jkY8f4IgM

In Aymara
Jiwasanaka   http://www.tvperu.gob.pe/programas/jiwasanaka
Televisión Aymara   https://www.youtube.com/watch?v=-BX1RpYfFK4

In Guarani
Red Guraraní   TV   https://www.youtube.com/user/TVREDGUARANI

In Mayan Languages
Baktun   http://www.ntd.tv/en/news/us/20130726/81849-mexico-releases-first-mayaspeaking-television-soap-opera.html

In Mapudungun
Mapuche Chile, TravelBook.TV
   http://www.travelbook.tv/playlist/mapuche-chile/PLE72B43704DC43C19
Wall Kintun TV   https://www.youtube.com/watch?v=t9WP9FRprdE

Films and Documentaries

Films and documentaries on/in Indigenous languages of Latin America
   http://www.youtube.com/results?search_query=documentales+en+lenguas+indigenas+de+America+Latina
Lenguas Originarias del Perú   https://www.youtube.com/watch?v=ueaqWXFb2yk
Movies featuring native peoples from Central and South America
   http://www.nativeamericanfilms.org/

Internet

Association for Teaching and Learning Indigenous Languages of Latin America (ATLILLA)
   http://www.iu.edu/~atlilla/
Acerbo Digital de Lenguas Indígenas
   http://lenguasindigenas.mx/acerca-del-acervo-digital.html
LANIC Indigenous Peoples   http://lanic.utexas.edu/la/region/indigenous/
NativeWeb – Resource Database Subcategories   http://www.nativeweb.org/resources/
The Archive of Indigenous Languages of Latin America
   http://www.ailla.utexas.org/site/lg_about.html
Atlas Sociolingüístico de Pueblos Indígenas en América Latina, Vol. 1 & 2
   http://www.unicef.org/honduras/tomo_1_atlas.pdf
   http://www.unicef.org/honduras/tomo_2_atlas.pdf
Instituto de Lengua y Cultura Aymara (ILCA)   http://www.ilcanet.org/
Lenguas Indígenas: una Red de Activistas en América Latina
   https://rising.globalvoices.org/lenguas/
Raising Voices   https://rising.globalvoices.org/
Instituto Nacional de Lenguas Indígenas   http://www.inali.gob.mx/
Primeros Pasos de Estudio Participativo: Lenguas Indígenas y Medios Digitales
   https://rising.globalvoices.org/lenguas/2016/01/12/estudio-addli-primeros-pasos/
Quechua at Penn   https://web.sas.upenn.edu/quechua/

photographs, music, news feeds and so on. In this way, they can carry on real-time interactive dialogues with many interlocutors simultaneously, in contrast to, for example, email's more static and unidirectional communication model ('Social Media,' n.d.).

Social media can be classified into five categories: collaborative projects, which include wikis, blogs and microblogs; content communities such as YouTube and Flickr; social networking sites, such as Facebook and Google+; virtual game worlds like World of Warcraft; and virtual social worlds such as Second Life (Kaplan & Hainlein, 2010). Kietzmann *et al.* (2011) assert that social media have become so rapidly successful because they fulfill many (or maybe even all) of the functional needs of social life – identity, conversations, sharing, presence, relationships, reputation and groups. For example, 'LinkedIn users care mostly about identity, reputation and relationships,' while YouTube devotees are more interested in 'sharing, conversations, groups and reputation' ('Social Media,' n.d.).

The presence of Indigenous languages of Latin America in social media is remarkable. Many of the media and technologies already mentioned, including social media, can be useful tools to contribute effectively to language preservation, promotion, and revitalization. Indigenous languages are crossing the digital divide thanks to native and second-language (L2) speakers who are making efforts to elevate, maintain, develop and invigorate them. Social media are also useful to connect speakers of Indigenous languages to one another, allowing them to interact, be involved in language documentation, share knowledge, ideas, projects and all kinds of information and initiatives in a fluid way regardless of geographical distances. Since young people are the driving force of language maintenance and revitalization, and social media are more commonly used by this new generation of speakers, they constitute a powerful force in keeping Indigenous languages alive. At the same time, these tools can help make these youngsters proud of their linguistic and cultural roots. In this way, Indigenous people are empowering themselves by appropriating these new technologies to organize themselves and communicate in their respective languages, sharing all kinds of information and knowledge. Table 4.2 offers specific examples of the presence of Quechua, Aymara, Guarani, Mayan languages, Náhuatl and Mapudungun in social media.

Software and Programming

Mobile technologies or transient technologies such as laptops, cellphones, iPhones and iPads constitute powerful tools for gaining access to and sharing all kinds of information and communication in many languages in general, and Indigenous languages in particular. In addition, through these mobile technologies, people have access to mass media and social media.

Other technological tools such as ATM machines, computers (One Laptop per Child), transient technologies such as cell phones, iPhones, iPods, iPads, CD-Roms and DVDs, and software such as spell-checking, video games, PowerPoint games, Rosetta Stone, machine translations,

Table 4.2 Latin American Indigenous languages in social media

Facebook

In several languages
Association for Teaching and Learning Indigenous Languages of Latin America on Facebook
   http://www.facebook.com/pages/Association-for-Teaching-and-Learning-Indigenous-
   Languages-of-Latin-America/172419129529535?sk=info
Latin American Indigenous Film/Cine Indígena Latino
   https://www.facebook.com/cineindigenalatino/?fref=ts
Suvival International (en castellano)   https://www.facebook.com/survivalesp/?fref=ts
Mozilla Nativo   http://mozillanativo.org/proyectos
Liberato Kani   https://www.facebook.com/LiberatoKaniPeru/

In Quechua, Spanish and English
Admiradores del Idioma Quechua (Runasimi)
   https://www.facebook.com/groups/admiradores.quechua/
Qichwa Simi/Runasimi   https://www.facebook.com/groups/grupo.runasimi/

In Aymara
Aymara Jaqupirinaka
   https://www.facebook.com/profile.php?id=100005531896935&fref=ufi
Aymara Facebook Utt'ayasxapxañani
   https://www.facebook.com/groups/1438682169781703/

In Guarani and Spanish
¡Firefox en guaraní está en la fase Beta!
   http://mozillanativo.org/2016/firefox-en-guarani-esta-en-la-fase-beta.html
Guarani Reko   https://www.facebook.com/guaranireko1/?fref=ts
Guarani Mbo'esyry   https://www.facebook.com/guarani.mboesyry?fref=nf
Ñe'ênguéra Sambyhyha   https://www.facebook.com/splparaguay/?fref=nf

In Mayan Languages
Facebook en idioma maya-k'iche'   https://www.youtube.com/watch?v=oXWVP0rmiMo
Wuqu' Kawoq – Maya Health Alliance   https://www.facebook.com/wuqu.kawoq

In Náhuatl
Nahuatlahtolli
   https://www.facebook.com/groups/nahuatlahtolli/1079997458699204/?notif_t=group_
   activity
Náhuatl   https://www.facebook.com/Nahuatl.mx/
Tlachamanaltianij Nahuatl   https://www.facebook.com/profile.php?id=100011605459144

In Ashaninka
Añaane Asháninka – 2016
   https://www.facebook.com/A%C3%B1aane-Ash%C3%A1ninka-2016-163907840367959/
Central Asháninka Río Ene   https://www.facebook.com/careashaninka/

In Mapudungun
Pu Chillkatufe: Talleres Mapudungun Equipo Kom Kim
   https://www.facebook.com/groups/365954196849308/
Aprender el Mapudungun   https://www.facebook.com/groups/aprendermapudungun/
Kimeltuwe, materiales de mapudungun   https://www.facebook.com/kimeltuwe/?fref=ts

YouTube

In Several Languages
Indigenous Languages of Latin America
   http://www.youtube.com/results?search_query=lenguas+indigenas
Andean Languages   http://www.youtube.com/playlist?list=PLD523D2FEA938B438
Amazonian Languages   http://www.youtube.com/results?search_query=lenguas+selvaticas

(continued)

Table 4.2 (*Continued*)

Blogs

In Quechua
CLACS Blog at New York University   https://clacsnyublog.com/tag/quechua/
Chaski Runasimi – Noti Quechua   http://chaski-runasimi.blogspot.com/
Atuqpa Chupan   http://atuqpachupan.blogspot.com/
Runa simi ñawpa willana   http://runasimiwillana.blogspot.com/

In Aymara
Jaqi Aru Blog   http://jaqi-aru.org/blog/
Aymara Yatiqaña   http://aymaryatiqana.blogspot.com/

In Guarani
Guarani Reko   http://www.guaranireko.blogspot.com/
Ñane Ñẽẽ Guarani   http://guaraniete.blogspot.com/

In Mayan Languages
Mayanglot: Modern Mayan Language Resources   http://mayaglot.com/blog/
Mayab T'aan   http://kanikmaya.blogspot.com/

In Náhuatl
Nahuatlahtolli – El Idioma Náhuatl: Aprendiendo Nahuatl
   https://www.pinterest.com/pin/574068283727439827/

In Ashaninka
Ashaninka Indian Language (Asháninka, Campa)
   http://www.native-languages.org/ashaninka.htm
Añaane Asháninka – 2015   http://deikybengee.blogspot.com/

In Mapudungun
Üñüm nütramelparkeenew   http://amaruquyllur.blogspot.com/
Fiostoforo: Guía para aprender en mapudungun   http://fiestoforo.cl/dungun.php

Twitter

In Quechua
Hablemos Quechua Twitter
   http://twitter.com/#!/hablemosquechua/statuses/79699459147169792

In Aymara
Jaqi Aru (Aymara) Tweets   https://twitter.com/#!/jaqiaru

In Guarani
Mozilla Paraguay   https://twitter.com/mozpy
#diadelidiomaguaraní   https://twitter.com/hashtag/diadelidiomaguarani

In Mayan Languages
#Kaqchikel   https://twitter.com/hashtag/kaqchikel
Indigenous Tweets – Kaqchikel   http://indigenoustweets.com/cak/

In Náhuatl
#nahuatl   https://twitter.com/hashtag/nahuatl
#náhuatl   https://twitter.com/search?q=%23n%C3%A1huatl
Mexikatlajtoli (@LenguaNahuatl) Twitter   https://twitter.com/lenguanahuatl
#Nahuatlahtolli   https://twitter.com/search?q=%23Nahuatlahtolli

In Ashaninka
#ashaninka   https://twitter.com/hashtag/ashaninka

In Mapudungun
#mapundungun   https://twitter.com/hashtag/mapundungun
Frases en mapudungun   https://twitter.com/Frasemapuzungun
Kimeltuwe on Twitter: 'Nütramkaiñ Mapuche zungun mew! Hablemos mapundungun
   https://twitter.com/kimeltuwe

(continued)

Table 4.2 (*Continued*)

Wikis

In Quechua
Wikipidiya Qhapaq P'anqa   http://qu.wikipedia.org/wiki/Qhapaq_p%27anqa
Qhichwa Simi   https://qu.wikipedia.org/wiki/Qhichwa_simi

In Aymara
Wikipidiya Nayriri uñstawi   http://ay.wikipedia.org/wiki/Nayriri_u%C3%B1stawi
Wikipidiya Chuqiyapu jach'a suyu   http://ay.wikipedia.org/wiki/Chuqiyapu_jach'a_suyu

In Guarani
Wikipedia in Guarani   https://gn.wikipedia.org/wiki/Ape
Wikitongues: Mba'éichapa! This week's #WeeklyTongue is Guarani
   http://wikitongues.tumblr.com/post/107979300019/mba%C3%A9ichapa-this-weeks-
   weeklytongue-is-guaran%C3%AD

In Mayan Languages
Mayan Languages Wikipedia   https://en.wikipedia.org/wiki/Mayan_languages

In Náhuatl
Ximopanōltih Huiquipedia   https://nah.wikipedia.org/wiki/Cal%C4%ABxatl

In Ashaninka
Asháninka people   https://en.wikipedia.org/wiki/Ash%C3%A1ninka_people

In Mapudungun
¡Kvmey tamvn akun Wikipedia mew!
   https://incubator.wikimedia.org/wiki/Wp/arn/%C3%91izol_Wvbgi%C3%B1
Mapuche language   https://en.wikipedia.org/wiki/Mapuche_language

Windows and Office, Open Office and AbiWord all make contributions to this effort as well, and are being actively used in Indigenous language preservation, documentation, promotion, and revitalization. Table 4.3 includes examples of software and programming in Quechua, Aymara, Guarani, Mayan languages, Náhuatl and Mapudungun.

Language Revitalization Agencies and Digital Activism in Cyberspace

Language planners and agencies are taking full advantage of these new technologies to maintain and revitalize Indigenous languages from the top down and the bottom up, and from local and global perspectives, enhancing the presence of Indigenous languages in social media in order to alleviate cyberdiglossic and cybermultiglossic situations. To a limited extent, a good number of Indigenous languages of Latin America and the rest of the world are already finding their way into media and technology, particularly radio, the internet, Facebook, YouTube, Twitter and blogs.[2]

National governments and NGOs are increasingly promoting literacy and developing multimodal pedagogical materials in Indigenous languages (in printed and digitals formats), and they are making available mass and social media (also in printed and digital modes) as well. The following language planning agencies and agents are involved in many LP

Table 4.3 Software and programming in Latin American Indigenous languages

In Quechua
Google Quechua   https://www.google.com/?hl=qu
Software Quechua   http://www.radioquechua.pe/2012/11/software-quechua.html
Hinantin   http://hinantin.com/home2/
Software for Learning Basic Quechua
    http://www.quechua.org.uk/Eng/Main/i_EuroTalkSoftware.HTM
RunasimiNet   http://facultad.pucp.edu.pe/ciencias-sociales/curso/quechua/

In Aymara
Ayni Bolivia: Juegos Educativos para la Alfabetización Digital
    http://www.aprendercreando.bo/
Ciberaymara (ILCA)   http://www.ilcanet.org/ciberaymara/
Jaqaru: Jueguemos a aprender aymara
    http://biblioteca.serindigena.org/index.php/es/centro-sur/mapuche/costumbres/109-
    biblioteca/animaciones/17887-jaqaru-juguemos-a-aprender-aymara

In Guarani
Diccionario Traductor Guaraní   http://www.iguarani.com/
Avañee (Diccionario Guarani)
    https://play.google.com/store/apps/details?id=py.com.twistedapp.avanee
Guaraní Online   http://liternauta.org/

In Mayan Languages
Google Translate   http://www.tiempo.com.mx/noticia/2567-crean_en_suiza_el_google_
    translate_para_la_lengua_maya/1
Firefox for Android in Purepecha (Tarascan) and Kaqchikel
    http://www.mozilla-mexico.org/
Wikimedia, Mozilla y Google traducen sus plataformas a la lengua maya
    http://mexico.cnn.com/tecnologia/2012/08/09/wikimedia-mozilla-y-google-traducen-la-
    lengua-maya-a-sus-plataformas

In Náhuatl
¡Videojuego en Náhuatl!   https://www.youtube.com/watch?v=mZhXU5i_3ns
Canal Nahuatl: curso en nahuatl   http://canalnahuatl.weebly.com/

In Mapudungun
Software Mapuche Williche
    http://www.futawillimapu.org/Llitu/Software-Mapuche-Williche.html
Windows in Mapudungun
    http://mapudunguyu.blogspot.com/2009/04/windows-en-mapudungun.html
El Mapu: El Diccionario Español Mapundungún para IOS
    https://www.wayerless.com/2011/03/mapu-el-diccionario-espanol-mapudungun-para-ios-
    creado-por-un-chileno/

and LR efforts: governments and government-authorized agencies and institutions, organizations with a public mandate for language regulation (e.g. language academies), grassroots (bottom-up) Indigenous organizations (e.g. feminist agencies on the issue of nonsexist language), and individuals from a variety of backgrounds, such as linguists, sociolinguists, language planners, teachers, language activists and Indigenous scholars in a variety of other fields.

Both Indigenous and non-Indigenous groups have joined to form virtual communities contributing to Indigenous language revitalization, so the presence of Indigenous languages of Latin America in cyberspace is considerable. However, most of the online communities that promote

Indigenous languages of Latin America use Spanish, English, or Portuguese, and these may be monolingual (e.g. only in Spanish or English) or multilingual (in English, Spanish, French and/or German, as well as Indigenous languages of Latin America). The virtual agents of Latin American language revitalization are composed of men, women, young people, Indigenous and non-Indigenous people (from diverse backgrounds), academic institutions, grassroots organizations, governmental and nongovernmental organizations, individual scholars, practitioners and language activists.

More and more Indigenous people are taking advantage of digital media to communicate with others in their Native languages. At the forefront of these movements are 'tech-savvy Indigenous internet users who have accepted the responsibility to ensure that their language and culture are reflected online' (Hivos.org., n.d.). Their pioneering work – their Indigenous language digital activism – helps to establish and augment rich digital content in Indigenous languages; in addition, their outreach and advocacy help to bring these media and technologies to a new generation of users who can help – consciously or not – revitalize their languages through these digital media technologies.

However, this work presents unique challenges to many of these digital activists. It could be, for instance, that there is no keyboard available with the necessary characters to type certain languages. Or perhaps there is a lack of consensus within the community with respect to orthographic norms or corpus modernization. For yet others, sociocultural considerations may limit what or how much information can be shared publicly online.

But resources are available to help language planners work through some of these difficulties. For instance, the Rising Voices initiative of Global Voices actively supports these efforts in several Latin American countries by offering microgrants and mentoring programs. In an effort to encourage the creation of networks and opportunities for peer learning, Rising Voices also co-organized the First Indigenous Language Digital Activism Gathering in Oaxaca, Mexico in October 2014. The meeting attracted 25 Indigenous language digital activists speaking 20 languages.

Hivos, an organization that promotes the use of ICT technologies to 'create and further promote, safeguard and anchor freedom of expression, freedom of information and internet freedom,' is funding Global Voices to expand this support in Ecuador and Colombia, where Indigenous language digital activists are already working with languages such as Kichwa, Achuar, Shuar and Wayuu online. With Global Voices facilitating, these digital activists will be able to create a space for peer-learning and for exchanging experiences through a local network, which will be affiliated with the group in Mexico. They also plan to initiate a new blog to track and share some of the best examples of Indigenous language digital activism in the region, focusing in particular on the Andean region (Hivos.org, n.d.).

In addition to the previously discussed Indigenous-language media and technology resources available in cyberspace, it is fundamental to develop all kinds of pedagogical resources and materials in Indigenous languages for different educational levels (preschool, kindergarten, elementary and secondary school, and college, if possible). Also, it is imperative that bilingual teachers be trained because they are the agents of language maintenance and revitalization in the educational domain. The issue is not only the implementation of educational programs in Indigenous languages for their communities of speakers; rather, these programs should also include the speakers of dominant languages, so they can develop linguistic and cultural awareness and learn to appreciate a wide range of invaluable knowledge and skills that the Indigenous languages bring with them. More importantly, the community of Indigenous language speakers needs support from diverse social sectors to ensure that intergenerational transmission of language and culture, which is a cornerstone in any linguistic and cultural revitalization effort, continues vibrantly in the future.

Last but not least, it is fundamental to create networks of LPP and LR at local and global levels. Planning, implementation, evaluation, outcome and sustainability are crucial facets of LPP and LR. After a language plan has been implemented, it is important to evaluate both the program and its outcome, so that efficacy and progress can be determined and the program can be modified as necessary to maintain progress towards the goals of the plan – and it must be sustainable to guarantee continuity for many years. If all this is carried out in a systematic way, language shift will be reversed successfully, and in the process the mosaic of linguistic landscapes and the rich repertoire of sounds and voices of many speakers of oppressed languages will still be heard and their knowledge and wisdom preserved for many years to come.

Some Stumbling Blocks

The examples in Tables 4.1, 4.2 and 4.3 demonstrate the wealth of opportunities that media and technology offer. However, there are still obstacles to be overcome. One of the most significant is connectivity. In earlier decades, the topography of Latin American countries made connectivity difficult, if not impossible. However, thanks to recent advances in satellite and wireless technologies, connectivity is now easier to achieve, and with greater ease and cost efficiency:

> Satellite-based Internet connections offer the same bandwidth and the same price whether they are located in an urban hub or in the most remote village. Inexpensive wireless units permit sharing of an Internet signal around a village. Costs continue to drop. Development projects must study the region to be connected carefully and choose the most practical connectivity options. (Lieberman, n.d.: 8)

Likewise, cost can frequently be a barrier. Often, the costs associated with the use of almost any technological resource are so great that most Indigenous communities cannot afford them, given the subsistence level of existence many of them still live. However, through planning and dialogue between the federal government, language planners, political leaders, teachers and Indigenous organizations, it has been possible to provide media and technology access to even the most remote communities.

In addition to accessibility and costs, the following questions also need to be taken into account during the planning stages:

> Will the particular group being served in a revitalization program have access to computers? Is there enough computer expertise in the community to maintain the computers and upgrade the hardware and software regularly and to migrate programs to newer systems as needed? Do the language revitalization goals of the community fit in with computer technology? Are the resources there that are needed to make programs or other software products that will be sufficient to achieve the language revitalization goals of the community? Will the fact that computer technology is nontraditional and reduces human interaction be problematic? (Hinton, 2001: 266)

It must certainly be kept in mind that any computer project should only be one component of the language revitalization plans, not the whole plan. With the above questions as guides, along with understanding other necessities of rural communities, it should be possible to incorporate technology, used with and for Indigenous languages, into the daily life of the community, including the education of the younger generations, preferably, of course, in their respective Indigenous languages. Such community planning should also include training programs in which community members of all ages can actively participate, to learn to take best advantage of these new resources in supporting their language use.

Perhaps one of the most difficult hurdles to overcome is the lack of access to print literacy in many Latin American rural communities, often the result of lack of funding and educational opportunities. Where solutions have been and continue to be found for the other issues discussed in this section, this problem continues to stymie efforts to resolve it, impeding the achievement, in rural contexts, of language revitalization goals that involve the use of newer technologies that require reading ability. Text-to-speech software, which reads aloud the words written on the screen, might be a temporary or partial solution to help to alleviate the more immediate concern of simply being able to make use of the technologies. This would, however, necessitate the existence or creation of such software in Indigenous languages, something that is not necessarily a given, and is not an insignificant undertaking in itself.

Social class has long been a divisive construct throughout Latin American history. There are many theorists (and perhaps idealists) around the world who argue that technology should serve to reduce such social divides. In practice, the often-drastic differences in economic resources and opportunities between social classes in Latin America contribute to the digital divide (who can afford it, and who cannot). This then becomes an endless loop, with the digital divide in turn contributing to an increasing division between classes, rather than the hoped-for creation of better opportunities for everyone. Careful, long-range planning for the implementation of pilot programs is thus essential to avoid growing social disparity, and should be carried out from multiple perspectives – technological, economic, linguistic, political and educational – and should include participation by (representatives of) all members of society. This is the best way to achieve favorable, long-lasting results.

Another aspect to keep in mind is the importance of self-ownership of the technology: It must 'belong' to the Indigenous people and be perceived as something desirable and useful – not something imposed by outsiders. Indigenous people need to control the technology for their own purposes, recognizing its relevance for their lives.

Another possible obstacle related to the implementation of technology is the possibility that it could interfere with cultural traditions and the transmission of the Indigenous language. Media and technology could constitute antitraditional tools that could appropriate some traditional practices, such as oral tradition and cultural memory, which are transmitted from generation to generation through storytelling. Hence, we need to be cautious about going overboard and assuming that the incorporation of technology will always be the best solution:

> [T]he Web is a technology we are only beginning to take advantage of. [...] Early indications, coupled with the rapid growth of Web technologies for audio and video, suggest that the Web is growing in its potential as a language revitalization tool. It is therefore probably best to take a balanced approach of experimenting with the new technology while maintaining a healthy skepticism toward it. (Hinton, 2001: 267–268)

This is why it is necessary to be aware of all kinds of software and mass and social media in Indigenous languages, and be willing to explore the possibilities, but also be willing to accept if a community decides it is not in their best interest.

Another modality to explore as a means of ensuring that the younger generations do not lose contact with their ancestral roots is to encourage them to stay in contact with the elders of the community through media and technology. From this suggestion, though, emerges another possible obstacle, this one having to do with the generational divide in terms of technology use. In some cases, elders do not have the same access to technological resources, or they simply feel intimidated by them and do not want to use them. 'This is a serious problem for language maintenance and revitalization efforts on the Web since elders [in certain contexts] are frequently the only fluent speakers' (Buszard-Welcher, 2001: 339). In reality, sometimes what they need is for someone to take time to teach them how to handle those technological resources. To make this happen, it is essential to implement a training program in order to alleviate the technological insecurities of the members of these generations, and the rest of the population as a whole.

Conclusions

Media, technology, computers and schooling can all play a significant role in language revitalization, but by no means do they constitute a panacea for language maintenance and revitalization. Intergenerational transmission of the mother tongue is still the most powerful and effective prescription for invigorating and preserving the functional domains of Indigenous languages (Fishman, 1991). Systematic language and policy and planning, solid technological planning and language revitalization from multiple angles and agents, including both top-down and bottom-up efforts, also play a part. To solidify the objectives of language teaching and learning and language revitalization, it is necessary to take robust measures at every level, and to consolidate, articulate, unite, and multiply efforts. It is also critical to develop, with top-down and bottom-up participation, a solid linguistic, financial, and technological plan, and institute genuine educational reform to allow Indigenous languages to take their rightful place in education and the broader society. All of this needs to happen with the active participation of Indigenous peoples themselves, along with other sectors and vectors of society. Otherwise, the Indigenous languages of Latin America will slowly decline in the years to come.

Media and technology offer some alluring potential benefits, but much still needs to be done to take full advantage of them. Throughout this chapter, I have outlined current efforts and suggested possible future directions for incorporating media and technology into the language maintenance and revitalization arsenal, including the necessity to gain the decisive support of and instill a positive attitude in the majority Spanish-speaking population for initiatives that revitalize, valorize, promote and spread Indigenous languages. To effectively revitalize and disseminate Indigenous languages, the social networks that connect home, school, community and the wider society must be taken into account.

Notes

(1) For comprehensive information on languages in Latin America, see Adelaar and Muysken (2004); Aikhenvald (2012); *Atlas Sociolingüístico de Pueblos Indígenas de América Latina*, vols. 1 and 2 (2009); Campbell and Grondona (2012); Cerrón-Palomino (2008); Cortina (2014); O'Connor and Muysken (2014); and Torero (2002), among others. For more targeted treatments, see Coronel-Molina (2015) on language

ideology, policy, and planning in Peru; Coronel-Molina and McCarty (2016) for a hemispheric macro-level treatment of Indigenous language revitalization in the Americas; Hornberger (1996) on Indigenous literacies in the Americas; Hornberger and King (2001) on reversing language shift in South America; King and Haboud (2002) on language planning and policy in Ecuador; King and Hornberger (2004); and McCarty (2012) for an insightful chapter on Indigenous language planning and policy in the Americas.

(2)   For Indigenous languages of Latin America in media and technology, see Albó (1998); Bernard (1996); Coler and Homola (2015); Coronel-Molina (1999, 2013, 2016); Coronel-Molina and McCarty (2011); Firestone (2006, 2012); Hornberger (1996); Hornberger and Coronel-Molina (2004); Hornberger and King (2001); Hornberger and Swinehart (2012); Sumida Huaman (2011); Luykx (2001); Swinehart (2012); Uribe-Jongbloed (2013); and von Gleich (2004). For media and technology in relation to Indigenous languages in general, see Dyson Grant and Hendriks (2015); Gruffydd and Uribe-Jongbloed (2013); Jones (2015); Salazar (2007); Warschauer (1999); and Warschauer and Chun (2002). For language revitalization in geneneral, see Fishman (1991, 2001); Grenoble and Whaley (1998); Hinton and Hale (2001), among others.

References

Adelaar, W. and Muysken, P. (2004) *The Languages of the Andes*. Cambridge: Cambridge University Press.

Aikhenvald, A.Y. (2012) *The Languages of the Amazon*. Oxford: Oxford University Press.

AILLA (Archive of the Indigenous Languages of Latin America) (n.d.). Retrieved from http://www.ailla.utexas.org/site/lg_about.html

Albó, X. (1998) Expresión indígena, diglosia y medios de comunicación. In L.E. López and I. Jung (eds) *Sobre las Huellas de la Voz: Sociolingüística de la Oralidad y la Escritura en Su Relación con la eEducación* (pp. 126–156). Madrid: Morata/PROEIB Andes/DSE.

Atlas Sociolingüístico de Pueblos Indígenas de America Latina (Vols. 1–2). (2009). Cochabamba, Bolivia: FUNPROEIB Andes/UNICEF.

Bernard, H.R. (1996) Language preservation and publishing. In N.H. Hornberger (ed.) *Indigenous Literacies in the Americas: Language Planning from the Bottom Up* (pp. 139–156). Berlin: Mouton de Gruyter.

Buszard-Welcher, L. (2001) Can the Web help save my language? In L. Hinton and K. Hale (eds) *The Green Book of Language Revitalization in Practice* (pp. 331–345). San Diego, CA: Academic Press.

Campbell, L. and Grondona, V. (eds) (2012) *The Indigenous Languages of South America: A Comprehensive Guide*. Berlin: Mouton de Gruyter.

Cerrón-Palomino, R. (2008) *Voces del Ande: Ensayos sobre Onomástica Andina*. Lima, Peru: Fondo Editorial PUCP.

Coler, M. and Homola, P. (2015) Rule based machine translation for Aymara. In M.C. Jones (ed.) *Endangered Languages and New Technology* (pp. 35–48). Cambridge: Cambridge University Press.

Coronel-Molina, S.M. (1999) Functional domains of the Quechua language in Peru: Issues of status planning. *International Journal of Bilingual Education and Bilingualism* 2 (3), 166–180.

Coronel-Molina, S.M. (2013) New functional domains of Quechua and Aymara: Mass media and social media. In J.F. Tollefson (ed.) *Language Policies in Education: Critical Issues* (pp. 278–300). New York, NY: Routledge.

Coronel-Molina, S.M. (2015) *Language Ideology, Policy and Planning in Peru*. Bristol: Multilingual Matters.

Coronel-Molina, S.M. (2016) New domains for Indigenous language acquisition and use in Latin America and the Caribbean. In S.M. Coronel-Molina and T.L. McCarty (eds) *Indigenous Language Revitalization in the Americas* (pp. 292–311). New York, NY: Routledge.
Coronel-Molina, S.M. and McCarty, T.L. (2011) Language curriculum design and evaluation for endangered languages. In P. Austin and J. Sallabank (eds) *The Cambridge Handbook of Endangered Languages* (pp. 354–370). Cambridge: Cambridge University Press.
Coronel-Molina, S.M. and McCarty, T.L. (eds) (2016) *Indigenous Language Revitalization in the Americas*. New York, NY: Routledge.
Cortina, R. (ed.) (2014) *The Education of Indigenous Citizens in Latin America*. Bristol: Multilingual Matters.
Crystal, D. (2001) *Language and the Internet*. Cambridge: Cambridge University Press.
Dyson, L.E., Grant, S. and Hendriks, M. (2015) *Indigenous People and Mobile Technologies*. New York, NY: Routledge.
Firestone, A.R. (2006) Runakuna Hatarinqaku. Revitalizing Quechua in Urban Ayacucho, Peru. Unpublished master's thesis, University of Illinois, Urbana-Champaign.
Firestone, A.R. (2012) Quechua and Spanish in the Urban Andes: A Study on Language Dynamics and Identity Construction Among Peruvian Youth. Unpublished Ph.D. dissertation, University of Illinois at Urbana-Champaign, IL.
Fishman, J.A. (1991) *Reversing Language Shift: Theoretical and Empirical Foundations of Assistance to Threatened Languages*. Clevedon: Multilingual Matters.
Fishman, J.A. (ed.) (2001) *Can Threatened Languages be Saved? Reversing Language Shift, Revisited: A 21st Century Perspective*. Clevedon: Multilingual Matters.
Gadelii, K.E. (1999) *Language Planning: Theory and Practice. Evaluation of Language Planning Cases Worldwide*. Paris: UNESCO.
Grenoble, L.A. and Whaley, L.J. (eds) (1998) *Endangered Languages: Current Issues and Future Prospects*. Cambridge: Cambridge University Press.
Gruffydd Jones, E.H. and Uribe-Jongbloed, E. (eds) (2013) *Social Media and Minority Languages: Convergence and the Creative Industries*. Bristol: Multilingual Matters.
Hinton, L. (2001) Audio-video documentation. In L. Hinton and K. Hale (eds) *The Green Book of Language Revitalization in Practice* (pp. 265–271). San Diego, CA: Academic Press.
Hinton, L. and Hale, K. (eds) (2001) *The Green Book of Language Revitalization in Practice*. San Diego, CA: Academic Press.
Hivos.org (n.d.) *Network of Digital Activism of Indigenous Languages*. Retrieved from https://hivos.org/activity/network-digital-activism-indigenous-languages
Hornberger, N.H. (ed.) (1996) *Indigenous Literacies in the Americas: Language Planning from the Bottom Up*. Berlin: Mouton de Gruyter.
Hornberger, N.H. and King, K.A. (2001) Reversing Quechua language shift in South America. In J.A. Fishman (ed.) *Can Threatened Languages be Saved? Reversing Language Shift, Revisited: A 21st Century Perspective* (pp. 166–194). Clevedon: Multilingual Matters.
Hornberger, N.H. and Coronel-Molina, S.M. (2004) Quechua language shift, maintenance and revitalization in the Andes: The case for language planning. *International Journal of the Sociology of Language* 167, 9–67.
Hornberger, N.H. and Swinehart, K. (2012) Bilingual intercultural education and Andean hip-hop: Transnational sites for indigenous language and identity. *Language in Society* 41 (4), 499–525.
Human Resources Development and Operations Policy (7 June 1993) Indigenous people in Latin America. *HRO Dissemination Notes, 8*. Retrieved from http://www.worldbank.org/html/extdr/hnp/hddflash/hcnote/hrn007.html

Jones, M.C. (2015) *Endangered Languages and New Technology*. Cambridge: Cambridge University Press.

Kaplan, A.M. and Haenlein, M. (2010) Users of the world, unite! The challenges and opportunities of social media. *Business Horizons* 53 (1), 59–68.

Kietzmann, J.H., Hermkens, K., McCarthy, I.P. and Silvestre, B.S. (2011) Social media? Get serious! Understanding the functional building blocks of social media. *Business Horizons* 54 (3), 241–251.

King, K.A. (2001) *Language Revitalization Processes and Prospects: Quichua in the Ecuadorian Andes*. Clevedon: Multilingual Matters.

King, K.A. and Haboud, M. (2002) Language planning and policy in Ecuador. *Current Issues in Language Planning* 3 (4), 359–424.

King, K.A. and Hornberger, N.H. (guest eds) (2004) Quechua sociolinguistics. *International Journal of the Sociology of Language* 67 (entire).

Lieberman, A.E. (n.d.) *Taking Ownership: Strengthening Indigenous Cultures and Languages through the use of ICTs*. Retrieved from http://learnlink.aed.org/Publications/ Concept_Papers/taking_ownership.pdf

Lieberman, A.E. (2002) Bringing Mayan language and culture across the digital divide. *TechKnowLogia* July–September, 80–83. Retrieved from http://TechKnowlogia.org

Luykx, A. (2001) Across the Andean airwaves: Satellite radio broadcasting in Quechua. In C. Moseley, N. Ostler and H. Ouzzate (eds) *Endangered Languages and the Media* (pp. 115–119). Bath: Foundation for Endangered Languages.

McCarty, T.L. (2012) Indigenous language planning and policy in the Americas. In B. Spolsky (ed.) *The Cambridge Handbook of Language Policy* (pp. 544–569). Cambridge: Cambridge University Press.

Montviloff, V. (2002, April) Meeting the challenges of language diversity in the information society. Paper presented at the Congreso Mundial sobre Políticas Lingüísticas, Barcelona, Spain. Retrieved from http://www.linguapax.org/congres/taller/taller5/Montviloff.html

O'Connor, L. and Muysken, P. (2014) *The Native Languages of South America: Origins, Development, Typology*. Cambridge: Cambridge University Press.

Salazar, J.F. (2007) Indigenous people and the cultural construction of information and communication technology (ICT) in Latin America. In L.E. Dyson, M. Hendriks and S. Grant (eds) *Information Technology and Indigenous People* (pp. 14–27). Hershey, PA: Information Science Publishing.

Social Media (n.d.) *Wikipedia*. Retrieved from https://en.wikipedia.org/wiki/Social_media.

Stewart, W. (1968) A sociolinguistic typology for describing national multilingualism. In J.A. Fishman (ed.) *Readings in the Sociology of Language* (pp. 531–545). The Hague: Mouton.

Sumida Huaman, E. (2011) Indigenous language revitalization and new media: Postsecondary students as innovators. *Global Media Journal* 11 (18), 1–15. Retrieved from https://www.researchgate.net/publication/265451186_Indigenous_language_revitalization_and_new_media_Postsecondary_students_as_innovators

Swinehart, K. (2012) Ayllu on the Airwaves: Rap, Reform, and Redemption on Aymara National Radio. Unpublished PhD dissertation, University of Pennsylvania, Philadelphia.

Torero, A. (2002) *Idiomas de los Andes. Lingüística e Historia*. Lima, Peru: IFEA.

Uribe-Jongbloed, E. (2013) Minority language media studies and communication for social change: Dialogue between Europe and Latin America. In E.H. Gruffydd Jones and E. Uribe-Jongbloed (eds) *Social Media and Minority Languages: Convergence and the Creative Industries* (pp. 31–46). Bristol: Multilingual Matters.

von Gleich, U. (2004) New Quechu literacies in Bolivia. *International Journal of the Sociology of Language* 167, 131–146.

Wagner, D.A. and Hopey, C. (1999) Literacy, electronic networking, and the Internet. In D.A. Wagner, R.L. Venezky and B.V. Street (eds) *Literacy: An International Handbook* (pp. 475–481). Boulder, CO: Westview.

Warschauer, M. (1999) *Electronic Literacies: Language, Culture, and Power in Online Education*. Mahwah, NJ: Lawrence Erlbaum.

Warschauer, M. and Chun, D. (guest eds) (2002) *Technology and Indigenous Languages*. Special issue, *Language Learning and Technology* 6 (2), entire.

5 Language Vitality In and Out of School in a Remote Indigenous Australian Context

Inge Kral and Elizabeth Marrkilyi Ellis

All too often it is assumed that Indigenous language learning should take place in the classroom. But such assumptions do not consider the socio-cultural aspects of language acquisition, particularly in settings where the Indigenous mother tongue is still the first language. In this chapter, Inge Kral and Elizabeth Marrkilyi Ellis draw on their experience as language educators and researchers to consider language vitality in and out of school in a remote Indigenous Australian context. They consider the history of language pedagogy in the 'Ngaanyatjarra Lands' desert region of Western Australia and critically reflect on language education policy locally and nationally. Highlighted in this chapter is the effect of changing modes of communication in the Western Desert and the impact on oral traditions. Addressed also is the ensuing erosion of culturally relevant traditional roles and the language practices that underpin social organization. Kral and Ellis argue that in the quest to maintain language vitality and ensure intergenerational language transmission, everyday language policies and practices are urgently required. Such community-based language maintenance strategies would include language use through digital communication technologies and social media.

Introduction

In this chapter we present two perspectives on Indigenous language learning in the region known as the Ngaanyatjarra Lands in the Western Desert of Australia – an area of some 188,000 square kilometres, three times the size of Tasmania, fanning out from the tri-state border region of Western Australia – with a population of approximately 2000 (Figure 5.1). Elizabeth Marrkilyi Ellis is an Indigenous linguist and speaker of multiple Western Desert dialects. She has worked as a Ngaatjatjarra/Pitjantjatjara language teacher, interpreter and translator, and dictionary worker over

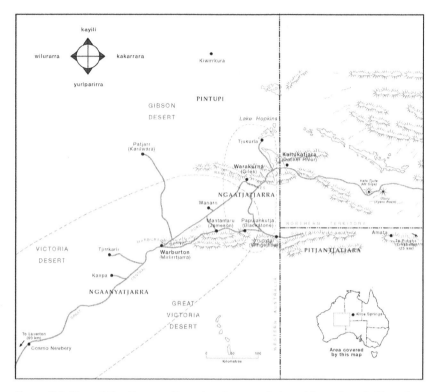

Figure 5.1 Map of the Ngaanyatjarra Lands, commissioned from Brenda Thornley, 2007, courtesy of Institute for Aboriginal Development, Alice Springs, NT, Australia

many decades. Having been awarded an Australian Research Council Discovery Indigenous Award at the Australian National University, Ellis is now documenting and analyzing the verbal arts of her speech community.[1] Inge Kral is a linguistic anthropologist at the Australian National University with some 30 years' experience as an educator and researcher in Indigenous language settings in Australia. Kral and Ellis have worked together over many years and recently collaborated on research documenting the changing modes of communication in the Western Desert and the impact of communication technologies on language use.[2]

Around the globe minority Indigenous languages are under threat, and as they disappear so too will the knowledge systems and worldview associated with each language (Evans, 2010; Woodbury, 1998). Of the originally estimated 250 Indigenous Australian languages plus dialects, only 13 are considered 'healthy' (Marmion *et al.*, 2014). Less than 20 will be passed on to the next generations and only a few will retain their full expressive richness. The majority language in the region is Ngaanyatjarra; however, speakers of the mutually intelligible Western Desert dialects Ngaatjatjarra, Pitjantjatjara, Pintupi and Manytjiltjarra also live in the

Ngaanyatjarra Lands. Ngaanyatjarra has been rated as 'critically endangered' (AIATSIS/FATSIL, 2005: 193).

Important aspects of the fragile communicative systems of Australian languages include ceremonial language, the use of respect registers and avoidance languages (Dixon, 1990; McConvell, 1982) and multimodal narrative (Green, 2014). The multimodal speech arts – oral narratives and other symbolic, visual and gestural modes of representation and communication – are a valued yet highly endangered part of the traditions of Western Desert people. Oral traditions are central to cultural practices and social interaction, and they embrace special respectful ways of speaking, sign language and the use of graphic symbols to accompany sand story narratives. Although it is evident that changed sociocultural factors have impacted on everyday spoken Ngaanyatjarra and child language socialization practices (Kral, 2012), the fact that these dialects are still used in everyday social interaction reveals much about the resilience of the language and its centrality to contemporary identity and ways of being. However, opportunities for Western Desert youth to acquire the full expressive potential of the oral traditions of their culture are decreasing dramatically.

In this chapter we begin by considering language learning from a pedagogical perspective by tracing the history of language teaching in the Ngaanyatjarra context. We show how, in instructional settings, language teaching has focused mainly on vernacular literacy. Ellis discusses the frustration of elders as they seek to find strategies to ensure that their language and culture are not lost. Together we ponder the role that the school can really play in 'saving' (Hornberger, 2008) endangered languages, and turn our attention to everyday language policies and practices (McCarty, 2011). We consider the connection between language endangerment and language socialization and the role of the family and community in the acquisition and transmission of cultural processes and practices, including language, over successive generations. We then shift to a focus on language vitality and resilience and discuss the dynamic hybridity of new youth language practices. We conclude by discussing a range of strategies in and out of school that could be considered to ensure that the full spectrum and richness of Western Desert dialects are transmitted to future generations.

Vernacular Literacy: A Short History of Formal Language Teaching

We begin with a short account of the history of alphabetic literacy learning in the Ngaanyatjarra region.[3] As was the situation in other locations in Australia (Gale, 1997) and around the globe, much early Indigenous language pedagogy was undertaken by missionaries, followed by a few *ad hoc* school initiatives from the 1970s.

The first phase: Adult vernacular literacy

The United Aborigines Mission (UAM) arrived at Warburton Ranges in 1934, attracting a small number of nomadic families who spoke no English. A school was soon established and English language and literacy teaching commenced (Figure 5.2). Virtually no linguistic or educational attention was paid to Ngaanyatjarra until 1952 when UAM linguist Wilf Douglas commenced the first serious study of Western Desert dialects (Douglas, 1964).[4] By 1957 he had compiled a grammatical analysis and developed a Roman alphabet orthography based on the Pitjantjatjara model from Ernabella Mission some 500 kilometers to the east. Simple primers developed to teach literacy provided the first accessible reading materials for adult vernacular literacy learners.

In 1963 linguists Amee Glass and Dorothy Hackett commenced a life-time vocation: learning Ngaanyatjarra, teaching vernacular literacy and translating scripture from English to Ngaanyatjarra and teaching vernacular literacy. Working in collaboration with newly literate Ngaanyatjarra speakers, they published a significant number of Christian texts in Ngaanyatjarra including the Old and New Testaments, the *Ngaanyatjarra/ Ngaatjatjarra to English Dictionary* (Glass & Hackett, 2003), and other secular texts and children's books. Christian literacy events were important as they modeled a purpose for vernacular reading outside pedagogical contexts. Church services and Sunday School activities were also textually mediated with Bible stories and hymns in Ngaanyatjarra as well as English.

Figure 5.2 Children at the first school at Warburton Ranges Mission early 1930s (*Source*: TJ-0000315 Tjumalampatju: Ngaanyatjarra Council Archive, used with permission from Ngaanyatjarra Council)

Additionally, services were held in the camps with hymn-singing and Bible reading led by family members. Hence, some members of the older generation are able to read and write Ngaanyatjarra. They in turn have passed vernacular literacy practices on to some in the next generation (Kral, 2012).

Significantly, throughout this period the mother tongue was strong; few adults spoke English and everyday life still pivoted around traditional practices and processes. Moreover, the emphasis was on introducing literacy in the vernacular as well as English. Since then, by contrast, little attention has been paid to Indigenous language teaching, apart from some informal Christian literacy activities, and in the schools a brief bilingual education initiative during the 1970s and subsequent LOTE initiatives. Simultaneously language change has increased at a rapid rate.

The second phase: School initiatives

In the 1970s, under the reforming agenda of the federal Whitlam Labor government, a policy turn introduced an ethos of self-determination across Indigenous Australia. Concordantly, policy emerged that took account of Australia's linguistic diversity and some bilingual education initiatives emerged in government and nongovernment schools in Aboriginal communities in Western Australia, South Australia and the Northern Territory (Disbray, 2015; Disbray *et al.*, 2017; Hartman & Henderson, 1994; Simpson *et al.*, 2009). Around Australia most official bilingual programs have ceased operating. Localized language programs have, however, continued in many locations, developed under the Languages Other Than English (LOTE) program or as Indigenous Language and Culture programs (Disbray, 2015), often in tandem with 'Learning on Country' activities in which elders take students out of the classroom and into the countryside to acquire ecological and linguistic knowledge (Douglas, 2015; Fogarty & Schwab, 2012).

At Warburton in 1973, in response to these broader national reforms, the UAM relinquished control of the mission to the government. Since the 1960s schooling at Warburton had been administered by the Education Department of Western Australia. In 1974 a second phase of vernacular literacy pedagogy commenced with the introduction of a pilot bilingual education program at Warburton School in tandem with training for Aboriginal teacher aides. The bilingual program provided a focus for increased Ngaanyatjarra literacy production. It was, however, short-lived and ceased in 1980. This period also saw Ngaanyatjarra people move out of Warburton and establish small outstation communities. By the 1990s the Ngaanyatjarra Lands encompassed some ten communities with a school in most communities.

Around this time a Ngaanyatjarra literacy program – taught by local Aboriginal Education Workers (AEWs), later termed Aboriginal and Islander Education Officers (AIEOs) – was evident in some schools. In 1998 Ngaanyatjarra language teaching came under the official LOTE program of the Western Australia Education Department (Glass, 2000). Jan

Mountney from the Summer Institute of Linguistics supported the program and her language teaching workshops provided an unusual opportunity for concentrated reading and writing in the vernacular as well as English. The LOTE program ceased some years ago. Nevertheless, the community desire to continue producing mother tongue reading material is evident in recent community-based book production initiatives.

The initiatives discussed above tended to focus on literacy. Then in 2002, the Education Department collaborated with the Ngaanyatjarra Council to develop a Ngaanyatjarra Language and Culture Curriculum (compiled by Kral and Ellis). It was not implemented until 2013 when aspects of the curriculum were introduced. Recently the Education Department has supported a Learning Day 'on country' with primary school students and teachers, as well as Daisy Ward, the school Community Liaison Officer, and Ngaanyatjarra Council anthropologist David Brooks. Such events are, however, still in their infancy. Although by 2018, Ngaanyatjarra language and culture was seeping into the school curriculum and early childhood programs were supported by children's books in Ngaanyatjarra.[5]

At this juncture, it should be mentioned that the first non-missionary linguist, Kazuko Obata, was appointed by the Ngaanyatjarra Council to work at a short-lived Language Center based at Ngaanyatjarra Community College in Warburton from 2000–2001 (Obata *et al.*, 2005). Notably, this community initiative stood apart from the school.

In the next section Ellis draws on her recent experience as a teacher and Area Director for the Ngaanyatjarra Lands schools to discuss what she perceives to be the stumbling blocks to language learning in the school setting, including the constraints for Aboriginal teacher and teacher aide training, and planning associated with language learning events on country and cultural activities with elders.

'We Do Not Want to Lose Our Language and Culture'

Currently, in the Ngaanyatjarra region the education focus, as in most remote Indigenous schools, is primarily on learning English language and literacy, and is laden with a rhetoric of failure. So what of the Indigenous voice in choosing how we want our children to be educated?

In the Ngaanyatjarra world it is understood that elders need to and must pass on traditional knowledge and customs to the younger generation within the education system, and many families currently do this in their own time, with their own resources (see also Douglas, 2015; Minutjukur *et al.*, 2014 for other Australian examples). Families want to work with the school to pass on traditional knowledge and culture because this is where the children are for the majority of the day when school is in. Elders and family members need to take students out on country because all the stories and knowledge that Ngaanyatjarra people have in their heads is there in the country. This is the Ngaanyatjarra people's teaching and learning methodology. This system was in place long before the coming of the White man. This traditional method of teaching and learning evolved out of the oldest culture on earth and has been taught continuously in the Western Desert for some 40,000 to 60,000 years.

Traditionally for us language and culture learning occurred on country within the extended family setting; therefore current language teaching must occur outside of schools. I am not saying that every vernacular lesson has to be outside of the school. What I am saying that there needs to be an acknowledgement of the extremely successful traditional Ngaanyatjarra teaching and learning methodologies and there has to be a balance between the Ngaanyatjarra way of teaching and learning and the mainstream approach. However, language learning in school settings rarely acknowledges traditional ways of teaching and learning. Elders want to teach, but they want to teach traditional knowledge, speech styles and registers on country and through narrative and cultural activities. Often elders are not accorded respect by the school for this approach. This marginalization of traditional learning practices is in part associated with school rules and regulations that work against such approaches, but also the fact that the national policy focus is now oriented specifically to English literacy learning. Thus, Aboriginal languages have mostly been pushed out of the school program and teachers tend to be fearful of challenging such national (and local) policy directives.

Importantly, I and other Ngaanyatjarra elders consider that one of the main reasons why children are not succeeding at school is language. In the Ngaanyatjarra Lands a student arrives at school at the age of five not speaking English, but rather his or her mother tongue: Ngaanyatjarra, Ngaatjatjarra, Pitjantjatjara, Manytjiltjarra or Pintupi. Most of the schools do not have preschool in the community; therefore the students are a few years behind before they start compared to an English first language-speaking child. On arrival at school Ngaanyatjarra students are given instructions and taught in English – a second or third language for most. A further critical reason why Ngaanyatjarra students are not succeeding at school is due to the fact that they do not see their family members working as teachers and little support is directed towards improving Aboriginal language teaching competence in the school environment – even though traditionally all adults were teachers and older children taught younger children.

Moreover, I consider that what is needed in these schools is a deeper understanding of the complexity of language and literacy instruction in this setting, as well as the development of appropriate curricula and training for local Ngaanyatjarra teachers. We do not have local Ngaanyatjarra people trained as teachers. We have local assistant teachers or AIEOs, but most are not literate in the Ngaanyatjarra language. AIEOs with literacy skills are hardly ever given free reign and assistance to deliver Ngaanyatjarra lessons.

Another issue is that the majority of the *walypala kuultiitja* (non-Aboriginal teachers) who come to teach in the Lands have little or no understanding of the complexity of this linguistic and educational context. The cultural divide is too great and requires teachers with special qualities, training and common sense to work and live in such a challenging environment. In terms of oral English language development, oftentimes the non-Aboriginal teachers are not modeling good Standard Australian English for the students as they speak to the students using a simplified English. Additionally, the majority of walypala kuultiitja do not know how to effectively utilize and interact with their AIEOs in the classroom. Many times I have gone into a classroom only to see the whitefella teacher at the front, teaching, while the AIEO sits silently at the back. The kuultiitja must encourage the AIEOs to perform at every level. Most of the time AIEOs are treated as crowd controllers and interpreters. The majority of walypala kuultiitja are not diligent in ensuring optimum input from their AIEOs, which would ensure optimum learning by the students. The coteaching environment between the AIEO and the teacher should be a respectful, comfortable one, where sharing, learning and teaching occurs to allow both to gain skills and knowledge from the other to ensure an exciting, inspiring, supportive and creative environment for the learner (cf. Bowman *et al.*, 1999).

In considering the ideal approach to language pedagogy in this context, I suggest that every community within the Ngaanyatjarra Lands should have a Language and Culture Center. Ideally this Center would be autonomous, independently funded and managed by the Indigenous peoples of the Ngaanyatjarra Lands. Within this Center children would attend sessions throughout the school term and holiday times where they are acquiring skills and knowledge of their mother tongue and their ancestors' culture. Topics taught in this Center would include those documented in the Ngaanyatjarra Language and Culture Curriculum, including: bush foods, waterholes, hunting, tracking, food preparation, kinship, and the ancestral home country, as well as the stories, songs and dances that belong to that country. The Center and the school staff would work together harmoniously and respectfully. The planning of language learning events on country would ensure that the correct protocols are implemented, that is, knowing where to go and who to include. This arrangement would advance the valuing of the mainstream language and culture plus Ngaanyatjarra language and culture. It would also enable elders to reclaim their traditional role as the educational institution, the library and the museum of Ngaanyatjarra society.

Language Endangerment and Language Policy

In Australia, schools and public policy relay important messages about the value, or not, of Indigenous languages and much public debate has been contested. A fundamental ideology that has been perpetuated is the notion that Indigenous languages hold youth back from academic and life success.[6] This became evident in the 1990s when the earlier language rights approach to Indigenous education was replaced by a discourse of crisis around the literacy 'problem' which linked unemployment and welfare dependency to poor education and lack of English. It was around this time that bilingual education programs in Indigenous schools waned (Simpson *et al.*, 2009), and the era of external benchmarking testing and a back-to-basics approach to literacy pedagogy was ushered in.

The commencement in 2008 of the National Assessment Program – Literacy and Numeracy (NAPLaN) – in Australian schools led to Indigenous students being assessed in accordance with the same developmental pathway for literacy achievement set by English first language students (McKay, 2001).[7] However, as researchers note (Wigglesworth *et al.*, 2011) while being suitable for most groups of Standard Australian English speakers, the NAPLaN test is linguistically and culturally unsuitable for Indigenous children living in remote communities. It is understood that Indigenous students need to be taught English to fully participate in society; however, schooling tends to reduce the linguistic complexity of students' everyday lives by privileging English and English literacy, and NAPLaN is now serving as a *de facto* language policy. Finally, it has been argued that 'English-only schooling as practised in most Australian Indigenous communities is destructive – it reduces children's ability to learn English, to learn other subjects, to learn about the verbal arts of their own societies' (Simpson, 2014).

In Australia a monolingual English mindset dominates and this continues to determine the direction of language policy in schools in remote regions where Indigenous languages are under pressure (Truscott & Malcolm, 2010). Scholars have argued that attitudes to language are of key importance in assessing the chances of endangered language survival (Austin & Sallabank, 2013). Often the groundwork for language shift is laid in language ideologies (Woolard, 1998) whereby negative attitudes toward endangered languages 'are both an outcome and a cause of shift to dominant languages' (Austin & Sallabank, 2013: 313). It has also been suggested (Wyman *et al.*, 2014a: 9) that various forms of policymaking – both formal and informal – may either drive endangerment and language shift or support language maintenance. So rather than relying on the implementation of language policies by the state or by schools to 'save' endangered languages, another approach is the implementation of informal or everyday language policy – that is, paying attention to everyday language choices and practices. Hence language policy can be viewed as a 'situated sociocultural process' whereby it is 'the complex of practices, ideologies, attitudes, and formal and informal mechanisms [that influence] people's language choices in profound and pervasive everyday ways' (McCarty, 2011: xii; Disbray, 2015; see also Chapter 3, this volume, describing the Māori experience of language resilience and everyday language policies).

Language socialization studies also indicate that experiences of language maintenance and endangerment are deeply rooted within local relationships, practices, knowledge systems, and geographical places and they can vary between individuals, peer groups and families (Wyman, 2014: 106). Ethnographic research has provided insights into the sociocultural processes underlying language maintenance and shift by illuminating what enables or stifles language learning (Granadillo & Orcutt-Gachiri, 2011; Wyman, 2012; Wyman *et al.*, 2014b), as well as youth language practices, attitudes and ideologies (McCarty, 2011). The focus on youth is crucial because 'the future of their Indigenous languages is in their hands' (Hinton, 2014: xi), as language choices made at this age will likely influence how they socialize their own children (Friedman, 2014).[8]

Language Endangerment and Youth Language Practices

Indigenous youth around the globe are trying to form their linguistic identities amidst tidal waves of sociolinguistic transformation and competing language ideologies (Harrison, 2007). Their everyday practices commonly embrace the coexistence of multiple languages and are often mediated by new information, globally circulating cultural forms, and communication technologies, resulting in the development of new cultural and related multimodal linguistic practices that intertwine with new intercultural or 'hybrid' identities (Duff, 2008). Scholars now talk of the notion of 'translanguaging' – that is, 'engaging in bilingual or multilingual discourse practices' (García, 2014: 209) – to better describe the actual ways that people, especially young people, adroitly move between languages. This perspective is one that affirms actual contemporary youth language practices.

In remote Australia the formation of youth linguistic identities is wedged between elders admonishing youth for codemixing and no longer speaking their ancestral languages properly, diminished opportunities to acquire complex grammatical forms and context-specific lexical knowledge, and the mainstream rendering of Indigenous mother tongues as invisible while prioritizing language and literacy learning in Standard Australian English. Youth are also negotiating new identities in response to the effects of globalized media on youth language and cultural practices (Kral, 2012), and we are seeing the emergence of hybrid linguistic repertoires and contemporary language varieties (Meakins, 2008; Morrison & Disbray, 2008; O'Shannessy, 2011). In the area of language documentation, however, most research has been focused on the older generation. Consequently we know little about the manner in which Indigenous youth are taking up the oral traditions of their culture or about how the communicative systems, speech styles, verbal arts, performance genres and inter-related knowledge systems are being acquired by youth.

Western Desert youth are living in this rapidly shifting linguistic ecology. For them, the introduced institutional pressures of schooling and employment have impacted their capacity to engage in cultural practices that previously enabled the acquisition of context-specific language forms and the acquisition of specialist knowledge. Despite these altered socio-cultural circumstances, language remains a strong identity marker and young people are transforming it to suit the contemporary context. They live in a speech community where the Indigenous mother tongue is still being transmitted to the next generation. Language change is apparent nevertheless, with older Ngaanyatjarra speakers noting that young people tend to use less complex sounds and many are not acquiring certain complex grammatical constructions. English codemixing is also evident, and younger speakers display a diminishing repertoire of communicative practices not only in the verbal artistry of oral narrative, but also in the use of respect and avoidance forms and special speech styles.

In research undertaken in 2012–2013, we filmed the female *mirlpa* or sand storytelling practices of old and young in Warburton Community and Tjukurla Community (see e.g. Ellis *et al.*, 2017).[9] In the Tjukurla examples the young storytellers are from families who encountered Anglo-Australians only in the 1960s; their grandparents were born into a nomadic hunter-gatherer existence and never went to school.[10] In these recordings adolescent girls display the traditional narrative style in their use of co-narration and certain prosodic features and vocal styles. They also employ complex grammatical Ngaanyatjarra structures and minimal English words.[11] By comparison, in the Warburton data the young narrators are from families who were already in the mission in the 1930s.[12] These girls are the third and fourth generation in their families to have learned English and are more distanced from traditional cultural practices. Their recorded narratives reveal a more stilted delivery style with fewer of the prosodic features of the traditional narrative style. Importantly, however, despite evident codemixing between Ngaanyatjarra and English lexemes, correct Ngaanyatjarra grammatical constructions are maintained. In summary, such data forecast the impending changes that will occur if steps are not taken now to prevent further language loss.

On a positive note, contemporary living is also giving Ngaanyatjarra youth a vast repertoire of symbolic, textual and media resources to draw on in their construction of altered local practices and new linguistic forms (see Chapters 4 and 6, this volume, for comparative evidence from Latin America and the United States). An emerging reality is evident where, via social media and digital communication technologies, young people in the Ngaanyatjarra communities are seeking to acquire new forms of multi-modal communicative competence. They are exploring the modes of cultural production enabled by digital technologies through song-writing and music recording, film-making, language documentation and sub-titling (Figure 5.3), as well as tagging and annotating in digital heritage archives. Youth are also participating in audio-visual media recording of country visits and cultural activities, thus acquiring language and socio-cultural knowledge from elders *in situ*. In social media, especially

Figure 5.3 Natalie O'Toole editing a Ngaanyatjarra sand story film (photograph by Inge Kral)

Facebook, the essentially social nature of communication favors the vernacular. In these technologically mediated modes of communication we are seeing a blurring of the boundaries between speech and writing. These young people live in an environment where they have been exposed to the emblematic use of the written vernacular in public spaces and are able to encode and decode in written Ngaanyatjarra, albeit often using non-standardized written forms in the social media messages.

We have outlined here examples of everyday community-based language policies that affirm contemporary Ngaanyatjarra youth identity through meaningful language use of relevance to youth practice. Youth and young adulthood constitute an important time in which ideological orientations associated with language and identity can change in accordance with everyday language policy. From this perspective, rather than consider the negative consequences of language endangerment and shift, we suggest that young people can hold multiple ideologies related to language and identity associated with traditional cultural values and globalized youth culture (see Chapters 8 and 9, this volume, for further explorations of similar themes). Accordingly, the discussion now turns to approaches that foster language vitality.

Fostering Language Vitality

Internationally in Indigenous regions the rhetoric of language endangerment and shift has changed to a focus on language vitality, sustainability and resilience (Grenoble, 2015). As Grenoble and Olsen note (2014: 7), drawing on Joshua Fishman (1991), a vital language is one used by *all* generations in *all* domains. They suggest that maintaining a high degree of cultural proficiency and communicative competence requires a rich documentation of language as culturally situated and culturally mediated practice. Furthermore, an 'indigenously defined metric for proficiency' is required to aid decision-making in regard to measures needed to foster language vitality (Grenoble & Olsen, 2014: 7). Drawing on the lessons learned in other Indigenous settings, we now discuss strategies to foster language vitality in Indigenous Australian languages.

We signaled above that the multimodal speech arts (encompassing narrative competence, oratorical skills and other symbolic, visual and gestural modes of representation and communication) are a valued, yet endangered, part of the traditions of Western Desert people. To be a competent language speaker entails not only using everyday speech, but also having proficiency in the cultural as well as linguistic practices of that community in different domains of use. This may entail understanding the social conventions of language use encompassing verbal and nonverbal communication modes (for example sign language), as well as having mastery of the verbal arts and speech styles used in everyday and ceremonial contexts, and having a broad-ranging understanding of traditional cultural practices and knowledge systems.

In the Western Desert, as elsewhere, oral narrative has long been central to instruction and learning in a manner that fosters attention to language, imagination and metaphoric thinking through the incorporation of core cultural concepts, moral themes, and proper ways of behaving for youngsters to emulate (Ellis & Wilkes, 2010; Klapproth, 2004; Kral & Ellis, 2008). Today however, the use of narrative for didactic purposes has waned alongside the dissipation of traditional knowledge and other language practices. Concomitantly there has been an erosion of culturally relevant traditional processes and roles that underpin social organization and have bound society together for generations. Yet as the future leaders of their communities Indigenous youth will need to be armed with the knowledge, stories and language that foster moral authority. Not having appropriate language practices, knowledge systems and connectedness to country will have long term consequences. For instance, not understanding one's affiliation to land may have implications for future claims to land ownership under Australian law through 'Native Title.' In this respect programs that support the intergenerational transmission of ecological, linguistic and land tenure knowledge are essential. Remote Indigenous Australians working with educators and researchers have explored methodologies that have proved successful in ensuring the maintenance of ecological knowledge systems and language (cf. Douglas, 2015; Fogarty & Schwab, 2012; Mooney, 2010).

Ceremonies and rituals such as funerals constitute a rich environment for the acquisition of respect registers and traditional modes of social interaction. Revitalizing and maintaining oral and cultural traditions to ensure that language forms are passed on to successive generations entails a local commitment to maintaining the narrative traditions and performing ceremonies, and thus to ensure that music and dance traditions are also not lost (cf. Grant, 2014; Treloyn *et al.*, 2013). Furthermore, youth need to be encouraged to participate in these events. Schools also need to understand the significance of these ceremonial events for reinforcing social organization and encourage attendance at ceremonies and funerals. Lack of respect by schools and public policy for these significant cultural learning activities and enduring asymmetrical social structures sends an important message to Indigenous people, particularly the younger generation, that their language and culture are not valued.

Earlier we described how new forms of cultural production such as music and film-making form a locus for oral and written language production. In addition, the motivation to communicate with kin enabled by Facebook is providing an avenue for everyday informal written communication. Around the world the rapid growth in individual ownership of small mobile digital devices has widened the scope for everyday self-directed language learning and maintenance strategies in minority language contexts (Petersen, 2013) through online dictionaries, spellcheckers, and apps and games for mobile phones and iPads (Carew *et al.*, 2015; First Languages Australia, 2015).

Conclusion

In this chapter we have described how, other than *ad hoc* attempts to offer Ngaanyatjarra literacy in schools, there have been no long-term school programs that address language maintenance. We have shed light on the obstacles and barriers that have stood in the way of optimum Indigenous language learning and teaching programs in one of the stronger Indigenous first language-speaking areas in Australia. However, given the ongoing reluctance at a local and national level to invest in language programs in schools, we question the assumption, as have others before us (cf. Hornberger, 2008; Skutnabb-Kangas, 2000), that schools can 'save' endangered languages. We have shown how language policy in Australia is no longer oriented around Indigenous language maintenance. Accordingly we have focused on the concept of everyday language policies and discussed the fact that attitudes to language are of key importance in assessing the chances of endangered language survival. We argue that rather than relying on national language policy initiatives, language vitality will require everyday language maintenance strategies and community-based initiatives.

In the Ngaanyatjarra Lands, one commonly hears Aboriginal people saying, 'We must keep talking our language so we can keep it strong forever.' However, such well-intentioned rhetoric is no longer sufficient without a commitment to everyday language policies. Language survival into the future will entail raising awareness of the importance of everyday language practices and performance, and a commitment to supporting community-based language maintenance initiatives. Community members must take responsibility for transmitting these sociolinguistic and cultural practices to the young, because *their* youth are *their* society's future. Elders must also become active in youth activities. These interactions will assist in the transfer of intergenerational knowledge and skills.

Such approaches must focus on youth as they are the agents of change. It is the youth generation who will be the adults of tomorrow, taking charge of the manner in which their language will be transmitted to the next generation.

Acknowledgements

This research was supported by ELDP (Endangered Languages Documentation Programme) Small Grant SG0187. Inge Kral was supported by an Australian Research Council (ARC) DECRA Award (DE120100720). Elizabeth Ellis was supported by the award of a Visiting Indigenous Fellowship from the Centre for Aboriginal Economic Policy Research at ANU in 2013, and is now on an ARC Discovery Indigenous Award (IN150100018). We thank the many Ngaanyatjarra people who have given their support over many years, especially the West and Smythe families at Warburton Community, and the Giles and Butler families at Tjukurla Community. Our gratitude goes also to Dr Jennifer Green (University of Melbourne) for our ongoing research collaboration on multimodal speech arts in the Western Desert. Lastly we thank the editors for their tireless dedication in pulling together this volume and the two anonymous reviewers for their useful comments.

Notes

(1) Elizabeth Ellis was awarded an ARC Discovery Indigenous Award (IN150100018), with co-investigators Jennifer Green, Inge Kral and Jane Simpson to investigate 'Western Desert speech styles and verbal arts.' Earlier research was funded by an ELDP Small Grant (SG0187).
(2) ARC DECRA (DE120100720), 'Connecting, communicating and learning through new media: Indigenous youth and digital futures in remote Australia' (2012–2014).
(3) This section has been sourced from Kral (2012).
(4) Ngaanyatjarra was the mother tongue of family groups living in and around the Warburton Ranges. By the 1960s speakers of other Western Desert dialects had begun entering the UAM mission at Warburton Ranges.
(5) The Indigenous Literacy Foundation has produced children's books and e-books in Ngaanyatjarra in collaboration with the Ngaanyatjarra Early Years Program.
(6) For instance in the *Forrest Review* (Forrest, 2014), Recommendation 3.2 situates 'English literacy and numeracy as the priority for all schools, by having an English language explicit instruction domain as the basis of each school day.' Here the

priority of English is in place until NAPLaN parity is achieved and *only then* can Indigenous children learn and become literate in ancestral languages.

(7) Under the National Assessment Program – Literacy and Numeracy (NAPLaN) – students in Years 3, 5, 7 and 9 are assessed using national tests in reading, writing, language conventions (spelling, grammar and punctuation) and numeracy. Data from NAPLaN test results give schools and systems the ability to compare their students' achievements against national standards.

(8) Recent studies in the language socialization literature that have addressed issues of language endangerment and shift include Meek (2007), Nonaka (2014) and Paugh (2012).

(9) By Ellis and Kral with Jennifer Green from the University of Melbourne on ELDP Small Grant (SG0187). Further recordings were made in 2016 under ARC-DI (IN150100018).

(10) During the 1960s nomadic Pintupi and Ngaatjatjarra people moved out of the Gibson Desert northwest of Warburton, and the Rawlinson Ranges around the NT border. At this time the Commonwealth Government, in cooperation with Great Britain, had established a program of testing long-range missiles to be fired from Woomera in SA in a trajectory northwest across the Central Aboriginal Reserves. As a consequence, desert groups still inhabiting this region were urged to move into settlements at Papunya in the NT, and Jigalong and Warburton in WA (Davenport *et al.*, 2005; Dousset, 2002).

(11) File #: MIR 20130906-JB + KG-03. See also Ellis *et al.* (2015).

(12) File #: MIR 20130912-PB + LS-01.

References

AIATSIS/FATSIL (2005) *National Indigenous Languages Survey Report 2005*. Canberra: Commonwealth of Australia.

Austin, P.K. and Sallabank, J. (2013) Endangered languages: An introduction. *Journal of Multilingual and Multicultural Development* 34 (4), 313–316.

Bowman, C., Pascoe, L. and Joy, T. (1999) Literacy teaching and learning in a bilingual classroom. In P. Wignall (ed.) *Double Power: English Literacy and Indigenous Education* (pp. 61–94). Melbourne: Language Australia.

Carew, M., Green, J., Kral, I., Nordlinger, R. and Singer, R. (2015) Getting in touch: Language and digital inclusion in Australian Indigenous communities. *Language Documentation and Conservation* 9, 307–323.

Davenport, S., Johnson, P. and Yuwali (2005) *Cleared Out: First Contact in the Western Desert*. Canberra: Aboriginal Studies Press.

Disbray, S. (2015) Spaces for learning: Policy and practice for indigenous languages in a remote context. *Language and Education* 30, 317–336.

Disbray, S., Devlin, B. and Devlin, N. (2017) (eds) *History of Bilingual Education in the Northern Territory: People, Programs and Policies*. Singapore: Springer.

Dixon, R.M.W. (1990) The origin of 'mother-in-law vocabulary' in two Australian languages. *Anthropological Linguistics* 32 (1–2), 1–56.

Douglas, J. (2015) *Kin and Knowledge: The Meaning and Acquisition of Indigenous Ecological Knowledge in the Lives of Young Aboriginal People in Central Australia*. Unpublished PhD thesis, Department of Anthropology, Charles Darwin University.

Douglas, W.H. (1964) *An Introduction to the Western Desert Language*. Oceania Linguistic Monographs. Sydney: University of Sydney.

Dousset, L. (2002) Politics and demography in a contact situation: The establishment of the Giles Meteorological Station in the Rawlinson Ranges. *Aboriginal History* 26, 1–22.

Duff, P.A. (2008) Introduction. In P. Duff and N. Hornberger (eds) *Language Socialization: Encyclopedia of Language and Education Volume 8* (pp. xiii–xix). New York, NY: Springer.

Ellis, E.M., Green, J. and Kral, I. (2017) Family in mind: Socio-spatial knowledge in a Ngaatjatjarra/Ngaanyatjarra children's game. *Research on Children and Social Interaction* 1 (2), 164–198, https://doi.org/10.1558/rcsi.28442

Ellis, E., Green, J., Kral, I., Simpson, J. and Stoakes, H. (2015) Desert clicks, taps and sound symbolism: Vocal style in Ngaanyatjarra narratives. Australian Linguistic Society Annual Conference presentation, Sydney, December.

Ellis, E. and Wilkes, M. (2010) What's in a word? Word form and meaning in a Ngaatjatjarra traditional story. *Ngoonjook: A Journal of Australian Indigenous Issues* 35, 6–18.

Evans, N. (2010) *Dying Words: Endangered Languages and What They Have to Tell Us.* Malden, MA: Wiley-Blackwell.

First Languages Australia (2015) *Angkety Map: Digital Resource Report.* First Languages Australia. Retrieved from http://firstlanguages.org.au/projects/digital.html.

Fishman, J. (1991) *Reversing Language Shift: Theoretical and Empirical Foundations of Assistance to Threatened Languages.* Clevedon: Multilingual Matters

Fogarty, W. and Schwab, R. (2012) *Indigenous Education: Experiential Learning and Learning Through Country.* CAEPR Working Paper No. 80/2012. Canberra: Australian National University.

Forrest, A. (2014) *The Forrest Review: Creating Parity.* Indigenous jobs and training review. Commonwealth of Australia. Retrieved from https://www.pmc.gov.au/indigenous-affairs/employment/indigenous-jobs-and-training-review

Friedman, D.A. (2014) Language socialization and language revitalization. In A. Duranti, E. Ochs and B.B. Schieffelin (eds) *The Handbook of Language Socialization* (pp. 631–647). Malden, MA: Wiley Blackwell.

Gale, M.-A. (1997) *Dhanum Djorra'wuy Dhawu: A History of Writing in Aboriginal Languages.* Adelaide: University of South Australia.

García, O. (2014) En/countering Indigenous bi/multilingualism. In L.T. Wyman, T.L. McCarty and S.E. Nicholas (eds) *Indigenous Youth and Multilingualism: Language Identity, Ideology and Practice in Dynamic Cultural Worlds* (pp. 207–214). New York, NY: Routledge.

Glass, A. (2000) History of Ngaanyatjarra Literacy. Alice Springs: Unpublished manuscript.

Glass, A. and Hackett, D. (compilers) (2003) *Ngaanyatjarra and Ngaatjatjarra to English Dictionary.* Alice Springs: IAD Press.

Granadillo, T. and Orcutt-Gachiri, H.A. (eds) (2011) *Ethnographic Contributions to the Study of Endangered Languages.* Tucson: University of Arizona Press.

Grant C.F. (2014) *Music Endangerment: How Language Maintenance Can Help.* New York, NY: Oxford University Press.

Green, J. (2014) *Drawn from the Ground. Sound, Sign and Inscription in Central Australian Sand Stories.* Cambridge: Cambridge University Press.

Grenoble, L.A. (26 February 2015) The hitchhiker's guide to documentation: Communicative practices, cultural competence and proficiency guidelines. Opening Plenary Address, International Conference on Language Documentation and Conservation 4, Honolulu, Hawai'i 2015. Retrieved from http://icldc4.weebly.com/plenary-address-information.html

Grenoble, L.A. and Olsen (Puju), C.C. (2014) Language and well-being in the Arctic. *Arctic Yearbook 2014,* 1–12.

Harrison, D. (2007) *When Languages Die.* Oxford: Oxford University Press.

Hartman, D. and Henderson, J. (eds) (1994) *Aboriginal Languages in Education.* Alice Springs: IAD Press.

Hinton, L. (2014) Foreword. In L.T. Wyman, T.L. McCarty, and S.E. Nicholas (eds) *Indigenous Youth and Multilingualism: Language Identity, Ideology and Practice in Dynamic Cultural Worlds* (pp. ix–xiv). New York, NY: Routledge.

Hornberger, N.H. (ed.) (2008) *Can Schools Save Indigenous Languages? Policy and Practice on Four Continents,* Basingstoke: Palgrave Macmillan

Klapproth, D. (2004) *Narrative as Social Practice: Anglo-Western and Australian Aboriginal Oral Traditions.* Berlin and New York: Mouton de Gruyter.

Kral, I. (2012) *Talk, Text and Technology: Literacy and Social Practice in a Remote Indigenous Community.* Bristol: Multilingual Matters.

Kral, I. and Ellis, E.M. (2008) Children, language and literacy in the Ngaanyatjarra Lands. In G. Wigglesworth and J. Simpson (eds) *Children's Language and Multilingualism: Indigenous Language Use at Home and School* (pp. 154–172). London: Continuum.

Marmion, D., Obata, K. and Troy, J. (2014) *Community, Identity, Wellbeing: The Report of the Second National Indigenous Languages Survey.* Canberra: Australian Institute of Aboriginal and Torres Strait Islander Studies.

McCarty, T.L. (ed.) (2011) *Ethnography and Language Policy.* New York, NY: Routledge.

McConvell, P. (1982) Neutralisation and degrees of repect in Gurindji. In J. Heath, F. Merlan and A. Rumsey (eds) *Languages of Kinship in Aboriginal Australia* (pp. 630–656). Oceania Linguistic Monographs 24. Sydney: Oceania Publications.

McKay, P. (2001) National literacy benchmarks and the outstreaming of ESL learners. In J. Lo Bianco and R. Wickert (eds) *Australian Policy Activism in Language and Literacy* (pp. 221–237). Melbourne: Language Australia.

Meakins, F. (2008) Unravelling languages: Multilingualism and language contact in Kalkaringi. In J. Simpson and G. Wigglesworth (eds) *Childen's Language and Mulitlingualism: Indigenous Language Use at Home and School* (pp. 283–302). London: Continuum.

Meek, B. (2007) Respecting the language of elders: Ideological shift and linguistic discontinuity in a Northern Athapascan community. *Journal of Linguistic Anthropology* 17 (1), 23–43.

Minutjukur, M., Patterson, V., Anderson, S., Gibson, F., Kitson, M., Martin, B., … and Larry, R. (2014) Voices from the Red Dirt on education. *Journal of Australian Indigenous Issues* 17 (4), 158–163.

Mooney, M. (2010) A small program under threat. *Dialogue* 10 (2), 76–78.

Morrison, B. and Disbray, S. (2008) Warumungu children and language in Tennant Creek. In R. Amery and J. Nash (eds) *Warra Wiltaniappendi = Strengthening Languages.* Proceedings of the Inaugural Indigenous Languages Conference (ILC) 2007 (pp. 107–111). Adelaide, Australia: ILC.

Nonaka, A.M. (2014) Language socialization and language endangerment. In A. Duranti, E. Ochs and B.B. Schieffelin (eds) *The Handbook of Language Socialization* (pp. 610–630). Malden, MA: Wiley Blackwell.

Obata, K., Kral, I. and Ngaanyatjarra Speakers (2005) *Ngaanyatjarra Picture Dictionary.* Alice Springs: IAD Press.

O'Shannessy, C. (2011) Young children's social meaning making in a new mixed language. In U. Eickelkamp (ed.) *Growing Up in Central Australia: New Anthropological Studies of Aboriginal Childhood and Adolescence* (pp. 131–155). Oxford and New York: Berghahn Books.

Paugh, A.L. (2012) *Playing with Languages: Children and Change in a Caribbean Village.* Oxford and New York: Berghahn Books.

Petersen, R. (2013) iDecolonize!: A review of Indigenous language-learning apps. *Rising Voices.* Retrieved from https://rising.globalvoicesonline.org/blog/2013/06/21/idecolonize-a-review-of-indigenous-language-learning-apps/

Simpson, J. (21 August 2014) The conversation. Retrieved from https://www.cdu.edu.au/laal/prof-jane-simpson-on-the-conversation/

Simpson, J., Caffery, J. and McConvell, P. (2009) *Gaps in Australia's Indigenous Language Policy: Dismantling Bilingual Education in the Northern Territory.* AIATSIS Research Discussion Paper No. 24. Canberra: Australian Institute of Aboriginal and Torres Strait Islander Studies.

Skutnabb-Kangas, T. (2000) *Linguistic Genocide in Education – Or Worldwide Diversity and Human Rights?* Mahwah, NJ: Lawrence Erlbaum.

Treloyn, S., Charles, R.G. and Nulgit, S. (2013) Repatriation of song materials to support intergenerational transmission of knowledge about language in the Kimberley region of northwest Australia. In M.J. Norris, E. Anonby and M.-O. Junker (eds) *Endangered Languages Beyond Boundaries: Proceedings of the 17th Foundation for Endangered Languages Conference* (pp. 18–24). Bath: Foundation for Endangered Languages.

Truscott, A. and Malcolm, I. (2010) Closing the policy-practice gap: Making Indigenous language policy more than empty rhetoric. In J. Hobson, K. Lowe, S. Poetsch and M. Walsh (eds) *Re-awakening Languages: Theory and Practice in the Revitalization of Australia's Indigenous Languages.* Sydney: University of Sydney Press.

Wigglesworth, G., Simpson, J. and Loakes, D. (2011) NAPLAN language assessments for indigenous children in remote communities: Issues and problems. *Australian Review of Applied Linguistics* 34 (3), 320–343.

Woodbury, A. (1998) Documenting rhetorical, aesthetic, and expressive loss in language shift. In L.A. Grenoble and L.J. Whaley (eds) *Endangered Languages: Current Issues and Future Prospects* (pp. 234–258). Cambridge: Cambridge University Press.

Woolard, K.A. (1998) Introduction: Language ideology as a field of inquiry. In B.B. Schieffelin, K.A. Woolard and P.V. Kroskrity (eds) *Language Ideologies: Practice and Theory* (pp. 3–47). New York, NY: Oxford University Press.

Wyman, L.T. (2012) *Youth Culture, Language Endangerment and Linguistic Survivance.* Bristol: Multilingual Matters.

Wyman, L.T. (2014) Youth linguistic survivance in transforming settings: A Yup'ik example. In L.T. Wyman, T.L. McCarty and S.E. Nicholas (eds) *Indigenous Youth and Multilingualism: Language Identity, Ideology and Practice in Dynamic Cultural Worlds* (pp. 90–110). New York, NY: Routledge.

Wyman, L.T., McCarty, T.L. and Nicholas, S.E. (2014a) Beyond endangerment: Indigenous youth and multilingualism. In L.T. Wyman, T.L. McCarty and S.E. Nicholas (eds) *Indigenous Youth and Multilingualism: Language Identity, Ideology and Practice in Dynamic Cultural Worlds* (pp. 1–25). New York, NY: Routledge.

Wyman, L.T., McCarty, T.L. and Nicholas, S.E. (eds) (2014b) *Indigenous Youth and Multilingualism: Language Identity, Ideology and Practice in Dynamic Cultural Worlds.* New York. NY: Routledge.

6 Task-Based Language Learning for Ojibwe: A Case Study of Two Intermediate Adult Language Learners

Mary Hermes and Kendall A. King

This chapter reports on a yearlong project using newly created conversa-
tion language archives, and how these are being productively used to
promote adult students' oral proficiency in Ojibwe, a Native American
language spoken in the upper-Midwest of the United States and in
Canada. Data reveal that conversational archives of fluent native speak-
ers provide an authentic conversational context for the study, use and
practice of challenging verb transitive animate (VTA) linguistic forms,
enabling adult learners to move from beginning to advanced speaker
status.

Introduction

A common challenge among second language learners of agglutinat-ing Indigenous languages is practicing and achieving target-like use of multiple, complex verb conjugations. Given that language courses are often grammar based and require learners to memorize verb paradigms, achieving oral proficiency through coursework is especially challenging for learners of these endangered languages (King & Hermes, 2014). As social contexts for learning and listening are rare, classroom pedagogies often have learners repeat patterns with substitutions. For agglutinating languages, this abstract and decontextualized process is demanding, even for full-time college students with extensive formal education. This gram-mar-based pedagogical approach can be even more overwhelming for adult Native community members who are not full-time students or have fewer experiences or fewer *successful* experiences in formal education. For many of these learners, their limited experience with metalinguistic, abstract analysis of objectified language forms means that accuracy with these verb forms is perceived as unattainable or extremely challenging (King & Hermes, 2014).

This reliance on grammar-based approaches is partly due to the lack of communicatively oriented materials for many Indigenous languages, and of course, the lack of speakers. In many cases, documentation-oriented work such as dictionaries, grammars and collections of narratives, produced by linguists, serves as the basis for teaching materials. Although the focus on naturalistic conversations in documentation work in recent years has productively supported the development of communicative teaching materials (Hinton, 2011), in contrast to English and other high-status languages for which a plethora of materials have been developed, tested and redesigned, the development of Indigenous-language learning materials for adults is in its infancy. Concomitantly, the push for language revitalization has brought to light the urgent need for more effective means of and materials for teaching and learning Indigenous languages.

As Hinton writes, 'language teaching and learning of endangered languages is a pioneering process that involves the development of new models of language teaching' (2011: 308). Working toward that end, the present research project examines the learning opportunities that resulted from two learners' engagement with communicative tasks. We documented the ways in which learning Ojibwe was potentially facilitated through use of communicative tasks and how that could contribute to new approaches to teaching Ojibwe language. For this chapter, we transcribe and analyze some of the language learning and use practices of two intermediate learners of Ojibwe in out-of-school, peer–peer interaction. Their intention was to pinpoint their learning needs and create learning opportunities for themselves. Our aim is to bring current perspectives on second language acquisition (SLA) to bear on the specifics of how Ojibwe might be learned, given the sociocultural context. Framed this way, this project draws from – and aims to contribute to – both language revitalization and SLA research. These are critical aims as language revitalization research has largely been ignored by mainstream SLA research, and language revitalization researchers, in turn, rarely draw from advances in applied linguistics (King & Hermes, 2014; King & Mackey, 2016).

Background: Ojibwe Language Revitalization

There are an estimated 50,000 'first speakers' of Ojibwe,[1] with most residing in Canada and a smaller number in the United States. An Algonquian language, Ojibwe belongs to one of the largest Indigenous language groups within North America. Speakers are geographically dispersed across more than eight US states and four Canadian provinces. Due to relocation, a majority of Ojibwe people in the United States are currently urban (Burt, 1986).

With only an estimated 500–700 'first speakers' in the US, there is a strong grassroots push for revitalization (Treuer, 2010). Encouraged by language immersion camps, Ojibwe classes, and a growing number of Ojibwe immersion schools, second language learners of Ojibwe are struggling to find more effective ways to learn a language that they rarely hear in everyday conversations. With the recent addition of a searchable, online dictionary (The Ojibwe People's Dictionary, 2015), Ojibwe learners are able to get assistance anywhere they have internet access.

A major line of US Ojibwe language revitalization work has been the development of Ojibwe immersion schools. Following the establishment of Waadookodaading Ojibwe Language Immersion School in 2001 and Niigaane Ojibwe Immersion School in 2003 (Hermes, 2004, 2007), three additional elementary/preschool immersion programs are in operation, and at least four more preschools or K-2 schools have recently opened. Due to these efforts, the growth in immersion schools is outstripping the ability to produce proficient speakers. This creates a shortage of qualified teachers with advanced proficiency in the language. Learners often plateau at the intermediate level and struggle to both practice and use the complicated verbal morphology.

In an effort to support Ojibwe language revitalization efforts, this project, called *Developing Fluency*, sought to document how usage of task-based learning materials might address the difficulty adult learners experience. Framed in the broader context of revitalization, we are focused on developing more efficient teaching methods. To this end, three adult participants agreed to engage in online communicative task work. This chapter addresses two questions with respect to that work: (1) What language use and learning opportunities do these tasks provide? and (2) What are the ways in which learners differentially engage with these tasks?

Study Design

We documented the work of a small group of adult learners as they engaged in communicative tasks to practice verb conjugations over 22 weeks. Learners met once or twice a week, mostly online, to engage in targeted practice of particular verb forms through pre-designed communicative tasks. Learners hoped to overcome the plateau they were experiencing and wanted to use some kind of structure in an informal setting.

Participants

Three adults initially participated: Mary Hermes (the lead author), Jenn (a recent college graduate) and Nibiiwanikwe (a language learner). The three learners knew each other as co-members of the Ojibwe language learner diaspora.[2] Further, all had participated in an intensive adult

Ojibwe language immersion camp just prior to the study in the summer of 2013 and in monthly weekend follow-up sessions as well (October 2013–April 2014, during the study period). All three were considered intermediate learners, having a basic conversational proficiency, but there were some important differences across the participants as well. For instance, while Mary's investment in the language is largely linked to symbolic capital, it also supports her professional and consulting work. As an Indigenous person, her language learning was driven by a desire to work with Ojibwe-speaking (and learning) elders and community members. It is an identity marker, but also a valuable engagement with community and an important spiritual commitment. In contrast to 'race'-based membership, speaking Ojibwe marks speakers as community members in a different way. On the other hand, Nibiiwanikwe, as a non-Indigenous learner, does not feel that learning the Ojibwe language affects her identity; she was not looking for any kind of validation of who she is through participation in the Ojibwe language community. Nibiiwanikwe began studying the language out of personal interest, and, as a gifted language learner, has become deeply enmeshed in social networks of Ojibwe users. As she remarked, 'If I were to stop speaking Ojibwe, I wouldn't have any friends in my life.' Ojibwe is a common point of interest, and drives many of her social networks. In this sense the language provides her with some social and symbolic capital but is not linked to her personal identity. At this point, she is known by other Ojibwe speakers and learners and hopes to have job opportunities using these skills.

Jenn dropped out of the project after ten weeks; for this reason, her participation is not included in our analysis. While this small number of participants makes the findings not generalizable in the technical sense, the findings here, and in particular the learning opportunities and affordances provided by the tasks, are transferable to many Indigenous language revitalization contexts.

Sessions and tasks

Sessions lasted approximately 30 minutes each. These were conducted via Google Hangouts and were both audio and video recorded. The focus of these sessions was on 'verb transitive animate' (VTA) paradigms, required for all transitive verbs that have an animate object (e.g. *I gave the bread to her*) (Nichols, 2015). In Ojibwe, some nouns, including, for instance, bread *(bakwezhigan)*, apple tree *(mishiiminaatig)*, or frog *(omagakii)*, are 'animate.' Transitive animate verbs are inflected differently depending on both the subject and indirect object (e.g. *I* to *her* vs *you* to *him*), if they are a subordinate or independent clause, and if they are part of a positive or negative clause. This results in more than 96 possible prefixes, infixes and suffixes for this verb class (VTAs) alone (see Table 6.1).

Table 6.1 Ojibwe VTA verb paradigm

	Independent Positive	Independent Negative	Dependent Positive	Dependent Negative
–	–	–	–	–
I → you (s.)	gi_in	gi_isinoon	_inaan	_isinowaan
I → you (p.)	gi_ininim	gi_isinooninim	_inagog	_isinowagog
I → her/him/(them)	ni_aa(g)	ni_aasiin	_ag(waa)	_aasiwag(waa)
You (s.)	–	–	–	–
You (s.) → me	gi_	gi_isin	_iyan	_isiwan
You (s.) → us	gi_imin	gi_isiimin	_iyaang	_isiwaang
You (s.) → her/him/(them)	gi_aa(g)	gi_aasiin (-aasiig)	_ad(waa)	_aasiwad(waa)
S/he	–	–	–	–
S/he/(they) → me	ni_ig(oog)	ni_igosiin (-igosiig)	_id > (-iwaad)	_isig(waa)
S/he/(they) → us (excl.)	ni_igonaan(ig)	ni_igosiinaan(ig)	_iyangid(waa)	_isiwangid(waa)
S/he/(they) → us (incl.)	gi_igonaan(ig)	gi_igosiinaan(ig)	_inang(waa)	_isinowang(waa)
S/he/(they) → you (s.)	gi_ig(oog)	gi_igosiin (-igosiig)	_ik(waa)	_isinok(waa)
S/he/(they) → you (p.)	gi_igowaa(g)	gi_igosiiwaa(ig)	_ineg(waa)	_isinoweg(waa)
3 → 4	o_aan	o_aasiin	_aad	_aasig

3 (p.) → 4	c_aawaan	o_aasiwaawaan	_aawaad	_aasigwaa
4 → 3	c_igoon	o_igosiin	_igod	_igosig
4 → 3 (p.)	c_igowaan	o_igosiiwaan	_igowad	_igosigwaa
4 → 5	c_aawaan	o_aasiwaawaan	_aanid	_aasinig
5 → 4	c_igowaan	o_igosiiwaan	_igonid	_igosinig
We (excl.)	–	–	–	–
We (incl.)	–	–	–	–
We (excl.) → you (s.)	ci_igoo	gi_igoosiin	_igooyan	_igoosiwan
We (excl.) → you (p.)	ci_igoom	gi_igoosiim	_igooyeg	_igoosiweg
We (excl.) → her/him/(they)	ri_anaanaan(ig)	ni_aasiwaanaan(ig)	_angid(waa)	_aasiwangid(waa)
We (incl.) → her/him/(they)	ci_aanaan(ig)	gi_aasiwaanaan(ig)	_ang(waa)	_aasiwang(waa)
You (p.)	–	–	–	–
You (p.) → me	ci_im	gi_isiim	_iyeg	_isiweg
You (p.) → us (excl.)	ci_imin	gi_isiimin	_iyaang	_isiwaang
You (p.) → her/him/(they)	ci_aawaa(g)	gi_aasiwaawaa(g)	_eg(waa)	_aasiweg(waa)
They	–	–	–	–
S/he (4th,they)	–	–	–	–

All sessions were organized around communicative tasks, defined here as an activity that has (1) an objective attainable only through the interaction among participants; (2) a mechanism for structuring and sequencing interaction; and (3) a focus on meaningful exchange (Lee, 2000: 32). At the onset, tasks were designed in advance of the online sessions by the participant-researcher (Mary Hermes) and the co-researcher (Kendall King). The intent was to use footage from the Ojibwe Conversations archives so as to have input from first speakers of Ojibwe.[3] As one researcher was also a participant, this created an excessive cognitive load (Hermes), and co-construction of loosely developed tasks around popular culture material such as Harry Potter was more common by the end of the 22 weeks.

Tasks varied each week depending on which VTA forms were the focus. For example, in the first month of the project, the movie called *Making Fry Bread* was used from the archives for content. Participants previewed a particular clip in advance of the online meeting. One task developed around this clip was getting the dough ready. Participants each had flour and water, and made balls of dough during the activity. Here the Google Hangout interface was important, as participants could not see each other's balls of dough. They had to communicate to find out, for instance, how many balls of dough were made? Are they sticky? What colors and sizes are they? This was a kind of task-based guessing game and interaction that forced participants to use animate verbs, as balls of dough are animate in Ojibwe.

Findings and Analysis

Findings are presented around our two research questions: (1) What language use and learning opportunities did these tasks provide for these learners? (2) What are the ways in which learners differentially engage with these tasks? After describing in detail the interaction and engagement in a task, we then move to discuss identity and engagement in learning.

Language use and learning opportunities

Across all sessions, we found that learners had multiple opportunities to use and practice a range of VTA inflections. However, given that there are more than 96 different combinations of prefixes, infixes and suffixes for VTAs (see Table 6.1), it was not possible to see evidence of development over the course of the study. Nevertheless, as illustrated in Table 6.2, learners attempted to use and had opportunities to practice many different VTA forms, including both positives and negatives, and subordinate and independent forms, as they engaged in the tasks. In other words, the tasks were successful in eliciting conversation and meaningful practice with low-frequency verb forms.

Table 6.2 Summary of tasks for developing fluency

Task One: Making Fry Bread

Pre-task: Watch the first 3 minutes of video 'Making Fry Bread.' Available at: https://www. youtube.com/watch?v=YQFpNhFmzB8

Warm up: Do you have him/them? (refers to small balls of bread dough)

Participants hold the balls of bread dough under the view of the camera, and so no one knows if you have it or not. Find out who has what by asking and guessing.

Task Two: Adding Water to Flour

Take turns adding water to flour, stirring and trying to get the right proportions to make a kneadable ball of dough. Only do what you are told to do by the other participants; you may ask questions.

Task Three: Knead the Dough

In this task you have to figure out how long you knead the bread dough in order to get the right consistency. Don't show the other participants what you are doing, or what the dough looks like. You can pretend to knead and not actually be kneading. They have to figure out what you are doing, and when the dough is done.

Task Four: Dinner Party

We are having a dinner party of Ojibwe language speakers and learners. First, we agree on the participants, and then together we must figure out an appropriate seating arrangement.

Task Five: Harry Potter (Rowling, 2002)

We are the characters in a Harry Potter book and (pretend you are a group) one group invites the other to attend a Quidditch game.

Task Six: The Subtle Knife (Pullman, 1997) and Your 'Dæmon'

As in the *Subtle Knife*, participants have 'dæmons' (an image of an animal who is your companion) attached to their lapel. Discuss who your dæmons like and don't like, and who the two of you together like and dislike.

Task Seven: Cartoons

Pre-task: View a cartoon clip sent to you. Do not tell the others what it is.

Task: One person describes the cartoon clip (60 seconds) while the other two draw what they hear. Discuss briefly then show the entire clip to the group.

Close analysis of transcripts also illustrates that the learners had many opportunities to negotiate for meaning. Negotiation, as defined within Long's (1996: 418) well known 'Interactional Hypothesis,' is the 'process in which, in an effort to communicate, learners and competent speakers provide and interpret signals of their own and their interlocutor's perceived comprehension, thus provoking adjustments to linguistic form, conversational structure, message content, or all three, until an acceptable level of understanding is achieved' (1996: 418). This process is integral to language learning as the 'negotiation of meaning, and especially negotiation work that triggers interactional adjustments by the native speaker or more competent interlocutor, facilitates acquisition because it connects input, internal learner capacities, particularly selective attention, and output in productive ways' (Long, 1996: 451–452). The online interface provided opportunities for only the speaker to know (or see) particular

Figure 6.1 Participants-in-person Mary Hermes (L) and Jordyn Flaada (R), speaking to a third participant over Google Hangout (photograph by Waabanang Lee Hermes, used with permission)

things that the others had to work to figure out. The physical distance might have made members of this particular group feel more comfortable in taking time to respond, and less pressured to respond correctly. Prior to this study, they all had established relationships in person. While these elements of negotiation were enhanced through online interaction, the downside was that some nuances of facial expressions, body language and pauses were distorted or made ambiguous by the computer interface and time lag (Figure 6.1).

Key components of negotiation include modified input, feedback and modified output. A large body of work over the last three decades has illustrated the ways in which these interactional mechanisms facilitate second language (L2) learning. First, input (the linguistic forms learners are exposed to), and in particular, interactionally modified input, has been shown to positively impact comprehension and learner development (Loschky, 1994; Mackey, 1999). Second, feedback, defined as 'a mechanism which provides the learner with information regarding the success or failure of a given process' (Leeman, 2007: 112), including implicit feedback, explicit feedback, and recasts, potentially draws learners' attention to language form (Ohta, 2001) and prompts more target-like use in response (which in some cases is linked to L2 development) (Mackey & Philp, 1998). And third, output (the language that learners produce), specifically output modified or reformulated by the learner, has been linked to L2 development (e.g. Loewen, 2004; McDonough, 2005) as well as to noticing of L2 forms (Mackey, 2006).

In short, a large body of research demonstrates that conversational interactions, in particular those involving the negotiation of meaning, promote language learning by bringing together input, feedback, and output in productive ways. Our data suggest that tasks such as those utilized here likewise have the potential to facilitate Ojibwe learner engagement with these same productive processes. We provide a close analysis to demonstrate how learners engage with these processes as they negotiate the meaning around directionality of ride-giving, and also the meaning of *boozi* (see Excerpt 1).

Excerpt 1: May 5, 2014 (Mary and Nibiiwanikwe)[4]

1	Mary	<u>Giga-wiijiiwimin</u> ina ogowedi[5] aam:
		Will you all go with us over there:
2	Nibiiwanikwe	iwidi.
		over there.
3	Mary	iwidi aa:
		over there:
4	Mary	What's that game called?
5	Nibiiwanikwe	Quidditch.
6	Mary	Quidditch, Quidditch odaminowin?
		Quidditch, Quidditch game?
7	Nibiiwanikwe	Ahaw. <u>Giwii-wiijiiwigoom.</u>
		OK. We will go with you all.
8	Mary	Aw:: Giishpin <u>wiijiiwiyaang</u> maagizhaa bimaadizi +/ bikaanizid bemaadizijig wii-dazhindaa +/ wii-dazhindaawaad.
		Oh:: If you all are going with us those people +/ different people will gossip +/ they will gossip.
9	Nibiiwanikwe	Gaawiin imbabaamendanziimin.
		It does not bother us.
10	Mary	Ahaw, <u>giga-boozi'imin</u> ina? non-target like
		Ninjiishada'ige. utterance
		Will you all give us a ride? I am sweeping (meant to say on my broom).
13	Mary	Boozig! <laughs>
		Get on! <laughs>
14	Nibiiwanikwe	I don't know if that makes sense ... but explicit
		OK. feedback
15	Mary	Get on the +/ our broom!
16	Nibiiwanikwe	What did you say?
17	Mary	Boozig.
		Get on.
18	Mary	To get into a vehicle.
19	Nibiiwanikwe	Isn't that like, ... I don't know. Can request for
		you repeat what you said? clarification
20	Mary	<u>Giga-boozi'imin ina</u>? ((slow rate of non-target like
		speech)) utterance

		Will you all give us a ride? ((slow rate of speech))	
21	Nibiiwanikwe	Isn't that like, … \<laughter\> I don't know what I'm agreeing to. \<laughter \>	explicit feedback
22	Mary	Oh you're so cautious around me. It's a good thing.	
23	Nibiiwanikwe	I know. I've learned that already.	
24	Mary	Aaniin danaa! *What the hell!*	
25	Mary	OK you're right. I don't need to use a VTA there.	
26	Nibiiwanikwe	Right.	
27	Mary	Gaawiin memwech aabajitoosiin. *It's not necessary to use it.*	non-target like utterance, unclear meaning
28	Mary	Giga-boozim nindoodaaban. *You all get into my car.*	
29	Nibiiwanikwe	Ahaw. *Right.*	
30	Mary	<u>Giga-izhiwininim.</u> *I will bring you all*	non-targetlike utterance
31	Mary	<u>Giga-izhiwinimin.</u> *You all will take us.*	
32	Mary	Izhiwin? *to bring someone?* ((izhiwizh, target))	root form of verb. asking for clarification
33	Mary	bring somebody?	
34	Nibiiwanikwe	You said that we're going to take you but we're taking your car.	explicit feedback
35	Mary	Giga-izhiwinigoom iwidi, ((slower rate of speech)) *We will take you all there,* ((slower rate of speech))	modified output
36	Nibiiwanikwe	Geget, giga-izhiwininim. ((makes sour face)) +/ min. *Sure, I will take you all* ((makes sour face)) +/ *you all will take us.*	non-targetlike utterance, self-corrected
37	Mary	Ahaw. *Right.*	

In this excerpt, Mary and Nibiiwanikwe are working out fictional plans for an outing within a *Harry Potter* context, drawing from characters and storylines of the novel. The goal of the task was to negotiate how they are going to get to the Quidditch game. The target forms here are the

VTAs needed for 'you-to-us' (*gi__imin or _iyaang*), 'you all-to-us' (*gi__ imin or _iyaang*) and 'we-to-you all' *(gi___igoom or ____igooyeg),* as well as their negative formulations.

In line 1, Mary sets the frame for the conversation by asking, 'Will you all go with us over there?' After some discussion of the name of the game (Quidditch), this is confirmed by Nibiiwanikwe in line 7 as she says, 'We will go with you all.' With this premise intact, Mary's question in line 10 ('Will you all give us a ride?') is problematic. The target-like statement here, in light of the agreed upon imaginary frame and Mary's subsequent statements ('on my broom') ('Get on!'), should have been, '**We** all will give **you all** a ride' (*Giga-boozi'igoom.*); instead, Mary says, 'Will you all give us a ride?' *(Giga-boozi'imin ina?).* Nibiiwanikwe (line 14) switches to English to ask for clarification, saying, 'I don't know if that makes sense.'

The confusion over the directionality of the ride, that is, who is taking whom, is further complicated by participants' understanding of *boozi'* ('give him or her a ride'). *Boozi* is an intransitive verb that means 'to board a vehicle.' However, *boozi'* (with a word final glottal stop) is a transitive verb that means to give a ride to someone. Nibiiwanikwe and Mary negotiate the meaning of *boozig* with Mary defining in English (line 18) and Nibiiwanikwe expressing doubt about Mary's formulation, requesting clarification and asking her to repeat in line 19. Mary again says, 'Will you all give us a ride?' instead of 'Do you all want to ride with us?' (line 20).

In line 21, Nibiiwanikwe again questions Mary's formulation, and they switch into English to tease each other about their differing approaches. Mary, in line 28, moves back to using the intransitive verb *boozi* (to board), perhaps doubting her earlier attempts at using the transitive *boozi'* (to give someone a ride). In line 28, she states, 'You all get into my car' in Ojibwe. This use of the intransitive verb is correct in that it keeps with the set-up agreed upon in lines 1–2 that Mary is driving. Nibiiwanikwe affirms this proposition in line 29. However, it is not incorporating use of VTA.

In line 30, Mary returns to use of the VTA ('You all will bring us') in Ojibwe. While this is properly formed, it violates expectations of task to work with 'we' and 'you all,' and thus the more appropriate statement would have been, 'We will bring you all.' Apparently recognizing this, in line 31, Mary attempts to reformulate. She says, 'You all will take us,' which is also not the target because it violates the established directionality of the ride. In line 32, she seeks clarification by restating the root form *izhiwizh-* in Ojibwe and in English. Nibiiwanikwe makes explicit the directionality problem by switching to English in line 34: 'You said that we're going to take you but we're taking your car.'

In line 35, Mary gets it right, modifying her output, stating *giga-izhiwinigoom iwidi* ('We will take you all'). In line 36, Nibiiwanikwe attempts to confirm. In her first try, she says, 'Sure, I will take you all.' She realizes her mistake of using the singular instead of plural, and as evident by a sour face, and reformulates by adding the suffix *imin,* which changes the meaning to 'You all will take us.'

Excerpt 1 illustrates engagement in processes known to support language learning as learners negotiate the meaning around directionality of ride-giving, and also around meaning of *boozi.* For instance, we see evidence here of both explicit feedback and modified output. In line 14, Nibiiwanikwe provides explicit feedback ('I don't know if that makes sense') in response to Mary's statement in line 10, which had inverted the directionality of previously agreed upon ride-giving. She does this again in English in line 34 by stating, 'You said that we're going to take you but we're taking your car.'

Furthermore, both learners have the opportunity to self-correct and produce modified output. For instance, in lines 30–33, Mary attempts to ask, 'We will take you all?' She makes two incorrect attempts, thinks it out in English, and then produces modified output in line 35, using the correct form. Furthermore, Nibiiwanikwe also has opportunity to modify her output. In line 36, she self-corrects, finally saying correctly, 'You all will take us.' In short, this excerpt illustrates the potential of task-based learning activities to promote negotiation of meaning, a process known to facilitate language learning, for endangered Indigenous languages such as Ojibwe.

Differential learning engagement with tasks

Across the data, it became evident that learners engaged very differently with the communicative tasks and seemed to make use of distinct language learning strategies. Mary was likely to try out new verb forms and to take risks by using forms that she was not completely sure were correct. For instance, in line 5, she confuses directionality by using the incorrect form. Mary was also most likely to self-correct and modify her own output in light of the feedback she received in interaction. In the present example, we saw that she uses the target form correctly in line 35 (correct modified output), after various (nontarget-like) attempts. In both this excerpt and across the sessions, she is persistent in working through this ambiguity and is willing to take the risk of not using Ojibwe perfectly in these practice sessions. As discussed below, this learning strategy might be linked to her investments in Ojibwe.

Nibiiwanikwe, in contrast, in both this excerpt and across the sessions, tended to use forms of which she is certain. Our quantitative analysis suggested that she made very few errors with the VTAs she did use (see Table 6.1 for an overview of accuracy rates). This could be due to the fact that she was already fairly confident and proficient in using these forms, and/or a function of her particular language learning strategies. Nibiiwanikwe reports being a visual learner, who can quickly and easily memorize verb conjugations once seen and copied in written form. She is able to produce these orally with high levels of accuracy. Mary's nontarget utterances were highly salient to her, and she often attempted to clarify, signal lack of comprehension, or provide feedback. At times this feedback was explicit (e.g. 'I don't know if that makes sense'); on other occasions this was more implicit (e.g. her recast in line 2).

Research on language learning strategies suggests strong positive correlations between the use of language learning strategies and language performance; furthermore, this body of work suggests that the 'use, choice and effectiveness of the strategy choice very much depend on who the learner is, what the task demands, and what context the learner is in' (Gu, 2012: 319). This task demanded that learners use particular verb forms to accomplish particular goals. This was a more demanding task in terms of accuracy for Mary than for Nibiiwanikwe. The learners were shaped by and situated within the task as well as the larger context of endangerment in which Ojibwe is located.

Discussion and Conclusion

These differences between how the learners engaged with the communicative tasks can be explained in part by viewing the negotiations here as sites of identity struggle. At a surface level, we could say that Mary creates or takes up more opportunities to use low-frequency forms by adopting a 'high-risk' strategy that entails repeatedly trying out different forms and often making mistakes. Nibiiwanikwe, in turn, tends to use only the forms which she is fairly confident she knows and can accurately produce. This difference in risk-taking might be explained by individual learner differences and varied proficiency levels, but it also might be linked to aspects of their identities and particular investments in Ojibwe language learning.

Applying Norton's idea of investment in language learning is potentially productive here; 'if learners invest in a language, they do so with the understanding that they will acquire a wider range of symbolic and material resources, which will in turn increase the value of their cultural capital and social power' (Darvin & Norton, 2015: 37). Of importance is the fact that 'conditions of power in different learning contexts can position the learners in multiple and often unequal ways, leading to varying learning outcomes' (Darvin & Norton, 2015: 37). In this context, and in many Indigenous contexts worldwide, the Indigenous language will not result in greater economic capital. In fact, in many Indigenous language contexts, this power difference is what positions 'choosing' to teach one's children the Indigenous language, rather than the language of wider currency, as a false or artificial choice (Skutnabb-Kangas, 2000). As there are limited economic and few professional incentives for learning Ojibwe, most learners invest in the language primarily for the symbolic capital that it provides within their social networks. As noted above, both of the learners here have invested heavily in learning Ojibwe, and have an identity stake both in the (individual) learning of the language and its (collective) revitalization.

The imagined futures and identities for Ojibwe language learners, the cultural capital, and the reclaiming and revenacularization of Ojibwe depend heavily on learners having an investment in symbolic capital, although for learners who persevere, there are more jobs becoming available in immersion teaching, second language teaching, or working for tribes or non-profits. In this way, social and economic capital are intertwined; by investing heavily in social networks, Nibiiwanikwe gained economic capital in a relatively small market. Although her original drive (investment) was not to gain Ojibwe language skills in order to have more job opportunities, it became a natural outcome of her time and effort. Although Ojibwe is not a 'cash language,' like English for example, pursuit of social capital may help revitalization efforts by creating a concurrent demand for people with Ojibwe language skills. A relevant question for revitalization, then, is, how important is economic infrastructure for revitalization, and is it possible for cottage industries to sustain this type of growth?

Another important aspect of identity in this context is the idea of authenticity (King & Hermes, 2014). Ideologies of language learning and intersecting ideas of 'authenticity' can impede interaction, communication and the negotiation of meaning. Heritage learners carry a high affective load (Heart & DeBuyn, 1998) and may be fearful of making mistakes (King & Hermes, 2014). This can often result in learning situations in which there is limited to no interaction (e.g. extended listening) or to abstracted grammar analysis. For instance, within one Ojibwe immersion camp setting (where the participants originally met), elders (first speakers of Ojibwe) are put in the position of determining both the content and structures for learning. Common activities include listening to elders' narratives; contextualized vocabulary presentations related to specific practices or objects; and creation and presentation of stories and skits. In these settings, there are limited structured opportunities for students to speak in spontaneous and interactive ways. For some, this compounds anxieties about accuracy and authenticity. In short, for a range of reasons, participants are not routinely engaged in communicative tasks that provide opportunity to negotiate for meaning. Because of the complicated and high level of symbolic investment among some of the learners, speaking at the camp (which inevitably entails making mistakes) can be difficult. In some instances, individuals say very little for the entire three weeks.

In this case study, we found that the learners, who all established relationships in person at camp, were in some ways freer to make mistakes in these tasks, as it was actually expected, as the stated purpose of the project was to examine learning language processes. As a kind of consciousness-raising move, the purpose was to practice (including expected mistakes) in a low-risk (three learners, no elders) environment. Participants could and did participate in transcribing the videos after the sessions, enabling them to also reflect on and notice their own errors as well as progress.

Task-based language learning potentially provides a productive alternative here as it allows learners (and elders) to focus on a non-language goal that demands meaningful communication. Elders working with second language learners in constructing tasks – that is, where language is actually necessary in order to facilitate communication – can provide a space where identity is negotiated through finding mutually agreed upon content and frames for the interaction. Since most of these elders acquired Ojibwe in their homes through everyday participation in life, there must be at this time and place a new way of acquiring Ojibwe, one that bridges all the cultural repertoires participants and elders bring to these instances of language reclamation (Leonard, 2008). As we have seen in the present case, tasks created opportunities for interaction where the stakes of cultural capital were not as high and risk-taking not as daunting. By definition, tasks demand interaction among participants, provide mechanisms for structuring and sequencing interaction, and focus on meaningful social activity in order to accomplish a non-linguistic goal (Lee, 2000). In the present case, we saw how tasks were taken up with teasing and humor, where learners had many opportunities to practice low-frequency forms, and with no risk of making embarrassing grammatical or cultural errors in front of an elder and larger community.

For a highly endangered language, the opportunity to engage with a fluent or even proficient speaker is rare. Pushing one's language skills in a meaningful context and receiving feedback on one's communicative effectiveness is even more rare. These communicative tasks were done online, and in a social and informal way. Developing more tasks like these that could be shared among budding revitalization efforts helps when learners are dispersed geographically and isolated in their efforts. The regular meeting for the tasks kept Ojibwe language in the forefront of learners' minds, offering a frequent social opportunity to practice, and yet the freedom to engage as we normally would (teasing, joking, getting off topic, gossiping). This socially enjoyable way of interacting meant that learners were willing to take risks and fully participate in the negotiation of meaning.

Overall, this single excerpt illustrates the ways in which simple communicative tasks can promote meaningful interaction in Ojibwe. We documented the ways in which learners negotiated for meaning using commonly identified interactional mechanisms that have been shown to facilitate second language development. This is important as it shows how for endangered Indigenous languages such as Ojibwe, conversational tasks: (1) provide learners with opportunities to practice less commonly used verb forms, (2) promote engagement with interactional processes that are known to facilitate second language development and (3) allow learners to practice in ways that correspond to their own comfort level and preference.

Of central importance from a revitalization perspective is the idea of social learning. To restore use and teaching of Ojibwe to a social domain, we need to think about how to create these contexts and what they might look like. These meetings represent learning in informal structures – structures that a participant and a participant researcher, or in other words friends, had in part designed. The environment made possible by the internet was their social means of communications and also a part of the environment that allowed a mutual language benefit.

For revitalization to be successful, we need to be able to teach each other Ojibwe in and through social networks, not relying on schools for this. Immersion schools have started the way, but families, ceremonies, places where we work, and especially places where we play are all important domains for teaching and learning as well. For Nibiiwanikwe and Mary, the 'rules' of the interactions were negotiated. In a sense, task-based communication is a replication of the social things we do outside of classrooms. For Ojibwe to be the means of communication in social spheres, one step is to think of this as the ideal teaching and learning context. Informal learning of Ojibwe through social networks offers many of the advantages that were detailed in this study.

Notes

(1) 'First speakers' is a term used in many communities to differentiate between those who have learned Ojibwe as a first language and those who have learned it as a second language, although there are many who fall somewhere in between, including those with passive or receptive skills only, latent speakers, and those who learned as a first language but have had to relearn it as adults. In many communities, 'first speakers' is often used instead of 'native language speakers,' which can be ambiguous (e.g. Native language vs native speaker of a language).

(2) The term 'diaspora' refers to the idea that although geographically dispersed as an artifact of colonization (in many cases from the reservations which could be considered homelands), there are Ojibwe language learners all over the geographic United States who come together at times online and at times in person, to form a community.

(3) Ojibwe conversations can be found at the Digital Conservatory, University of Minnesota library: https://conservancy.umn.edu/handle/11299/163235. The project was funded by the National Science Foundation "Documenting Chippewa [ciw] Conversation and Training Indigenous scholars" Award number 1346905.

(4) Discourse analysis transcription guidelines (based on Tannen *et al.*, 2007) are as follows:

((words))	Double parentheses enclose transcriber's comments, in italics.
/words/	Slashes enclose uncertain transcription.
+/	Indicates a truncated word or adjustment within an intonation unit, e.g. repeated word, false start.
?	A question mark indicates a relatively strong rising intonation (interrogative)
.	A period indicates a falling, final intonation
,	A comma indicates a continuing intonation
...	Dots indicate pause
:	A colon indicates an elongated sound

CAPS	Capitals indicate emphatic stress
`<laugh>`	Angle brackets enclose descriptions of vocal noises, e.g. laughs, coughs, crying.
Words [words]	Square brackets enclose simultaneous talk [words]
Italics	*Translation*
Underline	<u>VTA</u>
Bold	**grammatical or interactional notes**

(5) *Ogowedi* means 'these ones over here' rather than 'over there'; it is a demonstrative pronoun rather than a locative adverb (Jordyn Fladda, Ojibwe editor).

References

Burt, L.W. (1986) Roots of the Native American urban experience: Relocation policy in the 1950s. *American Indian Quarterly* 10 (2), 85–99.

Darvin, R. and Norton, B. (2015) Identity and a model of investment in applied linguistics. *Annual Review of Applied Linguistics* 35, 36–56.

Gu, Y. (2012) Language learning strategies. *Principles and Practices for Teaching English as an International Language* 318.

Heart, M.Y.H. and DeBruyn, L.M. (1998) The American Indian holocaust: Healing historical unresolved grief. *American Indian and Alaska Native Mental Health Research: The Journal of the National Center* 8 (2), 60–82.

Hermes, M. (2004) Waadookodaadging [the place where we help each other] Indigenous immersion: Personal reflections on the gut-wrenching years. In E. Meiners and F. Ibáñez-Carrasco (eds) *Public Acts/Desires for Literacies and Social Changes* (pp. 53–72). New York, NY: Routledge Falmer.

Hermes, M. (2007) Moving toward the language: Reflections on teaching in an Indigenous immersion school. *Journal of American Indian Education* 46 (3), 54–71.

Hinton, L. (2011) Language revitalization and language pedagogy: New teaching and learning strategies. *Language and Education* 25 (4), 307–318.

King, K.A. and Hermes, M. (2014) Why is this so hard?: Ideologies of endangerment, passive language learning approaches, and Ojibwe in the United States. *Journal of Language Identity and Education* 13 (4), 268–282.

King, K.A. and Mackey, A. (2016) Research methodology in second language studies: Trends, concerns, and new directions. *Modern Language Journal* 100, 209–227.

Lee, J.F. (2000) *Tasks and Communicating in Language Classrooms.* New York, NY: McGraw-Hill.

Leeman, J. (2007) Feedback in L2 learning: Responding to errors during practice. In R. DeKeyser (ed.) *Practice in a Second Language: Perspectives from Applied Linguistics and Cognitive Psychology* (pp. 111–137). Cambridge: Cambridge University Press.

Leonard, W.Y. (2008) When is an extinct language not extinct? Miami, a formerly sleeping language. In K.A. King, N. Schilling-Estes, L. Fogle, J. Lou and B. Soukup (eds) *Sustaining Linguistic Diversity: Endangered and Minority Languages and Language Varieties* (pp. 23–33). Washington, DC: Georgetown University Press.

Loewen, S. (2004) Uptake in incidental focus on form in meaning-focused ESL lessons. *Language Learning* 54 (1), 153–188.

Long, M.H. (1996) The role of the linguistic environment in second language acquisition. In W.C. Ritchie and T.K. Bhatia (eds) *Handbook of Research on Language Acquisition Volume 2: Second Language Acquisition* (pp. 413–468). New York, NY: Academic Press.

Loschky, L. (1994) Comprehensible input and second language acquisition. *Studies in Second Language Acquisition* 16 (3), 303–323.

Mackey, A. (1999) Input, interaction, and second language development. *Studies in Second Language Acquisition* 21 (4), 557–587.

Mackey, A. (2006) Feedback, noticing and instructed second language learning. *Applied Linguistics* 27 (3), 405–430.

Mackey, A. and Philp, J. (1998) Conversational interaction and second language development: Recasts, responses, and red herrings? *The Modern Language Journal* 82 (3), 338–356.

McDonough, K. (2005) Identifying the impact of negative feedback and learners' responses on ESL question development. *Studies in Second Language Acquisition* 27 (1), 79–103.

Nichols, J. (2015) Key to Ojibwe parts of speech. In *The Ojibwe People's Dictionary*. Retrieved from http://ojibwe.lib.umn.edu/help/ojibwe-parts-of-speech.

Ohta, A.S. (2001) *Second Language Acquisition Processes in the Classroom: Learning Japanese*. Mahwah, NJ: Lawrence Erlbaum.

Pullman, P. (1997) *The Subtle Knife*. New York, NY: Random House.

Rowling, J.K. (2002) *Harry Potter and The Sorceror's Stone*. St. Louis, MO: Turtleback Books.

Skutnabb-Kangas, T. (2000) *Linguistic Genocide in Education – or Worldwide Diversity and Human Rights?* Mahwah, NJ: Lawrence Erlbaum.

Tannen, D., Kendall, S. and Gordon, C. (eds) (2007) *Family Talk: Discourse and Identity in Four American Families*. Oxford: Oxford University Press.

The Ojibwe People's Dictionary (2015) Retrieved from http://ojibwe.lib.umn.edu/

Treuer, A. (2010) *Ojibwe in Minnesota*. St. Paul, MN: Minnesota Historical Society.

Williams, T. (13 April 2013) Quietly, Indians reshape cities and reservations. *The New York Times*. Retrieved from http://www.nytimes.com/2013/04/14/us/as-american-indians-move-to-cities-old-and-new-challenges-follow.html?pagewanted=all&module=Search&mabReward=relbias%3Aw&_r=1

7 Strengthening Indigenous Languages through Language Technology: The Case of Aanaar Saami in Finland

Marja-Liisa Olthuis and Ciprian-Virgil Gerstenberger

Increasingly, language documentation researchers and Indigenous people have come to appreciate the use of digital technology for endangered languages. In this chapter we report on the different stages of Aanaar Saami revitalization. The first efforts to enhance oral language competence involved establishing a 'language nest' for children in 1997. However, due to previous social and technological changes in the traditional life of the community, there was a deficit of middle-aged adults with sufficient oral competence. The CASLE program started in 2009 and was geared to adults with key roles in the community (teachers, pastors, journalists, civil servants). Yet, oracy is not enough for a language to survive in our time. Luckily, the digital world offers many possibilities to aid several needs for written language. In the context of a Machine Translation project between North Saami and Aanaar Saami initiated by Giellatekno, an academic research group obtained language resources from the Aanaar Saami language community. Through this project, language tools are being developed and scholarly research is being disseminated. But what happens with the resources and tools after the project is over? What is the benefit for the Indigenous community? We explore the Aanaar Saami community's needs for written resources and address how tools developed by the project can meet these needs in a dialogue with the language community.

Introduction

Indigenous peoples have increasingly begun to appreciate the value of digital technology to counter the loss of their cultures and languages. As pointed out by Hermes and King (2013: 126), technology can be effective in language reclamation in at least three ways: (1) communicative use, (2) production of materials and (3) documentation (see Coronel-Molina, Chapter 4, this volume and Hermes and King, Chapter 6, this volume, for related discussions of digital technology for Quechua and Ojibwe, respectively). Digital technology easily allows the creation of teaching materials by linking text to audio files, helping to bypass problems of relying solely on written materials and print literacy. Yet, in our modern world, a vital language needs a means to communicate in written form as well. Increased production of written language forms gives rise to the use of language technology, a specific domain of digital technology. Language technology can speed the creation and improve the quality of teaching materials. While language technology for languages of wider communication is a matter of course, for the languages of minorities, this is an exception.

Academic researchers interested in describing and documenting languages need both digital resources (e.g. texts or word lists) and the expertise of native speakers. In turn, research results can be exploited by language communities to boost their language revitalization work. But academia and Indigenous language communities are often like two different worlds. A close collaboration between them assumes two basic requirements: well-functioning communication and common formats for shared resources.

Based on language technology initially developed for North Saami, the Saami language with the most speakers, we report on the development of language tools for Aanaar Saami (AS), a Saami language with many fewer speakers. First, we sketch the development of the AS language community, then we provide an account of revitalization work that includes both oracy and literacy. In this context, we identify the needs for written language of a small community such as AS. We further describe two Saami Language Technology groups, Giellatekno and Divvun, which represent a successful collaboration between academia and Saami language communities. We discuss in particular one of Giellatekno's language technology projects, a Machine Translation (MT) project between North Saami and Aanaar Saami. We report on initial challenges for language activists and linguists working with language technology as well as for language technologists working with data sets that are not compiled for use in language technology.

During the MT project, many useful resources have been developed. But will they be used by the language community when the project ends? We conclude by considering how to use the resources developed in the MT project to most effectively support community-based language revitalization.

The Aanaar Saami Language Community

Saami is a Finno-Ugric language with nine subgroups spoken by Saami peoples indigenous to what are now Finland, Norway, Sweden and western Russia. Aanaar Saami is primarily spoken in the villages surrounding Lake Aanaar/Inari in northern Finland. With a surface area of more than 17,000 square kilometers, Aanaar/Inari is the largest municipality in Finland. Its population is about 6800, with a population density of 0.45 inhabitants per square kilometer. The Aanaar area is multilingual, having Finnish as a dominating language and Aanaar, North and Skolt Saami as minority languages, North Saami being the 'dominating' minority language (Olthuis *et al.*, 2013: 25). Traditionally AS people have lived from nature as hunter-gatherer-fisher people, but modern culture has also reached this area. The traditional ways of living have become a hobby for many people.

Before the intensive Complementary Aanaar Saami Language Education Program (CASLE) for adults began in 2010, the community counted 350 speakers (Olthuis *et al.*, 2013: 1). Six years later, there were approximately 450 speakers, including first- and second language speakers (Olthuis & Trosterud, 2015; Sarivaara *et al.*, 2016). The language community has always been relatively small, though, never counting many more than 1000 speakers (Olthuis *et al.*, 2013: 25).

The rapid decline of all Saami languages began when the traditional migrating school system was taken over by the contemporary school system in 1947. In the migrating system the teachers – primarily Saami – travelled from village to village, teaching a few weeks in one place before moving to the next one. Education was delivered bilingually in Saami and Finnish. In contrast, the modern school system removed children to distant schools and boarding schools, and due to lack of roads, children had to remain in the schools for long periods. Some children living 'not that far' were able to visit their homes during the weekend, but many children were able to go home only for longer holidays.

In the schools, the Saami language was either forbidden or in milder cases not supported (Rasmus, 2008). These traumatizing experiences nearly caused the destruction of the language. Therefore the present 'middle generation' of working adults, as well as their children, lost their language (Olthuis *et al.*, 2013). By the 1980s there was a clear break in the language transmission process: The Aanaar Saami language community counted only four child speakers in two homes (Olthuis *et al.*, 2013: 30). Thus, initial attempts to revitalize the language aimed at revitalizing oral language usage.

Spoken language

As with most small Indigenous languages, AS has mainly been used orally as a home language, having no official status in Saami communal life. By the 1980s the spoken language had nearly come to an end. Revitalization efforts began in 1997 with an AS 'language nest' established in the village of Aanaar and financed by the Finnish Cultural

Foundation. As with the Māori language nests begun in the 1980s (see Rau *et al.*, Chapter 3, this volume), the AS language nest was aimed at children under school age. Although the language nest was effective, re-evaluations in 2006 showed that one language nest could 'produce' approximately three new speakers annually, meaning that the number of speakers would still be in drastic decline over 20 years. There was a need to extend language nest activities. This was challenging because of the lack of AS-speaking nursery teachers. At the same time, the adults – that is, the 'lost' middle generation – expressed willingness to learn the language. However, there were no teachers for adult education, and there was a lack of teachers in the schools. With only a handful of people keeping the language alive, they were nearly drowning in work. Luckily, these well-educated individuals were able to plan the next steps to further revitalize the language (Olthuis *et al.*, 2013: 7–15).

This was the context for the CASLE program, designed to address the needs of AS revitalization (CASLE, 2013). In 2009–2010, 17 professionals (nursery-school teachers, school teachers, pastors, journalists and civil servants) were recruited and educated in AS, with the purpose of using the language in the workplace. Recruiting qualified Saami and non-Saami professionals in close contact with the community saved time in the revitalization process: The graduates could start working in AS immediately after finishing their AS education. CASLE was planned as an intensive one-year study program consisting of 1700 work hours for students. The first part of the program was classroom teaching. After learning the basics of classroom teaching, students were sent into the field to learn the language from other speakers through cultural courses (fishing, cooking and Saami media). This took place at students' workplace and from elderly language speakers who acted as language masters (see Olthuis *et al.*, 2013: 55–104). Later, the Saami Education Institute also employed younger Saami second-language (L2) learners as master teachers for adult students.

The revitalization process has returned the language back to elderly speakers as well. They actively serve as language masters for adult students, and *ákkukerho*, a 'grandmothers' club,' has been set up by one of the CASLE graduates, Teija Linnanmäki. The grandmothers' club attracts male speakers as well (Olthuis *et al.*, 2013: 137–138; Pasanen, 2015: 335).

After the CASLE study year, the language community expanded rapidly. Two new language nests were opened in 2010; education in schools expanded from two teachers to five; and the church offered ecclesiastical ceremonies in AS. Moreover, language education for adults began, and there were more AS speaking journalists at work. The Saami Parliament uses AS, and, since 2010 it has been possible to study AS as a primary subject at the university. All AS graduates after the CASLE year have been extremely talented and eager to learn the language. Since 2010, the language community counts approximately 100 new speakers from different backgrounds (Olthuis *et al.*, 2013: 129–166). Health care has become a new language domain. Many of these L2 speakers use AS as a home language as well, and there are approximately 50 homes using AS.

From these results it can be argued that it has been wise to concentrate on oral language transmission in the first stage of revitalization efforts. As the language is now in active oral use in the community, there is a clear demand to expand language usage into the written domain. This requires the help of language technology (Sarivaara *et al.*, 2016).

Written language

Historically very little had been written in Aanaar Saami. An orthography was created by linguists and pastors in the 1850s to 1890s. Some standardization was done in the 1950s and again in the 1990s, and there are occasional publications by native speakers such as fisherman Uula Morottaja, writing in the communal newspaper *Sabmelaš* in the 1950s (Olthuis, 2006).

As literary usage of the language was historically scarce, Petter Morottaja (2009) claims that the beginning of an AS literary tradition can be traced to the early 1990s, this also being the watershed period ushering in the digital world. AS has primarily been written in the communal newspaper *Anarâš*, issued five times a year. Modern AS literature barely existed prior to the introduction of digital technology. Only one of the 80 published fiction books dates back to the 1970s; the remainder have been published since digital technology was introduced (Anarâš čaabâkirjálâšvuotâ, 2016). Older literature consists primarily of ecclesiastical books. Schoolbooks have been launched during this 'digital period' (Saami Study Materials, 2016).

According to the Norwegian *bibsys* database (http://www.bibsys.no), at the time of this writing AS counted 120 publications, most being study books or literature. The most productive year for AS as a literary language was 2014, in which eight fiction novels and two study books were published – approximately 1500 pages total. (In a typical year 300–400 pages have been published.) The most active AS writer has been the *Anarâš* newspaper's editor-in-chief, Ilmari Mattus, who has also acted as a translator in the Saami Parliament. Approximately 90% of all texts published in AS have been influenced by him. At the same time, non-native speakers also publish in AS. The most active author has been the kindergarten teacher Riitta Vesala, who has written books for the language nest preschools in order to transmit the 'grammar' to children (Olthuis & Trosterud, 2015).

Presently there are five primary communal writing needs. First, texts need to be translated according to the Saami language law (Saami Language Act, 2004). The official municipal documents are translated from Finnish into all three Saami languages in Finland. The other factor is AS as a medium of instruction in schools since 2000. The constant need to produce study materials is significantly limited by the lack of linguists/ translators and financial resources. Some study materials for biology, mathematics and AS have been created (Saami Study Materials, 2016), but there is a long way to go to produce a 'full series' of materials. Larger projects, such as dictionary and grammar projects, have been carried out over the past 15 years, but are not yet completed. The dictionary project of the Saami Parliament included approximately 30,000 lemmas (words or phrases), without the usage context. However, present-day users have expressed the wish to have examples of the lemmas and to have them electronically available. Language technology is required to achieve this.

Secondly, the language is used in academic circles in scientific texts and presentations. Three master theses in linguistics were published in AS between 2013 and 2016, and more are expected. When possible, scientific presentations and lectures are conducted in AS.

Thirdly, news on the Saami Radio on the internet (http://yle.fi/sapmi) needs to be produced in AS. According to Pirita Näkkäläjärvi, head of Saami Radio, the plan is to multiply publishing on the internet, so each reporter should be able to write in AS. This is not the case at the moment.

Fourthly, semi-official writing needs involve producing written materials for the language nests. This kind of writing is highly recommended but not funded by the authorities. These projects have been funded with temporary grants.

Finally, there is a wish to read and write in one's spare time in genres such as the communal newspaper *Anarâš*, modern literature, magazines and comics (Sarivaara *et al.*, 2016). Short messages can be found on the communal Facebook site *Orroomviste* ('Living room'). There are also a few active blogs such as Marja-Liisa Mujo's blog http://tejablogi.blogspot. fi or Sammeli Valle's blog http://sammelin43.blogspot.fi. Elderly speakers do not usually write in Saami but with some encouragement, they are willing to do so. Another talented writer is Anni Sarre, an elderly AS woman, whose poetry book *Spejâlistem Heijastus* ('Reflection') was published in 2015 (Sarre, 2015; Kaarret & Niskanen, 2015). Both of these writers still act as language masters for adult students. Anni Sarre's apprentices have urged her to publish the poems, and have helped with standardizing the orthography. Together with his students, Matti Valle has learned to use a computer. He uses his personal orthography in AS writing.

As the CASLE program strongly stressed oral language learning, a follow-up revitalization program is needed to strengthen the written language used in modern society. The AS language technology team has begun a *Čyeti čälled anarâkielân* ('A hundred writers for AS') co-project in order to activate AS speakers in writing. The project was initiated by the AS language technology research group of the Arctic University of Norway and Lapland University. Its purpose is to increase the number of writers as well as having more texts in AS. The community still lacks writers, though, mainly in the middle generation, who are responsible for literacy transfer to younger generations. According to our questionnaire, approximately 40 people write short messages in AS, but only 20 of them are active writers. New speakers feel unsure in writing, and elderly native speakers, being the real masters of the language, have not learned to write in AS (Sarivaara *et al.*, 2016).

The plan for the near future is to have a writer's education program for AS, organized by the Saami Education Institute and the University of Oulu, beginning in autumn 2018. The details of the program need to be planned in consultation with the community. An internet-based survey was conducted in January 2016 in order to better understand their concrete writing needs. According to the results, community members would like to concentrate on the writing process, orthography, language revision and style questions. Workplaces need to produce professional texts and to use office hours for writing. These needs are related to the writing needs outlined above. People would like to have a spellchecker, an e-dictionary and e-grammar as well and digital help for word inflection (Sarivaara *et al.*, 2016).

An ongoing issue is the fact that elderly people are the masters of the language, on the one hand, yet they lack basic knowledge of using personal computers. Younger L2 speakers are less competent in the language but they have a far better knowledge of the newest technology. As for the CASLE-educated speakers, their problems in writing are different: they can master the orthography but need help with inflection and syntax (Olthuis & Trosterud, 2015). Our conclusion is that these generations increasingly need to learn from each other in order to successfully carry on both oral and written revitalization processes.

Saami Language Technology

Giellatekno, the Center for Saami Language Technology, was started in 2001 with the aim of building computational models for grammatical analysis of North Saami. In 2005, its closest collaborator, Divvun, the spellchecker project for North and Lule Saami, was funded by the Norwegian Saami Parliament. Based on language technology originally developed for Finnish, both groups work jointly to develop morphology analyzers by means of Finite-State Transducers (Beesley & Karttunen, 2003), initially for North and Lule Saami. A further important common point of interest was and still is the collection of texts in Saami languages, an activity that resulted in what is now referred to as SIKOR, the Saami International Korpus (SIKOR, 2015).

With considerable help from the language communities, Giellatekno and Divvun improved and extended the language analysis tools. The initial part-of-speech disambiguation with Constraint Grammar (Bick, 2000) led to full syntax analysis, i.e. parsing. The development of basic applications – automatic morphology and syntax analysis – enabled the development of more complex applications such as spellcheckers (Gaup *et al.*, 2006), Intelligent Computer-Assisted Language Learning programs (ICALL, Antonsen, 2013), and even rule-based MT systems as proof-of-concept (Tyers *et al.*, 2009).

The Giellatekno and Divvun projects have been successful, as measured by the number of downloads of downloadable tools and by their wide usage both privately and in public institutions such as schools or newspaper redactions. Moreover, the computational linguistic infrastructure built initially for North and Lule Saami attracted the interest of South Saami. Due mainly to the globalization of information via the internet, the Giellatekno and Divvun model attracted the attention of other research and language communities wishing to use the Giellatekno computational linguistic infrastructure.

Joint workshops and projects have been set up with researchers from different countries: with Komi in Russia, Kven in Norway, Kildin Saami in Germany and Norway, Skolt Saami in Finland, Pite Saami in Germany and Sweden, Greenlandic in Denmark and Greenland, and even with Plains Cree and Ojibwe in Canada. In addition, small projects with language activists have begun, such as the Meänkieli-Swedish-Meänkieli dictionary project in North Sweden.

Sharing the infrastructure for building language tools with so many groups working with different languages demanded a streamlined standardized platform. The result was a new infrastructure launched in 2014 (Moshagen *et al.*, 2014). Since almost all resources from Giellatekno are open source, anyone can download and use them for any language, regardless of the number of speakers. The bottleneck is that one has to have a good command of the formalisms used in the infrastructure.

The language tools themselves are low-level applications that perform basic word form analysis or generation operations and, normally, cannot be used by 'ordinary' people for the purpose of language revitalization. Yet they are essential tools for building higher-level applications such as:

(1) Spellcheckers (http://divvun.no/korrektur/korrektur.html);
(2) 'Intelligent' dictionaries, i.e. electronic dictionaries that can be used to look up not only the base form of a word, but also inflected forms or different spelling variants (http://saanih.oahpa.no);
(3) Intelligent Computer-Aided Language Learning (ICALL) tools (http://oahpa.no);
(4) MT tools (http://jorgal.uit.no).

In turn, these high-level applications are intensively used by different groups of North Saami speakers. At the time of this writing the North Saami *Oahpa* had registered more than 1 million question–answer drill exercises, and the North Saami-Norwegian *Bokmål* online dictionaries had been consulted more than 200,000 times, while the South

Saami-Norwegian *Bokmål* had been consulted more than 25,000 times. The Divvun spellcheckers was downloaded 11,425 times between 2008 and mid-2016.

To sum up, there is a fully developed infrastructure especially suited for Saami languages, which is indeed used for modelling North, South, Lule and Skolt Saami. The infrastructure is used also by researchers from the Komi Republic, Russia and researchers working with Ojibwe or Plains Cree in Canada, just to name a few. Yet, the most active Saami language community, which is also the most successful community in language revitalization, namely, the AS community, had not made use of the Giellatekno/Divvun platform at all.

The AS language community is situated in Finland, a modern country with a very good digital infrastructure. Finland has one of the best education systems in the world; in 2012, the country was even the Index leader of the World's Education System Ranking List (Lepi, 2014). AS meets all prerequisites for effortless processing by the language technology: It has a writing system, an alphabet adopted by the community, and absolutely no problems with keyboards or digital input of special characters. Unlike North Saami, there were no major orthographic reforms; unlike Kildin Saami (Rießler, 2013: 201), there were no disagreements on the adoption of the current alphabet. In August 2014, Giellatekno initiated an MT project between North Saami and other Saami languages. Fortunately, the choice for the target language to focus on was AS (Antonsen *et al.*, 2017).

The Machine Translation project between North Saami and Aanaar Saami

Since the overall goal of the project is to build a proof-of-concept MT system between North Saami and AS, low-level applications first had to be developed. Linguistic low-level applications are small programs that execute a specific task such as lemmatization, part-of-speech tagging, or morphosyntactic analysis. High-level applications usually rely on low-level applications, combining them in a purposeful way. An MT system, for example, needs analysis tools for the input of the source language but also generation tools for the output of the target language. Giellatekno uses the open-source MT system Apertium (Forcada *et al.*, 2011).

Any language technology project needs linguistic resources such as texts and dictionaries. Hence, for the initial work with AS, the question was to find out whether there were any resources to share with Giellatekno. Indeed, both a corpus – that is, a collection of monolingual texts in AS – and a bilingual AS-Finnish dictionary could be provided.

The corpus has been processed and is now offered for use as part of the Saami International Korpus (SIKOR). With its 1.56 million tokens, the AS corpus is fairly large relative to the number of speakers. It has been estimated that there is about the same quantity of corpus data, but not yet in digital form. For comparison, the Northern Saami corpus consists of approximately 22 million tokens while Sweden's language bank consists of 8.43 milliard tokens (Olthuis & Trosterud, 2015). One of the larger corpora in the world is the British National Corpus (BNC) with 100 million words and a collection of both written and spoken language (British National Corpus, 2001).

The current version of the AS corpus consists mainly of texts published in the communal newspaper *Anarâš*. In addition, the collection includes schoolbooks, modern literature as well as biblical and other ecclesiastical texts. However, it needs to be continuously extended. Measured against the corpus, the AS morphosyntactic analyzer under development has 93.3% coverage (April, 2016). Half of the omissions are due to open issues in the treatment of derivation and diminutives as well as foreign names and citations; the other half is due to lacunas in the Finite State Transducer (Antonsen *et al.*, 2016a).

As shown in Figure 7.1, the AS corpus can be used so that the user can type an inflection form of a specific word separately, such as the case forms of the noun *kandâ* (boy), *kaandân* (singular illative) and *kaandâst* (singular locative). It can be used advantageously in combination with a search in the online dictionary.

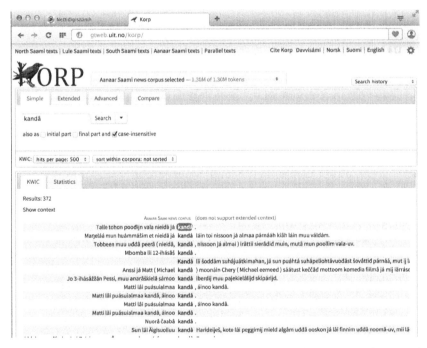

Figure 7.1 The noun *kandâ* ('boy') in singular nominative in the AS corpus. (Retrieved 27 April 2016 from http://gtweb.uit.no/korp/. Screenshot by authors.)

For an MT project, a monolingual corpus is not enough; a bilingual word list is needed. In this respect, the language community helped once again by providing Giellatekno with a Finnish-AS electronic dictionary. Since there were no North Saami-AS bilingual resources, a North Saami-Finnish dictionary has been composed with a Finnish-AS dictionary. Yet, due to the fact that the Finnish-AS dictionary was not machine-readable, the process of getting a usable bilingual dictionary for the MT project demanded a lot of time and effort.

But what does *machine-readability* mean? In order to have shareable data in digital format for language technology tasks – that is, data that can be used both by humans and by machines – the data must comply with a simple demand: It should be unambiguously processable.

Ambiguities can occur in any type of data. In the following, we give an example of ambiguity in lexical data stemming from the Finnish-AS dictionary:

aakkostaa *orniđ puustavij mild* [to alphabetize]
ahdistaa *atâštiđ atâštâm aatâšt* [to haunt]
aavistus avâštâs, kuommâm, ulme u'lme [premonition]
aivan aaibâs, (suorastaan) penttâ (ihan, juuri) [absolutely]

It is not easy to discriminate automatically between a multi-word expression such '*orniđ puustavij mild'* (literally, to organize alphabets accordingly) and the string '*atâštiđ atâštâm aatâšt'* denoting the infinitive form '*atâštiđ'* (to haunt) as the first part and the inflected forms '*atâštâm'* (I haunt) *and* '*aatâšt'* ((s)he haunts) as usage examples. Hence, the white space is ambiguous as separator in these two contexts. Furthermore, the comma in '*avâštâs, kuommâm, ulme u'lme'* separates different translations of the same Finnish lemma **aavistus**, which is also the case with the first comma in '*aaibâs, (suorastaan) penttâ (ihan, juuri).'* Yet, the second comma separates two synonymous adverbs put as additional bracketed information to the translation variant '*penttâ.'* Again, for automatic data processing, the first type of comma must be disambiguated from the second type.

Such disambiguation tasks are easy for humans but not trivial at all for automatic processing. These ambiguities could have been avoided from the very beginning of handcrafting the dictionary. With the personal experience of working with the AS lexicography, we highly recommend to have in mind machine-readability of handcrafted data while setting up new language material creation projects.

The AS dictionary data, in combination with the morphology analysis and generation tool, enabled the development of the online dictionary, (Johnson *et al.*, 2013), AS *Nettidigisäänih* (NDS), accessible for public use at http://saanih.oahpa.no. Not only does NDS provide information on inflectional paradigms, it also links the search to the AS corpus so that one can easily jump from the dictionary to the corpus to find all instances of a specific lemma or word form. Figure 7.2 shows the search of the noun *kandâ* (boy) in the NDS, whereas Figure 7.1 shows the instances of the same word found in the AS corpus via the dictionary. In this way, a word can be looked up in an efficient, easy way, both in the dictionary for inflection information and in the corpus for occurring contexts.

One might think that the corpus and the NDS are tools only for researchers, but this is not the case. Language users often face the problem of not knowing a certain word in AS or a fear of using a specific word in the wrong context. Key persons in language transmission especially fear transmitting their own mistakes to younger generations. In this context, language tools such as NDS play an important role as reference material. Users can submit direct feedback from within the application, proposing corrections or improvements of extant entries as well as additions of new data sets. Via Facebook and other social media, NDS and SIKOR are becoming more and more known in the language community.

Between January 2016 and May 2016, the dictionary had been accessed 15,865 times. Searches from Finland constituted 98% of the searches (15,539 searches); searches from Norway constituted 0.57% (91 searches). Even more interesting is that the 98% searches from Finland stemmed from 332 different IP addresses. This means not only that users from Finland consult the dictionary frequently but also that there are many different users consulting it. As for the AS corpus, the server log data show that it had been accessed 3177 times between January and May 2016.

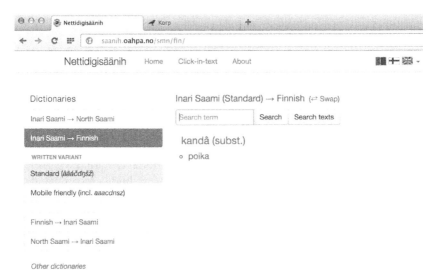

Figure 7.2 The noun *kandâ* ('boy') in the e-dictionary *Nettidigisäänih*. (Retrieved 27 April 2016 from http://saanih.oahpa.no/smn/fin/. Screenshot by authors.)

Beyond Machine Translation as proof-of-concept

The MT project brought together two different worlds with different goals – the Indigenous language community and the researcher community. Yet, the intensive and systematic work with the formal description of AS threw a different light on the language. What 40 to 50 years ago had been deemed extremely reliable and very good inflectional paradigms (see Bartens, 1988: 2), seems now to be insufficient both for computational analysis and for learners of the modern language. While finishing the formal AS paradigm implementation at Giellatekno, we assume that the old method of paradigm description covers only 15% of the real inflection system. It is too little to document the complete system. In order to produce the list of inflection types, one needs a thorough analysis of the word structures. Therefore one needs to have a dictionary with good coverage. Even though some smaller dictionaries exist and there is a need to produce a better grammar, we recommend taking the dictionary as a starting point and proceeding towards the grammar, taking into account frequency distribution of the lemmas.

Moreover, the language technology resources developed so far can be deployed even more fully to support the community's needs for language revitalization. Language revision is a basic task that must be done to all published materials such as official translations, schoolbooks, language teaching materials, literature, non-fiction, news and other journalistic texts as well as scientific texts. It is a challenging task, especially when non-natives need to take more responsibility for it. Besides NDS and SIKOR, a decent spellchecker is sorely needed in order to accommodate the ever-growing demand for written materials.

Yet, is it feasible to create a spellchecker for such a small language as AS at all? The technical development of an AS spellchecker is not a challenge because the main work has already been done for other Saami languages. From this viewpoint, AS can use the same implementations. According to our estimates, it would take less that one year of work to build a spellchecker of good quality.

Despite the fact that the MT system is still under construction, it can be of help for translators by speeding up the translation process. MT should be seen as a help for, not a replacement of, human translators. Post-editing of MT output by a human translator is always needed (Antonsen *et al.*, 2016a). The current version of the MT system has been evaluated by four professional linguists, who estimated that the translation process was quicker with MT (Antonsen *et al.*, 2016a). Due to the free availability of some parallel text from the Saami Parliament in Finland, the system is usually tuned for this domain. We have also translated some texts of children's literature. Our experience shows that the MT system suits these translation tasks, too, as the source text is narrative (see also Toral & Way, 2015). The main using arena would, of course, be the official translations required by the law and study materials. However, in practice, the translation is done from Finnish into AS, not from North Saami. The first reactions from the field have been somewhat complicated: The Saami languages in Finland are equal, and it is problematic to lift one Saami language above others, even if most texts will be produced in North Saami. However, if MT would address literature, for instance, it would be of great help.

MT can also be helpful in creating neologisms for AS. The emergence of new domains in modern society calls for new terms (see also Coronel-Molina, Chapter 4, this volume). Therefore, terminological gaps will appear while taking language use into new domains. As it is very time-consuming to construct neologisms from scratch (see Olthuis, 2007: 82–110), a useful language technology implementation would be using MT for translating the lacking concepts word by word from a further developed source language. This is the case specifically with compounds. At the time of this writing, the first attempts for AS were under way to construct the terminology of (world) history needed in schools. Thereafter, the automatically generated neologisms will be revised by language experts. To our knowledge this implementation has never been done for other languages.

Concluding Remarks

In this chapter we have put forward the idea of sharing digital resources between two rather different worlds – an Indigenous community and researchers working in the field of language documentation and language description – arguing that these two worlds should create a symbiosis by sharing language resources. While there are a growing number of language revitalization projects using digital technology (see, e.g. Jones & Ogilvie, 2013), language technology is still limited in use. Yet, language documentation researchers and linguists working with formal methods who are interested in less-studied languages need language data. For minority languages with a writing system, language activists create teaching materials in written form – most often today in digital form. Hence, the same material that is handcrafted for language revitalization purposes could be shared with the researchers.

In turn, the tools and resources built with the help of language technology could be shared with the language community in order to speed language material creation and check its quality. Furthermore, ICALL programs can be used for language learning tasks such as patterned drills that can be easily automated, freeing up time for teachers to focus on more challenging language learning tasks.

A functioning cooperation between researchers and language activists requires the following:

(1) shared (handcrafted) data should be machine-readable (unambiguously processable by computer);

(2) language activists, teachers, translators and other language professionals should be instructed on the effective use of specific language tools;
(3) in using the tools implemented during the MT project, AS speakers could give feedback for improvement and extension of the resources;
(4) community members should be encouraged to use their mother tongue (instead of Finnish, the majority language) in writing and in social media, email correspondence and SMS;
(5) more people with AS writing skills need to be recruited to strengthen the writing components of revitalization.

We fully agree with Crystal (2005: 520) that the internet 'offers an unprecedented degree of written public presence to individuals and small-scale community groups, and thus a vast potential for representing personal and local identities.' In today's world, a truly living language is used across all types of social media and digital communication channels, including text messaging and email. Without diminishing the importance of orality for the vitality of Indigenous languages, we claim that in these contemporary times, the AS community needs both orality and literacy.

Acknowledgements

We wish to thank Trond Trosterud as well as three anonymous reviewers for their careful reading of an earlier version of this chapter and their insightful and constructive comments and suggestions. This helped us improve the quality of the chapter. Any remaining errors in the chapter are, of course, our own responsibility.

References

Anarâš čaabâkirjálâšvuotâ (2016) Retrieved from http://nettisaje.wikidot.com/anaras-caabakirjalasvuota

Antonsen, L. (2013) Constraints in free-input question-answering drills. Proceedings of the Second Workshop on NLP for Computer-assisted Language Learning at NODALIDA 2013, 22–24 May, Oslo, Norway (pp. 11–26). NEALT Proceedings Series 17, 11–26.

Antonsen, L., Trosterud, T., Olthuis, M.-L. and Sarivaara, E. (2016a) Modelling the Inari Saami morphophonology as a finite state transducer. In T.A. Pirinen, E. Simon, F.M. Tyers, and V. Vincze (eds) Proceedings of the Second International Workshop on Computational Linguistics for Uralic Languages (pp. 3–13). Retrieved from rgai.inf.u-szeged.hu/project/iwclul/proceedings/pdf

Antonsen, L., Gerstenberger, C.V., Olthuis, M.-J., Sarivaara, E., Seurujärvi, M., Trosterud, T. and Tyers, F. (2016b) Dihtorjorgaleami Hástalusat. Davvisámegielas Anárašgillii. Tromsø: Sámesymposiet.

Antonsen, L., Gerstenbergers, C., Kappfiell, M., Rahka, S.N., Olthuis, M.-J., Trosterud, T. and Tyers, F. (2017) Maching translation with North Saami as a pivot language, Proceedings of the 21st Nordic Conference of Computational Linguistics

(NODALIDA 2017), 22–24 May 2017, Gothenburg, Sweden. *Linkping Electronic Conference Proceedings* 131, 123–131. Linköping University Electronic Press.

Bartens, R. (1988) Tieteen moninkertaisen työmiehen merkkipäivänä. Erkki Itkonen 75 vuotta. *Virittäjä* 92 (1), 1–7.

Beesley, K.R. and Karttunen, L. (2003) *Finite State Morphology.* Stanford, CA: CSLI Publications.

Bick, E. (2000) *The Parsing System Palavras – Automatic Grammatical Analysis of Portuguese in a Constraint Grammar Framework.* Oakville, CT: Aarhus University Press.

British National Corpus, version 2 (BNC World) (2001) Distributed by Oxford University Computing Services on behalf of the BNC Consortium. Retrieved from http://www. natcorp.ox.ac.uk

CASLE (2013) Complementary Aanaar Saami Language Education. Retrieved from http://ww.casle.fi.

Crystal, D. (2005) *The Stories of English.* Penguin Books.

Forcada, M.L., Ginesti-Rosell, M., Nordfalk, J., O'Regan, J., Ortiz-Rojas, S., Pérez-Ortiz, J.A., Sánchez-Martínez, F., Ramírez-Sánchez, G. and Tyers, F.M. (2011) Apertium: a free/open-source platform for rule-based machine translation. *Machine Translation* 25 (2), 127–144.

Gaup, B., Moshagen, S.N., Omma, T., Palismaa, M., Pieski, T. and Trosterud, T. (2006) From Xerox to Aspell: A first prototype of a North Sámi speller based on TWOL technology. In A. Yli-Jyrä, L. Karttunen and J. Karhumäki (eds) *Finite-State Methods and Natural Language Processing. Lecture Notes in Computer Science 4002* (pp. 306–307). Berlin and Heidelberg: Springer-Verlag.

Hermes, M. and King, K.A. (2013) Ojibwe language revitalization, multimedia technology, and family language learning. Retrieved from http://llt.msu.edu/issues/february2013/hermesking.pdf

Jones, M.C. and Ogilvie, S. (eds) (2013) *Keeping Languages Alive: Documentation, Pedagogy and Revitalization.* Cambridge: Cambridge University Press.

Johnson, R., Antonsen, L. and Trosterud, T. (2013) Using finite state transducers for making efficient reading comprehension dictionaries. Proceedings of the 19th Nordic Conference of Computational Linguistics (NODALIDA 2013), 22–24 May 2013, Oslo University, Norway. *NEALT Proceedings Series 16*, 59–71.

Kaarret, A. and Niskanen, E. (2015) Anni Sarre čäällim tihtâkirje almostui. Retrieved from http://yle.fi/uutiset/anni_sarre_caallim_tihtakirje_almostui/7761117

Lepi, K. (2014), *The Top 10 (And Counting) Education Systems in The World.* Retrieved from http://www.edudemic.com/learning-curve-report-education/

Morottaja, P. (2009) Kirjálâšvuotâ jottáá já symboleh kirdâčˇeh fantasia suájáiguin. In K. Ruppel (ed.) *Omin Sanoin, Kirjoituksia Vähemmistökielten Kirjallistumisesta* (pp. 65–70). Helsinki: Kotimaisten kielten tutkimuskeskus.

Moshagen, S., Rueter, J., Pirinen, T., Trosterud, T. and Tyers, F.M. (2014) Open-Source Infrastructures for Collaborative Work on Under-Resourced Languages. Workshop: Collaboration and Computing for Under-Resourced Languages in the Linked Open Data Era. LREC 2014, 71–77.

Olthuis, M.-L. (2006) 1800-luvun inarinsaame ja inarinsaamen kirjakielen synty. [The Aanaar Saami in the 19th century and the birth of the Written Aanaar Saami Literary Language]. In T. Nordlund, T. Onikki-Rantajääskö and T. Suutari (eds) *Kohtauspaikkana Kieli. Näkökulmia Persoonaan, Muutoksiin ja Valintoihin* (pp. 386–412). Suomen Kirjallisuuden Seuran Toimituksia 1078. Helsinki: Suomen Kirjallisuuden Seura.

Olthuis, M.-L. (2007) *Inarinsaamen Lajinnimet.* Avveel: Anarâškielâ servi ry.

Olthuis, M.-L., Kivelä, S. and Skutnabb-Kangas, T. (2013) *Revitalising Indigenous Languages. How to Recreate a Lost Generation.* Bristol: Multilingual Matters.

Olthuis, M.-L. and Trosterud, T. (2015) *Inarinsaamen Lingvistinen Suunnittelu Kieliteknologian Valossa* [Aanaar Saami Language Planning from the Viewpoint of Language Technology]. Retrieved from http://agon.fi/article/inarinsaamen-lingvistinen-suunnittelu-kieliteknologian-valossa/

Olthuis, M.-L., Sarivaara, E., Gerstenberger, C.V. and Rosterud, T. (2016) *Čyeti Čälled Anarâškielân. Kirjálistemohjelm Huksim Uhkevuálásii Kielâ Várás.* Tromsø: Sámegiela ja sámi girjjálašvuođa dutkan- ja bagadansymposia.

Pasanen, A. (2015) *Kuávsui Já Peeivičuová 'Sarastus ja Päivänvalo'. Inarinsaamen Kielen Revitalisaatio.* Helsinki: Suomalais-ugrilainen seura ja Helsingin yliopisto.

Rasmus, M. (2008) *Bággu Vuolgit, Bággu Birget. Sámemánáid Ceavzinstrategiijat Suoma Álbmotskuvlla Ásodagain 1950–1960 Logus.* Oulu: Giellagas-Institute.

Rießler, M. (2013) Towards a digital infrastructure for Kildin Saami. In E. Kasten and T. de Graaf (eds) *Sustaining Indigenous Knowledge: Learning Tools and Community Initiatives for Preserving Endangered Languages and Local Cultural Heritage* (pp. 195–218). Fürstenberg/Havel: Kulturstiftung Sibirien.

Saami Language Act from 1 January 2004. Retrieved from http://www.finlex.fi/fi/laki/ajantasa/2003/20031086

Saami Study Materials Provided by the Saami Parliament (2016) Retrieved from http://www.samediggi.fi/index.php?option=com_content&task=view&id=158&Itemid=61&lang=english

Sarivaara, E., Olthuis, M.-L., Gerstenberger, C.V and Trosterud, T. (2016) *Čyeti Čälled Anarâškielân. Kirjálistemohjelm Huksim.* Umeå: Aktasne II 10.3.2016.

Sarre, A. (2015) *Speijâlistem. Heijastus.* Aanaar: Sämitigge.

SIKOR (2015) UiT The Arctic University of Norway and the Norwegian Saami Parliament's Saami text collection, Version 01.03.2015. Retrieved from http://gtweb.uit.no/korp

Toral, A. and Way, A. (2015) Machine-assisted translation of literary text. *Translation Spaces* 4 (2), 241–268.

Tyers, F., Wiechetek, L. and Trosterud, T. (2009) *Developing Prototypes for Machine Translation between Two Sámi Languages. Proceedings of the 13th Annual Conference of the European Association of Machine Translation*, EAMT09. Allschwil: European Association for Machine Translation.

Part 3

Prospects and Possibilities for Indigenous Language Reclamation

8 Without the Language, How Hopi Are You?: Hopi Cultural and Linguistic Identity Construction in Contemporary Linguistic Ecologies

Sheilah E. Nicholas

Contemporary Hopi society reflects significant change brought about by modernity and contact with Western society. Nevertheless, village life revolves around a rich calendar of traditional secular and ceremonial ritual activities which has helped to preserve much of the culture in its traditional form. Thus, Hopi remains a vibrant, living culture, one in which the people continue to carry out ceremonial and traditional responsibilities through their ancestral language, Hopilavayi, the Hopi language. This chapter voices a critical consciousness by the Hopi community of a fundamental difference in how today's Hopi youth are growing up from those of previous generations – Hopi youth are not acquiring the Hopilavayi as their first language. A worrying concern centers on Hopilavayi as essential to the construction of a culturally distinct identity with inherent responsibilities learned in the process of 'becoming Hopi.' Findings from an ethnographic case study of Hopi language shift and vitality (2003–2004) focus on the intergenerational pattern of Hopi identity construction among three Hopi youth amid changing sociocultural and sociolinguistic ecologies. The family case studies exemplify the ways in which parents and grandparents ensure their children and grandchildren come to know the Hopi world as their first world in the course of 'living and experiencing' Hopilavayi through the practice of culture. Reciprocally, the youth demonstrate that they 'have their hearts in the Hopi way of life.'

The world looks at the Hopi with great admiration because of our culture. If we don't work on this language issue, we're just going to be Hopis in name only. There will be no meaning beyond that. Because of our language and culture, we have a lot to contribute to the world. When you learn about Hopi, you learn about that balance between your responsibilities to yourself, your society, your whole world. That's how Hopis think about it. *This is passed through the language.* (HLAP Orientation Meeting, 23 December 1996; emphasis added)

Introduction

The Hopi people, *Hopìit,* are the westernmost of the Puebloan peoples in the US Southwest and continue to reside in village communities on their Aboriginal lands in the Black Mesa Plateau region of the state of Arizona. This northeastern region of high, arid plateau lands, described as barren and desolate, 'has produced a people who have devised a reciprocal, ethical and spiritual relationship with this environment' (McCarty *et al.*, 2012: 82). The landscape is a reminder to the Hopi people that their epistemological origins are intimately tied to the traditional subsistence practice of *natwani* – planting the short blue ear of corn by hand, a practice which stems from a distinct Hopi identity and a practice carried out today (Figure 8.1).

This region, known to the Hopiit as *Hopitutskwa*, Hopi lands, is also referred to as the Hopi Reservation, a politically designated area of 1.6 million acres, situating Hopi as a geographic, cultural, linguistic and political enclave within the multiple enclaves of the Navajo Nation,[1] state of Arizona, and United States (Figure 8.2). The Hopi are one of the 22 Arizona and the 566 US federally recognized tribes. About 14,000 are enrolled members, of which 7000 are permanent residents of 12

Figure 8.1 Hopi cornfield, *Hopitutskwa*, Hopi lands (photograph by Sheilah E. Nicholas)

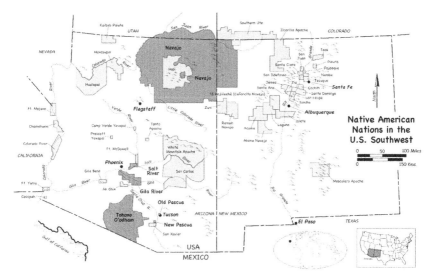

Figure 8.2 Native nations in the US Southwest (graphics by Shearon Vaughn, from McCarty 2011; used with permission)

traditional villages and small communities located on and below three mesas – First Mesa, Second Mesa and Third Mesa. Another 7000 members have migrated to off-reservation communities and cities locally (in-state), nationally and internationally for economic, academic and myriad other opportunities; many make frequent returns to maintain connection and carry out cultural and ceremonial responsibilities. Residents include non-Hopi and non-Indian employees of the tribal government, health and education service facilities as well as in-married individuals.

Contemporary Hopi society reflects significant change brought about by modernity and contact with Western society. Vehicles and buses criss-crossing the reservation landscape carrying residents to work and school are evidence of the incorporation of a cash economy, a Western education system and a form of governance established to conduct tribal, state and federal affairs with external entities. State and US highways have opened access to and from the mainstream world. A less visible change in this kinship-based matrilineal and matrilocal society is the composition of the family household.

Traditionally, the Hopi household comprised immediate and extended family members (maternal grandparents, and in-married son-in-laws), while today's Hopi households are primarily nuclear family units. Nevertheless, each village continues to function as a social, cultural and ceremonial autonomous unit and village life revolves around a calendar of traditional secular and ceremonial ritual activities. Some of the Hopi villages are among the oldest continuously occupied settlements on the North American continent. The nearest urban centers are located from 45 to 90 miles away and this remoteness has helped to preserve much of the culture in its traditional form. Thus, Hopi remains a vibrant, living culture, one in which the people continue to carry out ceremonial and traditional responsibilities through their ancestral language, *Hopilavayi*, the Hopi language.

Hopilavayi is a member of the Uto-Aztecan language family – a family of languages that extends from what is now the western US to southwestern Mexico – yet also as a 'separate branch within Northern Uto-Aztecan' (*Hopìikwa Lavàytutuveni*; Hopi Dictionary Project, 1998: xv). There are four distinct Hopilavayi varieties in usage: First Mesa, Second Mesa, Third Mesa and Musangnuvi Village. Hopilavayi continues to be the medium of intergenerational use in *kiva* (an underground or partially underground ceremonial chamber) activities, at ceremonial performances and in cultural practices. Hence, the contemporary sociocultural and sociolinguistic world of Hopi youth includes village life and active participation in the cultural traditions and institutions as well as experiences in and with the Western/mainstream world through off-reservation excursions, on-reservation Western education systems, and the influence of digital and mass media.

The expression that opens this chapter voices a critical consciousness by the Hopi community of a fundamental difference in how today's Hopi youth are growing up from those of previous generations – Hopi youth are not acquiring the Hopilavayi as their first language. A worrying concern centers on Hopilavayi as essential to the construction of a culturally distinct identity with inherent responsibilities learned in the process of 'becoming Hopi' (Nicholas, 2008). The process is defined by the Hopi expression, *Hopiqatsit ang nùutum hintsakme, Hopisinoniwtingwu*, When one participates along with others in the Hopi way of life, one becomes Hopi. Thus, the Hopi identity formation process and Hopilavayi are pinpointed as the customary way and primary mechanisms through which each generation of Hopi has learned to carry out the overarching and expanding responsibilities to self, family and community in the Hopi world and beyond.

'Becoming Hopi' – a morally behaving one; one who is mannered, civilized, peaceable, polite; who adheres to the Hopi way; who is fluent in the language (*Hopìikwa Lavàytutuveni*, Hopi Dictionary Project, 1998) – begins at birth. Through birthright into one's mother's clan, the individual acquires the marks of identity and belonging – clan membership, maternal village affiliation, and ceremonial names – along with one's ascribed roles and responsibilities established within the clan-kinship social system. Birthright affords the privileges of participation in the Hopi world through which one acquires the knowledge about her/his responsibilities. Today, however, the phenomenon of linguistic shifting from Hopilavayi to English as the predominant language of use in the cultural Hopi way of life has positioned Hopilavayi as facing an ominous future. Without Hopilavayi, how will the younger and succeeding generations of

Hopi learn the implicit ethics and principles – 'humility, cooperation, respect, and universal earth stewardship' (Kuwanwisiwma, 2002: 16) – inherent in the construction of a Hopi cultural identity?

In this chapter I respond to this concern. I focus on illuminating the Hopi perspective of: (1) a culturally distinct identity and the intrinsic meaning attributed to that identity; (2) Hopilavayi and the role it assumes in the construction of a Hopi identity; and (3) the inherited responsibilities which each generation of Hopi is socialized to uphold. I draw on the findings from my case study of Hopi language shift and vitality (Nicholas, 2008) centering on the intergenerational pattern of Hopi identity construction among three Hopi youth – Dorian, Jared and Justin – amid changing sociocultural and sociolinguistic ecologies. Parent and grandparent generation participants were included to ascertain the influence of the philosophical foundations of the Hopi way of life, the cultural and linguistic ideologies held, the core principles, values and practices that remain salient and why. The findings revealed that each family and household affect how language learning, language shift and language maintenance are divergently shaped by the context in which one learns and uses language: Dorian and Jared used words and short phrases but were unable to carry on a conversation in Hopilavayi, whereas Justin self-identified as a proficient Hopilavayi speaker.

The family case studies exemplify the ways in which parents and grandparents demonstrate they 'have their hearts in the Hopi way of life, *Hopiqatsit aw unangvakiwyungwa*,' and ensure their children/grandchildren come to know the Hopi world as their first world through the course of 'living and experiencing' the Hopi way of life. While Dorian asserts that 'Most of the time when you're growing up, it's English [that is used] … in learning the basic things [cultural practices] we [the Hopi people] do,' it is the privileges of participation in Hopi traditions that cultivate and nurture the development of a Hopi identity. However, each youth aspired to learn (Dorian and Jared) and continue learning (Justin) Hopilavayi contending its role as fundamental to accessing the deeper meaning of their Hopi identity – the 'missing pieces' that elude them.

I use the notion of language as cultural practice (Nicholas, 2008, 2018) as the conceptual framework to discuss *Hopivötskwani*, the Hopi path/way of life and Hopi oral tradition as intimately linking language, culture and identity. The late Hopi elder and research anthropologist Emory Sekaquaptewa, asserts that, 'There are many ways that one can experience culture; [spoken] language only being one of them' (cited in Nicholas, 2018: 305). He contends that language 'lives' in the context of culture – in the daily routines of life as well as in social institutions such as marriage practices and baby naming ceremonies; language has meaning within these contexts. Thus, the Hopi people view active participation and increasing involvement in traditions throughout one's cultural life as 'taking the place of [spoken] language to instill the sense of belonging and connection' toward the construction of a Hopi identity (Nicholas, 2018: 305).

Hopivötskwani is philosophically grounded in the concept of *natwani* – the practice of growing corn by hand; the metaphor for practicing life – encoded in and conveyed through the Hopi oral tradition (Nicholas, 2009). Through an array of language forms – teachings, story, prayer, song words, performance, ritual language and symbolism – the Hopi oral tradition manifests in ritual practices, religious ceremonies and cultural institutions to inculcate the Hopi people with the cultural knowledge, history, ethics and values of their communal society. Hopilavayi is maintained in these conventions of a traditionally oral society. Hopivötskwani and Hopilavayi are further illuminated as transporting a distinctly Hopi 'linguistically and socioculturally structured environment' (Ochs, 1988: 21) from a remote past to the present. Both convey the conditions for what adults do with the language and how children/youth access, participate in, and thus develop a particular orientation toward life that produce specific behaviors, attitudes, and character.

I begin with a discussion of the research methodology. Next, I describe the changing Hopi sociocultural and sociolinguistic ecologies drawing on the life histories of the grandparent and parent study participants. Against this backdrop, I introduce and briefly discuss the Hopi life plan, Hopivötskwani,[2] to offer context for its saliency as providing the deeply internalized cultural foundation among generations of Hopi people. Following this, I describe the ways the parent participants demonstrate they have 'their hearts in the Hopi way of life,' *Hopiqatsit aw unangvaki-wyungwa* (Nicholas, 2010) in assuming the role of the first teachers of the Hopi way for their children. The saliency of Hopivötskwani is maintained through the privileges of participation and language as cultural practice and reciprocally manifest in the ways their children express their allegiance to the Hopi way. I conclude with a look to the 'next steps' premised on the role of schools as critical sites where the Hopi people can empower themselves in determining the trajectory of their reclamation efforts.

Research Methodology

Investigating Hopi language shift and vitality evolved with a critical consciousness of the pronounced language shift from Hopilavayi to English in my community and in my personal life. Although Hopi was my first language, it was displaced by English in the course of my schooling; however, I retained a receptive ability in the language into adulthood.[3] The larger study from which this chapter is derived came about as I assisted Emory Sekaquaptewa in providing Hopilavayi literacy lessons[4] to students in Hopi language classes at a reservation middle/secondary school. I was intrigued by the circumstances leading these youth to enroll in Hopi language classes;[5] despite 'living and experiencing Hopi' throughout their lives, many had not acquired Hopilavayi. I viewed their enrollment in Hopi language classes as expressing a yearning to learn their ancestral language.

Study site and data collection

Hopi language shift is both an unprecedented and complex phenomenon, a lived experience of a traditional oral society. This study situates the Hopi community as the research site (see Figure 8.3) and focused life histories collected through in-depth interview inquiry as method (Seidman, 2009/2013). Secondary data sources included conversations with Emory Sekaquaptewa[6] regarding the Hopi way of life and comments

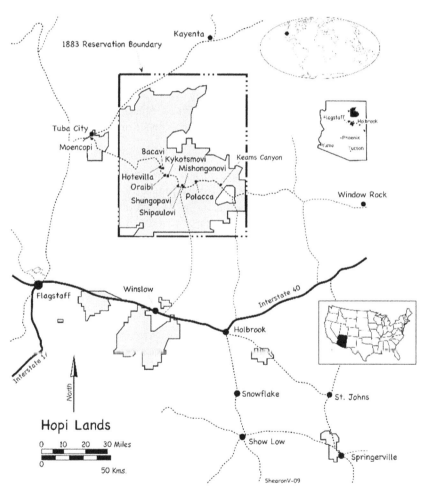

Figure 8.3 Research setting (shaded areas indicate Hopi lands; the current Hopi Reservation area is within the bold boundary) (graphics by Shearon Vaughn; McCarty, T.L., 2011, p. 52, used with permission)

documented at the HTCPO village forums (January–October 1996 through January 1997).

Study participants

Youth

Dorian (female), Jared and Justin (males) are the focal youth study participants. From birth, each experienced a childhood upbringing immersed in the Hopi culture – traditions, practices and social institutions. Thus, as young adults, they expressed a strong affinity for their heritage culture. By birthright, each had acquired cultural marks of identity – maternal clan identity, maternal village affiliation, birth and ceremonial names – and the privileges of participation in the Hopi way of life. At the time of the study, all were aged 19 and recent high school graduates having attended only schools located on the reservation. Dorian was living with her mother and younger brother and attending to her duties as the reigning Miss Indian Arizona,[7] Jared was in his first semester of community college off the reservation and Justin was living with his mother, stepfather and younger sister while tending to the family's cornfield, participating in kiva activities and helping his stepfather with construction work.

Parents

Parent study participants were: Dorian's parents, Anna and Doran;[8] Justin's parents, Lillian and Marshall (stepfather to Justin); and Jared's mother, Charlene. All were residing and working on the reservation at the time of the study. Anna was employed as a teacher aide and taking courses toward a teacher degree at a local community college branch site. Doran was an entrepreneur-founder of a solar energy business. Lillian was a tribal employee while Marshall was self-employed in construction work, a Hopi farmer and actively involved with kiva activities and his religious duties. Charlene was employed in the tribal legal system.

Grandparents

In Hopi culture, a matrilineal society, the maternal grandmother plays a significant role in the cultural world of Hopi children. However, prior to interview scheduling, Dorian's and Justin's maternal grandmothers passed away, and Jared's maternal grandmother withdrew from the study. The family intergenerational model was modified for the grandparent generation to include: (1) Vivian (estimated age 73), Dorian's paternal grandmother; (2) Clara (82), a resident of Jared's maternal village; and (3) Marie (estimated age 65), from the same Mesa as Justin, but a resident of a different village (see Table 8.1). At the time of the study, each was a resident in her maternal village. Vivian, mother of four, was caring for a younger adult sibling, tending to her field and gardens, and a participant but not highly active in Hopi traditional activities. Clara had one daughter

Table 8.1 Study participants. The [*] identifies the participants who are first-language Hopilavayi speakers.

Youth generation focal study participants	Dorian (female)	Jared (male)	*Justin (male)
Parent generation	*Anna	*Charlene	Lillian
	Doran	—	*Marshall (stepfather)
Grandparent Generation	*Vivian (Paternal grandmother)	*Clara	*Marie

and was active in the tribal elders program as well as her village *Maraw*, Women's Society. Marie, mother of five, cultural knowledge keeper and literate in the Hopi language, was assisting the Hopi Tribe in various capacities. Three grandchildren were living with her.

Changing Hopi Sociocultural and Sociolinguistic Ecologies

Participant life histories

This study established a picture of changing sociocultural and socio-linguistic ecologies that was generational in nature. With the advent of compulsory Western education and policies along with the dominant White wage economy, 'getting schooled' for these changes of life positioned Western education and English as critical for cultural survival, integrity and self-determination in the eyes of the Hopi. The following life histories give voice to these lived experiences of change.

Grandparent life histories: Vivian, Clara, Marie

Marie recounted her own parents' words about an inevitable change:[9]

> For certain, we [Hopi] would be living two ways of life. It is unlikely that the White man will ever simply leave us alone [isolated from the mainstream]. On account of this, we will be living here [on our own lands, co-existing] with them. [To us, their children, they stated,] 'You will come to know things like them [through their education], and then you will come to understand things like them so that you do not find yourselves in an unfortunate situation.' I think that they [my parents] meant that if we learned what the *Pahaana* [White man] was all about, we would be better able to survive the kind of life [wage economy] that was coming. ... and the better prepared at knowing what was coming, then we would be able to make better lives for ourselves. (Interview, 15 October 2003)

Marie's parents suffered tremendously in the initial Hopi experience with Western education, as she reflected: '... They [agents of the school] did not ask their parents; they just took them [her parents as children] and placed them somewhere [schools]. And they [my parents] did not understand English.' Yet, her parents remained resilient and applied as well as modeled for their children the 'benefits' of their experience on behalf of family and community thus 'planting' the perception of English and Western education as essential to the continued survival of the Hopi as a sovereign people. However, Marie also recalled,

> But the most important thing is … when they [my parents] came back [to Hopi], they never forgot their language, or the customs and practices and the values of Hopi. … My mother always said it [the schooling and mainstream experience] strengthened what she already had [her cultural foundation]. (Interview, 15 October 2003)

For this grandparent generation, local access to Western education was provided from grades 1 to 8; thereafter, Hopi youth attended off-reservation secondary schools (grades/levels 9–12) during adolescence, a critical period in identity formation. Marie boarded with White families while attending schools in Phoenix, Arizona and Provo, Utah; Clara was sent to boarding school in Phoenix, and Vivian attended various off-reservation schools. Clara and Vivian did not complete grade 12; Vivian later entered a nursing program. Following secondary schooling, each secured employment (nonexistent on Hopi at the time) and remained in mainstream society. All married and had children. Marie made a permanent return home for the birth of her first child and assumed her role as a married in-law and mother; Clara and Vivian remained in urban settings raising their children as 'town people' who spoke English and lived the mainstream lifestyle until retirement when both made a permanent return to Hopi. Having acquired Hopi as their first language, each asserted they did not 'forget' the language and upon their return, 'just began speaking [Hopi] like them [family].'

At the time of data collection (2003), Marie and Clara described the visible and disconcerting impact of change among the Hopi:

> Our languages [Hopi and English] are mixed together. We are now interjecting English into our Hopi. Therefore, we are speaking a truly different language. And then we are no longer accustomed, it seems, to speaking the Hopi language. It appears as though we are embarrassed [to speak our language] … If we were not like that, we would be holding on to it. (Marie, Interview, 15 October 2003)

> It [the prominence of the Hopi language] has really changed. They [the Hopi people] are always speaking English. (Clara, Interview, 15 October 2003)

Clara targeted younger 'educated' Hopi women – with advanced schooling – as modeling this 'English only' behavior while Marie contended that elder speakers of Hopi were complicit in this behavior by also speaking only English thereby normalizing English and diminishing the integrity and prominence of Hopilavayi. Vivian pointed out that as grandmothers/elder speakers, they themselves did not speak 'good' Hopi nor had a command of *wukwlavayi*, the linguistic repertoire of elders containing wise council or prophetic opinion (Hopìikwa Lavàytutuveni, 1998:

748). They observed how language shift had severed the intimacy shared through language among generations. Often, older Hopi admonished and/ or implored younger Hopi to speak to them using Hopilavayi. Clara recalled an incident when an elder in the audience addressed a young Hopi giving a presentation in this way, '… We [elders] are not understanding you [your discourse]; therefore, you need to speak in Hopi [to us]. You are Hopi. Therefore, we implore you to think on this and then begin to speak in that way [using Hopilavayi] to us.' Vivian recalled her own behavior: 'My grandkids speak only English and I say to them, "I don't speak very good English like *you* kids. You kids know a lot [of English], yet you don't speak Hopi."'

Marie spoke about the loss of respect for the value and integrity of the Hopi way of life increasingly observed in the manner with which the younger generation carry out Hopi practices and customs. Hopi tradition dictates one to work with conviction and sacrifice toward a goal wherein lies the 'value' of and 'respect' for the custom and tradition; the reward of communal spiritual benefits is thus 'earned.' Instead, the younger generation were taking 'shortcuts' to save time and expend minimal effort or altogether neglecting cultural practices. She exclaimed, 'Look how many generations there are now [of young Hopi] who have not once gone to their fields. [Consequently] they have no knowledge of these things [cultural practices].' Such behaviors were contributing to the erosion of Hopi family and communal values. According to Vivian, the traditional practice of communal living when grandparents played a vital role in the household had succumbed to changes she cited as: nuclear family units, interracial marriages, mixed heritage children of non-Hopi mothers, and urban lifestyles.

All cited modern times and circumstances, including schools and Western education as having positioned the Hopi people in a perplexing situation, one filled with conflict and tension. Nevertheless, these grandmothers offered hope and optimism about the vitality of the Hopi way of life in the fact that many Hopi continue to adhere to the Hopi way of life. In a moment of self-reflection, Marie stated, 'I believe I have moved our language along a little; my children at least have learned some. Now, if my grandchildren plant corn, then that [tradition] will also be carried into the future. Therefore, when I look at myself from this point of view, I have *almost* set it right.' Collectively, these grandmothers suggest the resolution to the current dilemmas lay in the philosophy and teachings embedded in the Hopi way of life as presenting the most reliable guide toward an uncertain future.

Parent life histories: Anna and Doran (Dorian); Charlene (Jared); Lillian and Marshall (Justin)

The out-/in migration pattern for Western education and economic opportunities among this parent group differed with an earlier return to

Hopi, but also divergently lived. Anna, Charlene and Marshall experienced a traditional Hopi childhood upbringing – an extended family household, Hopilavayi as their first language, participation in Hopi traditions guided by significant kin – while Doran and Lillian experienced childhood off-reservation. Schooling began in reservation schools followed by off-reservation schooling for Charlene and Anna. For Marshall, off-reservation schooling started when he was sent with an older sibling to Utah. He recounted the memory:

> I had just finished second grade. I didn't know I was going [to school in Utah] until I got on the bus with them [my sisters]. And at the top of the hill, I turned and [saw] my village go [disappear from sight]. That's when it hit me that I'm going away and so I cried all the way up to Utah. I only spoke ... the Hopi language. ... [so] I had to learn the English language [rapidly, because] that's all they spoke [at the school]. ... I had to shut my Hopi tongue off completely. ... [But] when I was alone, I would speak out loud to myself; I would speak to myself in Hopi. (Marshall, Interview, 23 April 2003)

Charlene attended a federal Indian boarding school in Phoenix while Anna experienced private secondary schooling far from Hopi on the US northeastern coast in New York City and at Dartmouth College in New Hampshire. Their experiences – loneliness as the most profound and the struggles with learning English – resonated with those of their parents. All had higher education aspirations; Doran pursued a pre-med/engineering program and Anna subsequently attained a teaching degree.

For Charlene, Marshall and Anna, Western schooling played a significant role, as Marshall put it, in 'becoming accustomed to speaking English,' also divergently experienced. For Marshall, the shift to English began early, was traumatic, abrupt and rapid and had negative repercussions on his summer returns to Hopi. No longer able to respond with Hopilavayi to others, he was made fun of and called a Pahaana (White person). For Charlene, the long absences from family and culture impacted her ability to maintain a Hopilavayi speaking proficiency: '... it just kind of drifted off [out of use].' For Anna, her eldest child brought the English she learned in school into their home which she as well as her mother and her husband, a non-speaker of Hopilavayi, reinforced. Perplexing for Anna is to find herself using Hopilavayi with family members who are Hopilavayi speakers quite easily, but not so with her children. Lillian and Doran attended off–reservation public schools and were non-speakers of Hopilavayi. Doran stated, 'I never really learned Hopi ... It was never really encouraged ... my mom always talked to us in English.' However, after 16 years of self-learning mentored by a colleague and motivated by his first job as a family counselor, his participation in kiva activities, and a run for political office that required Hopilavayi fluency, Doran had achieved conversational Hopilavayi proficiency. Nevertheless, Doran acknowledged that he remained limited in expressing the deeper levels of Hopi thought and accessing the same in the religious realm.

Economic development on the reservation – largely in the educational, health, tribal and federal agencies as well as entrepreneurship – now offered economic security. Moreover, the 1985 construction of the Hopi Junior/Senior High School allowed Hopi youth to remain on Hopi for their K-12 educational journey and participate in Hopi cultural traditions. For these parents, life circumstances and 'choice' strongly influenced by tradition initiated an early and permanent return to Hopi: Anna and Charlene for the birth of their first child; Lillian to assist in the care of her maternal grandmother; Marshall to attend to his inherited religious duties; and for Doran, personal well-being. Nonetheless, cultivating and nurturing a Hopi identity for their children was made daunting against the contemporary backdrop of an upheaval in the customary way of doing and being Hopi. Anna best described the 'change,' stating, 'We're living the life of a Pahaana [a White person living at Hopi] now,' mirroring the urban style and pace of mainstream society. 'City life' had seemingly become superimposed on the Hopi way of life; the Hopi people had become 'accustomed to speaking English,' and the schools, now established institutions within Hopi reinforced this trajectory. Embracing the Western lifestyle had transformed Hopi youth into strangers to their immediate family, extended kin and village communities in self-discipline, self-respect and respect for others and traditions. Additionally, these parents found themselves in competition for their children's time and attention to cultural practices lured away by television, social media, school, and school-sponsored sports activities.

Marshall, Doran and Anna reflected on *navoti,* cultural knowledge/beliefs about the ominous consequences of diverging from the Hopi path. One belief forewarned that the Hopi people themselves would initiate the end of Hopi culture by abandoning the Hopi way of life. Another belief foretold the consequence of language loss when the *katsinam,* spirit beings, would no longer sing their songs with reminders of staying on the Hopi path.[10] Ultimately, entry into the Hopi afterlife/spirit world would not be realized for every family member if these forewarnings were not heeded. Such oral traditions compelled these parents to provide their children with a strong cultural foundation in order to confront what Marshall depicted as 'what kind of situation we will leave for them.' Collectively, the grandparent and parent life histories allude to the philosophical foundation of the Hopi way of life, Hopivötskwani, to which they turned for guidance.

Hopi Oral Tradition: Carrying Forward the Hopi Way of Life

Hopivötskwani, the Hopi path/way of life, is encoded in the oral tradition of the Emergence Story. Recurrent retellings of this Hopi genesis narrative have kept this philosophical foundation indelible in the minds of the Hopi people, as encapsulated here:

> We [the Hopi people] at that place [of Emergence] received our path of life; what kind of life we were to lead was made known to us. It was by means of corn, cultivating corn, that we would live [subsist, endure], and where [geographic environment] we were to undertake this life sustaining practice. This way of life would be one of hard work; survival would be a struggle. However, by means of our belief [in and *acceptance* of this way of life], and because of our faith, a greater power [the Creator] would take pity on us and bestow upon us [life sustaining] drops of rain. (E. Sekaquaptewa, personal communication, 30 November 2003)

The story of Emergence further narrates the epistemological origins of the Hopi people,

> ... the Hopi emerged from a layer under the earth into this, the fourth, world by climbing up inside a reed. Upon arrival, they met a deity, *Maasaw*,[11] who presented them with a philosophy of life based on three elements: maize seeds, a planting stick, and a gourd full of water. *Qa'ö*, 'maize,' was the soul of the Hopi people, representing their very identity. *Sooya*, 'the planting stick,' represented the simple technology they should depend on. There was an explicit warning against over-dependency on technology, which had taken on a life of its own in the third world below, producing destruction through materialism, greed and egotism. *Wikoro*, 'the gourd filled with water,' represented the environment – the land and all its life forms, the sign of the Creator's blessing, if the Hopis would uphold Maasaw's covenant and live right. Maasaw told them life in this place would be arduous and daunting, but through resolute perseverance and industry, they would live long and be spiritually rich. (Whiteley & Masayesva, 1998: 189)

The story of Emergence conveys the fundamental tenets for the construction of a distinct Hopi identity – becoming a human being.[12] In effect, the practice of growing corn by hand, natwani – practicing the core values of humility and reciprocity; acting on and in faith; maintaining unity and leading a moral existence – is the embodiment of the instructions toward this end for a people intimately involved in the communal pursuit of life in this high, desert landscape. Hopivötskwani entails living in harmony with others, sharing life's fulfillment – physical sustenance and spiritual contentment – and a commitment to maintaining the cohesiveness of the community. Keeping the community at the forefront reflects a moral existence and is in keeping with the moral image that a people maintains of itself (Leon-Portilla & Spicer, 1975). In the broader sense, Hopivötskwani, is anchored in the principle of humanness and of sharing this humanity with others captured in the Hopi words, *nami'nangwa, sumi'nangwa*, to live with mutual love toward one another, and in this mood, united in common purpose, proceed in the manner of togetherness (Nicholas, 2005).

I turn to describing the ways in which the parent and youth participants of this study were enacting their faith and commitment to the tenets
of Hopivötskwani amid significant sociocultural and sociolinguistic
change.

'From Parents to the Child from Forever': Balancing Responsibilities

Anna, Doran and Dorian

Anna consistently encouraged and reminded her daughters to participate in 'whatever I'm doing' culturally, *naapa'angwantotangwu*, helping
each other – preparing food for the dances, weddings, baby namings – and
being physically and visibly present at these activities. She modeled this –
'that's how I was raised.' Anna believed that 'as long as they're participating and carrying on what they learned like making bread, making *piiki*,
blue-corn wafer bread, *poota*, coiled plaque, and like [my son] learning
about farming,' her children will acquire the Hopi values embedded in
these activities. She upheld, 'they know the culture, the values of being
Hopi, who they are and where they come from (identity), but not as ...
speaker[s].' Affirmatively, Doran stated, 'The thing that makes us Hopi is
our core value system; that's what needs to stay intact – the teaching of
respect for one another, the teaching of helping one another, the teaching
of doing things together as [a] people. That is what need[s] to continue to
happen – more so than language. ... [So] I talk to them about different
things about Hopi; I've only done it in English at this point.' He pointed
out that nurturing a cultural identity required a parent to spend time with
one's children, do things with them, to be patient with them so that they
'start to figure you out,' – your level of commitment to and respect for
them. Their children reciprocated with an 'inquisitiveness' that led Anna
and Doran to believe 'that Hopi is real important to them.'

Dorian reflected on her upbringing asserting, 'I was taught what
things [cultural practices/traditions] meant; why we do this, why we do
that [therefore] I had ... respect [for these],' despite learning these through
English. In particular, Dorian's parents and extended family were a supportive force as she pursued, won, and held the title of Miss Indian
Arizona, an achievement attained by knowing 'more about my [tribal]
traditions than any other [pageant] contestant.' Members of her family
provided the Hopilavayi for introducing herself (Hopi identity), for the
prayers and songs she performed as well as her knowledge about Hopi
culture in presentations as a 'tribal ambassador' to other tribal nations.
Importantly, she represented the Hopi culture as a 'living' culture and
strongly advocated for language maintenance imploring other tribal
youth, 'if you know it, speak it, use it; you don't learn it for nothing.'
Alluding to a deeper link between language, identity and responsibility,

she stated, 'They [parents] didn't teach us how to introduce ourselves in Hopi for nothing,' because at the core of constructing a distinct cultural identity is to 'know who you are. ... and your responsibilities' of belonging.

In 2017 (Nicholas, 2018),[13] at 33 years old, Dorian had a 12-year old son and a career in medical administration. Both were members of the family household that included Dorian's parents and a younger adult sibling. Although residing in an urban setting necessitated by employment, they remained firm in sustaining cultural practices: Hopi was the language of interaction between her parents so Hopilavayi was heard daily; Dorian continued to listen to Hopi songs, transcribing the words in order to learn their deeper meanings through discussions with her parents; and, her parents were a significant and influential cultural presence in her son's life – he accompanied them on regular trips to know and experience Hopi.

Charlene and Jared

A single parent, Charlene established a strong foundation of unconditional love and support for her children in the form of firm parental guidance and discipline to instill core Hopi cultural values – 'to respect others ... not to ... think they're better than somebody else ... [but to] be humble.' She consistently reminded her children that to live at Hopi required a particular conduct; this was an expectation of the community and must be visibly demonstrated: 'You have to be involved in your religious practices and present yourself as somebody that knows a lot about Hopi and being Hopi. You have to maintain that status by taking part [in cultural activities].'

Jared's upbringing was significantly shaped by his female maternal kin – mother, maternal grandmother and great-grandmother. These intimate bonds instilled a strong sense of responsibility and accountability to them in terms of his behavior against the constant lure of *qa hopi*, not hopi/unhopi sociocultural change – increasing destructive/self-destructive behaviors among youth: domestic violence, substance abuse and gang membership. Resisting the intense peer pressure came with focused thoughts on what impact his 'choices' would have on these women, 'How would they react to me [if] I got in trouble? How would [others] react to my parents? I don't want my parents having a bad name because of me. [These thoughts] kept me out of trouble.' This implicit sense of conduct owed to family, and commitment to the Hopi way, extended to his participation in ceremonial activities. His ceremonial duties were also preparation for assuming his future role as *taha*, maternal uncle to his sister's children and others through clan and ceremonial relationships. Importantly, the trajectory toward initiation into the male priesthood society, *Wuwtsim*, positioned the essentiality of Hopilavayi, 'Now that I want to join [be a Wuwtsim initiate], I need to ... speak Hopi.'

At this writing, Jared resided away from Hopi. Nevertheless, social media kept him connected as did recollection of times spent on Hopi. An especially poignant recollection was of spending one year on Hopi when he not only planted corn but participated in an important ceremony; the reward was the 'gift' of heavy rains and a subsequent bountiful harvest: 'It brought my heart back to peace; it felt good.' Additionally, he and his partner were committed to using Hopilavayi as an everyday language practice in their interactions. This long-term relationship is moving toward marriage and they are ready to have a family; he wanted his own children to experience, as he did, the gift of time spent with a grandmother.

Lillian, Marshall and Justin

Marshall was adamant that parents 'need to be involved in the cultural doings, practiced in the household'. 'That's a big factor right there,' he asserted. Learning the culture is 'taught down from the grandfather to the father and to the sons and nephews. ... They're the ones that should be instilling the respect for ... the meanings of things. ... and so it's always [like] a ladder you're climbing up ... [and] you need to be taught in those stages as you [grow],' he expounded. He likened the cultural education process to 'feeding/nourishing' one's children. 'They won't take it all in [at once], but those are just the learning blocks they're just absorbing yet; just little crumbs you're feeding them. And as they think on that, as the years go by, then they'll be asking for more and then you just keep feeding them,' he explained. Marshall's adherence to Hopi traditions was guided by a strong belief that these traditions are carrying the Hopi people toward their intended destiny – spiritual fulfillment and immortality: 'It's [the sense of duty and obligation to one's children instilled] in us from our fathers and grandfathers, and then now, we're teaching our nephews and sons. [And so] we don't have to struggle with our boys.'

Marshall emphasized one's attitude and behavior when participating in religious or cultural customs as critical: 'It is having one's heart in it;. ... this is central to our [religious, spiritual] being. And even though one does not speak Hopi, if you go to the kivas and bring in your offerings [thoughts and prayers], be humble and, *pay taawi've* [learn the songs] ... it's [about] you and your thoughts *paasat* [then].' The implication is that one is affected in heart, thought, and behavior through experiencing the religious and secular rituals conducted through oral tradition. Songs, especially, continue to be perceived as the most powerful spiritual form of language. This was confirmed for Marshall through Justin's behavior and use of Hopilavayi in their kiva activities: 'It goes right here [pointing to his heart] and [confirms that] I'm doing something at least.' He also maintained, 'I couldn't have gone to school for it [to learn Hopilavayi]. ... It should always be in the home, to me. That's where I stand and so we're [the family] going to try and keep it going [in that way].'

At the time of the study, Justin had made a critical life decision – to remain on Hopi to attend to his and his family's cornfields rather than leave Hopi to pursue higher education. He rationalized that he was 'born and raised' to be a Hopi farmer stating, 'For me, leaving this place, and my farming, the culture; that just got to me … [and] I just left that [the idea of leaving] just to be out here.' He recounted the philosophical foundation, values, skills and knowledge of the Hopi practice of dry farming he had acquired. He understood that tending to the corn was at the core of existence for the Hopi people – physical, economic, intellectual and spiritual, expressed frequently by his late maternal grandmother and enacted by male kin. The act of planting corn by hand using a hand-held planting stick, sooya, symbolically engaged each man to uphold the tenets conveyed in the Hopivötskwani. Beyond planting, concern for the well-being of the plants was incessant in ensuring their very survival against life's challenges, much like attending to one's biological children (Black, 1984). As well, their growth was nurtured through the language of song and talk: 'You can talk to the plants; they're like your children. [You tell them], "Just be strong as you're growing up. Don't let anything bother you." And they'll hear you,' he explained. Justin observed the reciprocal commitment to this tradition on the part of women – husking, shucking, drying, sharing and storing for the next year's planting as well as preparing the corn for consumption and ceremonial use. He acknowledged that his family and kin had guided him to 'becoming Hopi,' and he was prepared to do the same for his own children: 'I just want to put it [carrying out the Hopivötskwani] on them; have 'em learn it too, just keep it going and just don't let it go.'

Recently, Justin shared that since participating in the initial study (2003–2004), employment took him away from Hopi, but never more than 90 miles away. At the time of this writing, Justin was working with Hopi and Navajo/Diné students in multiple roles at a school located about 50 miles away from his maternal village. While Navajo language classes are a curricular offering at this school, Hopilavayi is not; so he used Hopilavayi with the Hopi students, most of whom he described as understanding Hopilavayi. He was maintaining his involvement in the kiva activities and the upkeep of his own cornfield and 'corn children' (see Black, 1984; Nicholas, 2009, 2010); in these contexts, Hopilavayi is the medium. In addition, he has assumed lifelong commitments to his female sibling's children as *taha*, maternal uncle, to whom he has clan responsibilities, and through his kiva activities responsibilities to a godson as his father, *na'at*, and extending to his godson's son as his grandfather, *kwa'at*. Justin has also established new connections with his partner's family for whom Hopilavayi is the prominent medium. Justin continues to assert a strong allegiance to his heritage, community and language stating, 'I just want to influence as many people as I can.'

Next Steps: *Itamyani* – We Will [Carry the Hopi Way of Life Forward]

> It is said, that in a time when life becomes difficult [tested, testing], one has to be very discerning in order to choose the right way [the Hopi way]. (E. Sekaquaptewa, personal communication, 25 October 2000)

The study participants' life histories illuminate that the Hopi way of life, a trajectory established at the time of Emergence, remains the reliable guide in adapting to change. How – birthright and the privileges of participation – and by whose hands – kin – the course continues to be maintained is expressively captured by each of the youth participants: Dorian who stated 'The language is supposed to be on the part of the parents' efforts ... this is how it's always been passed on, from parent to child, for forever!'; confirmed by Jared's perspective that 'it's just the way they're [children are] raised'; and Justin's poignant rendering, 'Since you're Hopi, you're brought up that way [and] you can't let it go [abandon or ignore one's upbringing].' Justin's words, in particular, suggest that youth will continue to hold tightly to the Hopi way/path of life they are bound to by habit, security, intellect, and choice instilled by significant kin.

Amid change, Doran aptly acknowledged, 'It's a matter of figuring out ... how we go about changing, taking in and accepting of the modern society those things that are good, and using it along with Hopi [cultural beliefs/knowledge and traditions].' These life histories suggest that the Hopi people must resume their collective journey forward by *re*-centering their cultural map, Hopivötskwani, and *re*-newing their commitment to the communal ethics of nami'nangwa, sumi'nangwa – with mutual concern and care for one another, and with the mood of unity on the part of 'everybody ... the Hopi people' (HLAP, 1998).[14] The family and community serve as the foundation from which supportive spaces and structures/institutions are established that cultivate and nurture cultural identity and linguistic development. Today, such spaces and structures include schools which have been institutionalized in contemporary Hopi communities. Schools, cited as initiating and playing a continuing role in a shift away from Hopi, ironically, through tribal mandates (Hopi Tribal Consolidated Plan of 1995), signify a 'proactive' initiative and perspective of the schools' vital role in language and culture maintenance. However, in this realm, schools need direction and assistance, wherein lies the potential for a collective *re*-turn to the 'path' set at Emergence as well as the community's role in the education of their children. Fundamentally, this involves engaging the Hopi people in a *re*-search/research of the instructions vis-à-vis Hopivötskwani to inform a community-approach to planning with the goal of spearheading language reclamation on 'all fronts' – home, community, cultural domains, and schools. Hopilavayi inclusion/program development offer the 'next steps': to position the community (parents, grandparents, significant kin) in establishing the institutional 'conditions' that go beyond merely 'allowing' Hopilavayi in the school, and to act from and on the principles of sovereignty toward empowering ourselves and taking *agency* in determining the steps toward resuming our shared journey. Moreover, it is about gaining *voice* – being heard and 'hearing ourselves' – reasserting the collective will, 'Itamyani,' '*We* will [carry the Hopi way of life forward]' (Ruiz, 1991). To do so has been the communal ideology and imperative toward continuity, spiritual fulfillment and immortality 'from forever.'

Notes

(1) The Navajo Nation is geographically the largest federally recognized Native American Indian tribe in the US. Their reservation is spread throughout northern Arizona and New Mexico, and southern Utah. The Navajos' self-referential term is Diné, meaning The People (see http://www.navajoindian.net/).

(2) The first excerpt is a recorded retelling by E. Sekaquaptewa; the second excerpt is a published account.

(3) I have achieved a strong proficiency through which I have learned about my roles as a clan member and a Hopi woman. Hopilavayi is fundamental to my current scholarship and work as a language educator in the field of Indigenous language reclamation.

(4) Although Hopilavayi has a written history and a tribally adopted orthography, it remains primarily an oral language.

(5) The course goals included: Short-term – building a speaking vocabulary, sentence formation based on real-life situational activities, comprehension of spoken Hopi, and introduction to Hopi literacy; Long-term – awareness of Hopi identity through language, a basic knowledge of the language to provide motivation toward a speaking ability, and encouragement of using the language in the home with family members and in the classroom (Nicholas, 2000).

(6) The late Emory Sekaquaptewa (1928–2007) was also my mentor, clan uncle and co-chair of my dissertation committee.

(7) Miss Indian Arizona History – This is an annual pageant founded in 1961, which since 2000 has been sponsored by the Intertribal Council of Arizona (ITCA) and the Miss Indian Arizona Association officially becoming the Miss Indian Arizona Scholarship Program focusing on academic and community service (see http://www.missindianarizona.com/history.html).

(8) Pseudonyms are used for all study participants with the exception of Dorian and her parents. Dorian and her father, Doran, wanted their actual names to be used; Anna later gave her permission.

(9) The English translations of the grandparents' original quotes in Hopilavayi reflect the Hopi narrative style which I worked to retain.

(10) In the spiritual world of Hopi, katsinam (pl.) are a central feature of the Hopi identity. Through their songs, the katsinam metaphorically remind, inform, advise, admonish, and inspire the Hopi people about adhering to the Hopi way of life (Nicholas, 2008).

(11) A spirit being, lord of the Fourth world, god of life and death (*Hopi Dictionary/ Hopìikwa Lavàytutuveni*, 1998: 219).

(12) Hopi, as a term, has multiple meanings: human being, behaving one – civilized, peaceable, polite, adhering to the Hopi way, fluent in the language (*Hopi Dictionary/ Hopìikwa Lavàytutuveni*, 1998: 99–100).

(13) In 2017, I contacted each of the youth participants as a follow-up to the initial study.

(14) Hopilavayi revitalization initiatives at the tribal, community and individual levels have been undertaken and ongoing; however, these efforts have not realized a cohesive and unified movement nor measurable, effective and sustainable outcomes.

References

Black, M.E. (1984) Maidens and others: An analysis of Hopi corn metaphors. *Ethnology* 234 (4), 279–288.

Hopi Dictionary Project (1998) *Hopi Dictionary/Hopìikwa Lavàytutuveni: A Hopi- English Dictionary of the Third Mesa Dialect*. Tucson: The University of Arizona Press.

Hopi Language Assessment Project (1998) *Presentation of Hopi Language Survey Results*. The Hopi Tribe, Hopi Culture Preservation Office; Bureau of Applied Research and Anthropology. Tucson: University of Arizona.

Hopi Language Assessment Project Orientation Meeting (n.d.) Unpublished document.

Hopi Tribe (1995) 'Hopit Pötskwaniat' Hopi Tribal Consolidated Strategic Plan of 1995.

Kuwanwisiwma, L. (2002) *Hopit navotiat,* Hopi knowledge of history: Hopi presence on Black Mesa. In S. Powell and F.E. Smiley (eds) *Prehistoric Culture Change on the Colorado Plateau, Ten Thousand Years on Black Mesa* (pp. 161–163). Tucson: University of Arizona Press.

Leon-Portilla, M. and Spicer, E.H. (1975) *Aztecs and Navajos & Indian Identity Versus Assimilation*. New York: The Weatherhead Foundation.

McCarty, T.L., Nicholas, S.E. and Wyman, L.T. (2012) Re-emplacing place in the 'global here and now' – Critical ethnographic case studies of Native American language planning and policy. *International Multilingual Research Journal* 6 (1), 50–63.

Nicholas, S. (2000) Hopi language I, II, III. Field report for Indigenous Language Institute. Unpublished document.

Nicholas, S.E. (2005) Negotiating for the Hopi way of life through literacy and schooling. In T.L. McCarty (ed.) *Language, Literacy, and Power in Schooling* (pp. 29–46). Mahwah, NJ: Lawrence Erlbaum.

Nicholas, S.E. (2008) Becoming 'Fully' Hopi: The Role of the Hopi Language in the Contemporary Lives of Hopi Youth – A Hopi Case Study of Language Shift and Vitality. Unpublished PhD dissertation, American Indian Studies Program, University of Arizona, Tucson, AZ.

Nicholas, S.E. (2009) 'I live Hopi, I just don't speak it' – The critical intersection of language, culture, and identity in the lives of contemporary Hopi youth. *Journal of Language, Identity, and Education* 8 (5), 321–334.

Nicholas, S.E. (2010) Language, epistemology and cultural identity: 'Hopiqatsit aw unangvakiwyungwa.' 'To have one's heart in the Hopi way of life'. *American Indian Culture and Research Journal* 34 (2), 125–144.

Nicholas, S.E. (2018) Practicing being and living Hopi Language and cultural practices of contemporary Hopi youth. In G. Wigglesworth, J. Simpson and J. Vaugh (eds) *Language and Practices of Indigenous Children and Youth*. London: Palgrave.

Ochs, E. (1998) *Culture and Language Development: Language Acquisition and Language Socialization in a Samoan Village*. Cambridge: Cambridge University Press.

Ruiz, R. (1991) The empowerment of language-minority students. In C.E. Sleeter (ed.) *Empowerment Through Multicultural Education*. Albany: State University of New York Press.

Seidman, I.E. (2006/2013) *Interviewing as Qualitative Research: A Guide for Researchers in Education and Social Science*. New York: Teachers College Press.

Whiteley, P. and Masayesva, V. (1998) Paavahu and paanaqso'a: The wellsprings of life and the slurry of death. In P.M. Whiteley *Rethinking Hopi Ethnography* (pp. 188–207). Washington, DC: Smithsonian Institution Press.

9 Transformation from the Bottom Up: Ideological Analysis with Indigenous Youth and Language Policy Justice in Nepal

Prem Phyak

While activists struggle to promote greater space for Indigenous languages in education, dominant language policies and practices continue to implicitly and explicitly pose ethical and ideological challenges in Indigenous peoples' attempts to claim and reclaim their linguistic and cultural identities. Central to this struggle is uncovering and addressing the ways in which alternative ideologies, voices and participation are peripheralized in education policy processes. Building on recent work on 'engaged language policy' (Davis, 2014; Davis & Phyak, 2017; Phyak & Bui, 2014), this chapter portrays my work with Limbu Indigenous youth in Nepal. These efforts involve engaging Limbu youth in critical consciousness-raising to counter two hegemonic ideologies – neoliberalism and 'one nation-one language' – towards building spaces for Indigenous languages and epistemologies in education. More specifically, I portray how Limbu Indigenous youth develop critical awareness of linguistic discrimination, engage in dialogic intervention and take grounded actions towards equitable policies that recognize Indigenous languages as both a right and a resource.

Introduction

We're all Nepali … . Nepali must be learned … . We've more than 100 languages … how is multilingual education possible? … .You know Indigenous youth and parents don't want their own mother tongue in school … . (Field notes, 06/13/2013; informal discussion with a Nepali social worker)

… Why do you, an educated person, talk about small languages? …We should talk about quality education in this modern age, right? … .We should teach English to get *jagir* [job] … to go *bidesh* [abroad]. (interview with head teacher 06/25/2013)

194

The perspectives on English, Nepali and Indigenous languages (known as mother tongues) in the above excerpts are not simply the personal views of a head teacher and a social worker. In Nepal, they are indeed 'common sense' notions about Nepalese language policy and practices. As Gramsci (1971) argues, such commonsensical ideas are formed when the individuals or groups unquestioningly embrace the ruling ideology as a natural social condition. Hegemony occurs as an organizing principle in which beliefs, ideas, values, and worldviews of one class or group dominate other views as explanations of social realities. The idea that Nepali nationalism can only be enacted through the Nepali language; that learning English helps students obtain *jagir* and go *bidesh*; and that mother tongues are inappropriate for quality education are 'common sense' ideas that reproduce the existing sociopolitical power relations and dominant groups' *habitus* (Bourdieu, 1991), or 'set of dispositions which incline agents to act and react in certain ways' (Thompson, 1991: 12). Rooted in the social structure, habitus includes practices, perceptions and attitudes that are formed without conscious critical engagement in understanding the social world. To create spaces for Indigenous/minoritized languages in public spheres, it is necessary to uncover and denaturalize such commonsensical assumptions through 'ideological clarification' (Dauenhauer & Dauenhauer, 1998; Fishman, 2001; Kroskrity, 2009).

As seen in the above excerpts, two seemingly contradictory ideologies – linguistic nationalism and neoliberalism – are dominant in language policies and sociopolitical discourses of Nepal. Until 1990, the state strictly enforced a Nepali-only policy in education, the courts and government offices. Although some space was provided for Indigenous languages in education after 1990, languages other than Nepali are not considered legitimate official languages. While Indigenous peoples' movements for language, educational and political rights had just begun in the 1990s, the nation-state adopted a neoliberal ideology for nation-building. Privatization, deregulation and market-based competition have now become the principal features of national development discourse (Pandey, 2012). As the World Bank and International Monetary Fund (IMF) are becoming more influential in shaping the country's structural reform plans, education, health, industry and other social services have been privatized and the state is continually withdrawing its responsibility to ensure equal access to public services.

As global market-based discourses influence policymakers' perspectives on development, national policies continue to promote neoliberal ideologies such as competition, individualism and a free market in educational and other policies. Consequently, the general public, policymakers and even Indigenous people unquestioningly accept the global dominance of English as a necessary means to go abroad and find jobs. The idea that English language ability is essential for socioeconomic upward mobility is an example of ideological hegemony, which rejects, as Blommaert (2008) argues, alternative views about language policies and practices. The same kind of ideological hegemony is also embedded in the assumption that all must speak Nepali to show their Nepali national identity.

Against this backdrop, this chapter portrays the ways in which Limbu Indigenous youth are engaged in analysis of ideologies that marginalize Indigenous languages, cultures and values. In taking language policy as a site of ideological struggle (Kroskrity, 2009), I argue that it is necessary to engage the Indigenous people who have endured historic and ongoing oppression and marginalization, in challenging ideological hegemony and developing a new alternative ideology, which Gramsci (1971) calls a 'good sense.' My perspectives are informed by an 'engaged language policy' perspective (ELP) (Davis, 2014; Davis & Phyak, 2015, 2017) that keeps social justice at the center of analysis while engaging language policy actors in 'dialogic exploration of language policy as non-linear processes,' recognizing that covert ideologies and policies are potentially marginalizing and multilingual policies are often 'desirable, effective and possible' (Davis & Phyak, 2015: 147). In other words, ELP undertakes the process of conducting ideological analyses *with*, not *for*, parents, educators, and all concerned others (Indigenous youth in this case), towards raising awareness of ideological adversity such as neoliberal commodification through privatization of education, monolingualism and standardization (Davis, 2014; Phyak & Bui, 2014). Further, an ELP perspective calls for *language policy justice*; the Indigenous people must be given space to fully participate in critiquing and transforming dominant policies. I further argue that language policy justice can only be ensured with the marginalized people's critical consciousness/awareness, as opposed to *false consciousness* and *common sense*, about ideologies embedded in sociopolitical and educational discourses.

Language Ideologies and Indigenous Youth Research

Language policy scholars such as McGroarty (2006), Pennycook (2013), Ricento (2015), and Tollefson (2013) keep language ideologies at the center of analysis as a means of uncovering how language policies and practices are interconnected with sociopolitical inequalities and racial/ethnic discrimination. Silverstein (1979: 193) defines language ideologies as 'sets of beliefs about language articulated by users as a rationalization or justification of perceived language structure and use.' For Woolard and Schieffelin (1994: 55–56), language ideologies 'envision and enact links of language to group and personal identity, to aesthetics, to morality, and to epistemology.' Indeed, language ideologies are the assemblages of commonsensical ideas and attitudes about language; moral and political interests of social and linguistic groups; and social inequalities and discrimination emanating from linguistic hierarchies and historical oppressions (Blommaert, 1999; McCarty et al., 2011). A language ideological perspective provides an interdisciplinary lens to explore and analyze how language inequalities are constructed and reproduced, and to scrutinize participation, voice and agency of multiple actors in language policy.

Recent studies have focused on how Indigenous youth negotiate multiple language ideologies. Wyman *et al.* (2014) unravel how Native American youth negotiate contested ideologies and build activism to counter hegemonic ideologies. By participating in humanizing, counter-hegemonic and praxis-driven activities, these youth become aware of the complex sociolinguistic existential reality and ideologies that constrain Indigenous languages. Although Indigenous youth are deeply affected by language shift, Wyman *et al.* (2014) characterize them as potential agents for transforming historical and contemporary sociolinguistic inequalities. In another study, McCarty *et al.* (2009) examine how the language ideologies of Indigenous youth are shaped by larger sociopolitical conditions and linguistic markets. Influenced by the domination of English, these youth describe English as a 'business language' of high social status, 'the 21st century language,' and a 'language of survival.' 'On the other hand, they also recognize it as 'a tool of assimilation and conquest' and 'a language of colonization.' These Indigenous youth also demonstrate 'sentimental attachments' to their heritage language, viewing it as part of a 'unique indigenous identity.' Lee (2009) analyzes Navajo and Pueblo youth's competing ideologies of Indigenous language loss and identity and examines how they negotiate their identities with and without heritage language ability. Lee shows that while these youth recognize the importance of Indigenous languages for cultural continuity and identity, they also consider English as a necessity for success in American society.

While it is necessary to uncover the multiple ideologies of Indigenous youth, what is more important is to engage them in making explicit the ideological meanings of local and language policies and practices. Indigenous youth must be engaged in ideological analysis – a synthesis 'of linguistic awareness, linguistic beliefs, feelings, and practices, and relations of political economic power' (Kroskrity, 2009: 52) – for raising their critical consciousness about marginalizing and hegemonic ideologies. As Kroskrity (2009: 72–73) notes, this includes a critical examination of how people's 'perception of language and discourses are constructed in the interest of a specific social or cultural group.' It is important for Indigenous people to engage in decolonizing hegemonic projects with the potential to build alternative policies and practices that support the use of Indigenous languages and epistemologies in education (Gegeo & Watson-Gegeo, 2013). Such ideological analysis pays particular attention to how political, economic and historical positionings of communities and individuals are interconnected with their views about language and language policies and practices.

Engaging Indigenous youth in ideological analysis focuses on their ideological clarifications of past and contemporary language policies and practices (Dauenhauer & Dauenhauer, 1998; Fishman, 2001). Studies have shown that lack of ideological clarification is detrimental to creating a sustainable space for Indigenous and minoritized languages in dominant public spheres (Fishman, 2001; Kroskrity, 2009; Sallabank, 2013). Fishman (2001: 17) highlights the importance of ideological clarification in movements aimed at reversing language shift (RLS) as follows:

> RLS movements must realise from the very outset of their ideological clarification that ethnolinguistic authenticity and identity must be associated with Xish versions of modern Yish-dominated pop-culture and consumerism (...) but, even more importantly, with a continuing ethnohumanistic, ethnoreligious and ethnocultural constellation of beliefs, behaviours and attitudes. Only such a constellation will ultimately provide a rationale going beyond the economies of scale inherent in the materialist view of those who have essentially concluded that 'if you can't beat them, join them'. It is only the conviction that one's own-language-in-culture is crucially different ... that makes RLS worthwhile ... .

Kroskrity (2009) argues that Indigenous peoples' conscious efforts to challenge and transform dominant commonsensical beliefs must be an integral part of efforts to create space for Indigenous and minoritized languages in language policies. Keeping social justice at the center, Davis (2014) forefronts an engaged language policy approach to reconceptualize language policy as a non-linear space for critical dialogue in which multiple actors are engaged in challenging and transforming hegemonic ideologies. Davis and Phyak (2015) portray their ongoing efforts to engage teachers, youth, community members, policymakers and parents in ideological analysis for promoting equitable multilingual education in Hawai'i and Nepal. They argue that that the marginalized people who are often considered objects, not citizens, must develop critical agency to transform ideological hegemonies through dialogue in which they collectively uncover ideologies concerning language policies and practices that affect their lives.

Critical ideological analysis helps marginalized people awaken from *a sense of injustice* (Stoudt *et al.*, 2011), and engages them in denaturizing dehumanizing racial/ethnic ideologies through on-the-ground activism. However, ideological clarification is not only about locating ideological hegemonies, but also engaging participants in dialogue toward action (Freire, 1970). In what follows, I discuss how Limbu Indigenous youth develop a critical awareness of multiple ideologies that may in fact challenge the legitimacy of their own language practices. My analytical approach is informed by Stoudt *et al.*'s (2011) idea of engaging youth in awakening sense of injustice.

Setting the Scene for Dialogue: Limbu Indigenous Youth Interrogating Existential Reality

The Indigenous youth discussed in this chapter are affiliated with the Limbu Students Forum, the Limbu Indigenous students' organization in

Tribhuvan University in Kathmandu, Nepal. The Forum was established by Limbu graduate students in 1998 to promote the Limbu language, culture, script, literature and history. Initially, the Forum's scope was limited to organizing an annual picnic to establish a network among Limbu students in various colleges in Kathmandu. However, after the 2006 People's Movement, the Forum has been actively involved in political activities concerning Indigenous rights and identity, including language rights.

Critical dialogues in this chapter are drawn from a collaborative project, Indigenous Youth and Critical Language Policy, undertaken with Limbu students from 2011 to 2014. The major goal of the project was to engage Limbu youth in dialogue to raise their critical awareness about ideological issues and activate their self-empowerment toward taking necessary actions to create space for the Limbu language, culture and knowledge system in education and other public spheres. I met these youth in 2011 at Tribhuvan University, Kathmandu, where I worked as a lecturer. Because we share the same cultural, ethnic and heritage language identity, we have participated together in various Limbu Indigenous programs, cultural festivals and carnivals where we have engaged in dialogue about language, culture, history and politics.

Dialogue – an emancipatory process of learning, knowing, and consciousness raising – remains at the center of our engagement (Davis, 2009; Freire, 1970; hooks, 1994). Critical dialogue with the Limbu youth covered a wide range of interlocking issues such as nationalism, identity, development, ethnic marginalization, historical oppression, and the commodification of education and language. First, we collectively documented and shared our own *existential reality* of language policies and practices during various formal and informal meetings at the national and local levels. For example, in a focus group discussion, one youth, Chalan, who came from a remote part of the Terhathum district, shared the status of the Limbu language in education in his own village: 'Limbu was taught **especially** [up to] **three class** [third grade]. The Limbu people don't know what to do after **third grade** … and these days Nepali **domination** begins at home from childhood.[1] So people think that Limbu must not be taught as far as possible.' Similarly, another youth, Abodh, mentions that 'the Indigenous youth feel inferior [to others] if they speak their home language outside home.' Abodh contended that Indigenous languages are *bahishkrit* [excluded] from *sarkari jagir* [government jobs], education and other domains, so Indigenous youth have a feeling of *laj* [shame] when they speak their own home language in public spaces. Another youth, Muksam, recounted that English is considered the language of *ijjat* [prestige], quality education, and *jagir* [job]. All the youth connected English with globalization, 'competitive age,' private schools and job markets.

Limbu youths' observations of their sociolinguistic existential reality reflect two major ideologies – linguistic nationalism and neoliberalism. The ideology of linguistic nationalism – the assumption that all people must speak the same language to confirm their national identity and patriotism (Anderson, 1991; Blommaert, 1999) – has been the most dominant ideology since the mid-18th century creation of the nation-state. Although 123 languages are spoken by 126 different caste/ethnic groups (Census, 2011), only the Nepali language in Devanagari script is the country's 'legitimate' official language. While the 2007 Interim Constitution ensures basic education in the mother tongue as a fundamental right, the dominance of Nepali in the wider sociolinguistic landscape forces Indigenous youth to self-silence their mother tongue. The Limbu youth say that they felt *laj* [linguistic shame] due to the low sociopolitical power and prestige of their mother tongue in Nepalese society.

The creation of the nation-state has played an important role in the construction of this linguistic nationalism ideology. Following the annexation of multiple tribal states, the Gorkha Kings legitimized their own native language, the Gorkha/Khash language, as the national language and strictly enforced a one nation–one language policy (Sonntag, 2007; Weinberg, 2013). The modernization of the Khas/Gorkha language was supported through various state mechanisms such as schools, mass media, the courts, and government offices. The ideology of linguistic nationalism became more prominent in the Panchayat System (1960–1990) in which multiparty democracy was banned and the education system and Indigenous lands were nationalized and modernized. Considering Indigenous languages a threat to nationalism and inappropriate for modern education, a Nepali-only policy was strictly implemented. Thus, modern education became a mechanism to assimilate Indigenous people into the mainstream Hindu culture and Nepali language dominance.

As resistance against this oppressive linguistic and cultural history grew in the early 1990s, a new powerful ideology – neoliberalism – entered Nepal's nation-building discourse of *bikas* (development). Heavily influenced by the structural reform plans of multilateral agencies such as the World Bank, the International Monetary Fund (IMF) and the Asian Development Bank, the national policies have focused on the Western concept of bikas as an approach to improve people's economic status. The bikas plans, which primarily address donors' interests, have paid much attention to poverty reduction and infrastructure development through modernization, a free-competitive market economy, privatization and foreign investment and debt (Pandey, 2012). These policies, however, do not recognize the traditional knowledge embedded in Indigenous peoples' lived experiences; they categorize Indigenous people as 'poor' – waiting for external support, but not a source of knowledge.

As public services are being privatized, Indigenous people have the least access to socioeconomic and political resources (Figure 9.1). Recent data show that 47% of national resources are consumed by the wealthiest 20% of people, while only 8% of national resources are distributed among the poorest 20% of the population (Census, 2011). Approximately

Figure 9.1 Limbu people making paddy. As privatization has increased, Indigenous people in Nepal have the least access to socioeconomic and political resources (photograph by Prem Phyak)

one-quarter of Indigenous people are living under extreme poverty and are deprived of equal access to educational and economic resources. For example, the literate population of the Indigenous people – those with a School Leaving Certificate or higher degree – is only 11.1%, while 54.3% of upper caste (hill Brahmins-Chetris) people are literate with the same degree. Moreover, while about 20% of Indigenous students (excluding Newari) attend private schools and colleges, 41% of hill Brahmin students attend such schools (Subba *et al.*, 2014: 101). Private schools are more expensive, concentrated in urban cities and focus on English as a subject and the medium of instruction.

In the remainder of this chapter, I discuss how Limbu Indigenous youth develop critical awareness of these ideological issues.

Awakening the Sense of Injustice: Documenting and Naming Hegemonic Ideologies

After engaging the Limbu youth in critically examining their own existential sociolinguistic reality, they were further engaged in observing language policies and practices in schools and communities. The youth participated in various interactive programs on Indigenous politics, language policy and education. They closely observed interviews and informal discussions with policymakers, Indigenous activists, teachers, parents and other youth at the local and national levels. Some youth also participated in online discussions. Most importantly, they participated in the

2012 Indigenous street movement in Kathmandu. After each observation, we sat together in the youths' office, in village settings, and in other places to critically reflect on what we had learned from our observations and interactions in the field.

In these 'extraordinary conversations' (Fine & Weis, 2003), the Limbu youth interrogated power, ethnicity, education, poverty and social class as intellectual and activist work towards countering hegemonic ideologies. At the center of these conversations was the notion of *awakening the sense of injustice* (Duetsch, 1974, cited in Stoudt *et al*., 2011), which involves knowing, talking, and raising critical awareness about social injustices. Awakening the sense of injustice 'unveils and provokes critical conscious-ness and action' among marginalized groups (Stoudt *et al*., 2011). First, the Limbu youth were engaged in collectively unveiling and naming the hegemonic ideologies in a series of dialogue. These youth identified lin-guistic oppression rooted in the history of monolingual policy and domi-nation of neoliberalism in the guise of modernity and bikas. While narrating his observations and interviews with teachers, Muksam recounted, '[Most Limbu parents in villages are **uneducated** ... they aren't **aware** of political issues ... they aren't in **power** to make decision.' He made explicit that 'a monolingual policy' is responsible for the erasure of Indigenous languages in education. While reporting about the teachers with whom he talked, Muksam argued that teachers' 'negative ideology' towards Indigenous languages and Indigenous peoples' lack of awareness are major forces that diminish the importance of Indigenous languages. Another youth, Abodh, expressed a similar opinion: 'I talked to some teachers ... they cannot justify why Indigenous languages mustn't be used in school ... they just say that students don't like to learn.' Abodh called this phenomenon 'narrow thinking' and considered it an 'unwillingness' to accept Indigenous languages and cultural identities.

The negative attitude towards Indigenous languages, which Dorian (1998) relates to a colonial 'ideology of contempt,' is linked with the domi-nant discourse of Nepali nationalism and nation-building. In dialogue sessions, the Limbu youth frequently referred to the oppressive history of monolithic nationalism. For example, based on his discussions with com-munity elders and Indigenous activists in his village, Jalan contended that Limbu people were 'illegally' integrated into Nepal and forced to adopt Hindu culture and speak the Gorkha/Khas language. With this aware-ness, the youth argued that 'internal colonization' – Nepalification and Hinduization – contributed to the erasure of the Limbu language from public spaces.

The counter-history, which has not been taught in school, shows that until 1774, the Limbu Indigenous people had their own land, Limbuwan, ruled by ten Limbu tribal kings. After an unsuccessful three-year battle, the Gorkha King Prithvi Narayan Shah negotiated with the Limbu kings and, in 1774, they signed a treaty to end the war. Accordingly, Limbuwan became part of Nepal, but the Limbu people retained the right to use their ancestral land without any government control (Caplan, 1970). For them, Kipat was not simply land for subsistence, but an embodiment of language, culture, and ancestral linkage. Breaching the 1774 treaty, the nation-state continually attacked the Limbu people's right to self-determination and formally ended the Kipat system in 1964 by enforcing a modern land reform policy. With the nationalization of land, Limbu and other Indigenous people in Nepal lost their ancestral and pastoral lands; as a Limbu youth said, they became 'alienated in their own homeland.' The National Federation of Indigenous Nationalities (NFIN) estimates that about 65% of Indigenous peoples' ancestral lands in Nepal are now occupied by national parks and conservation areas.

These youth's critical consciousness builds on the counter-hegemonic histories they collected from Indigenous activists and community elders. In an informal group discussion, Abidg shared what a local Limbu language teacher and the founder of a community school told him. In the 1980s, when languages other than Nepali were banned, the teacher and his friends established a mobile night school to teach the Limbu language and Mundhum (the Limbu people's oral scripture). These youth continue to build awareness of how linguistic nationalism discriminates against Indigenous people (Bauman & Briggs, 2003; Kroskrity, 2009). Another youth, Rajendra, contended that the Limbu people's Nepali language practices are considered 'bad,' 'uncivilized' and 'substandard' in the mainstream society. He illustrated this with the language practices in his own village, where Limbu people are mocked when they replace 'gh' with 'kh' and 'p' with 'ph'.[2] Most Limbu people, particularly those who are dominant speakers of Limbu, feel embarrassed, as they are ridiculed for their 'nonstandard' language practices. The youth thus agree, as Rajendra said, that rejection of the Limbu language and language practices by the state is the 'rejection of the Limbu peoples' identity.'

Although the 1990 Constitution allowed the Indigenous people to establish their own ethnic organizations to revitalize their languages and cultures, their representation in the state executive, judiciary and legislature is disproportionate; their absence in decision making mechanisms contributes to the erasure of their voices and rights from national policies (Lawoti, 2010). Despite the objections of Indigenous peoples, Nepali has been the only official language and the use of other local languages in government offices was ruled 'unconstitutional' by Nepal's Supreme Court in 1999.

With an increased sense of injustice, Limbu youth are also analyzing how a mother tongue-based multilingual education policy that has opened some space for Indigenous languages (Ministry of Education, 2010) is not receiving proper attention from schools and the state. While the youth blamed *ekal bhashi manasikata* (a monolingual mentality), they also identified *angreji moha* (English craze) throughout the country. Uncovering an unequal 'order of indexicality' (Blommaert, 2005), Muksam explained that because the wealthy send their children to private schools, English is indexed as the 'language of wealthy and modern people,' and the 'language of quality and modern education.' Since Indigenous languages are ignored in the guise of both nationalism and modernity/privatization/globalization, these youth name the current situation 'super-injustice' (a free translation of *anyaya mathi anyaya*] – a process in which (Indigenous) people are tempted towards the materialistic world without being aware that they are disconnected from their own land, language, and culture. This super-injustice occurs through what Harvey (2006) calls 'accumulation by dispossession' – a process in which a few wealthy people and corporate entities accumulate capital by dispossessing others from their land and language. While Harvey's capital includes monetary capital, following Bourdieu (1991), we consider the term in a generic sense, which includes social, linguistic, cultural and symbolic capital.

Denaturalizing and Transforming Hegemonic Ideologies

Having a greater sense of injustice, we participated in the Indigenous street movements that took place in Kathmandu in May 2012 and collectively engaged in denaturalizing ideological hegemonies and the superinjustices mentioned above. The organizer of the protest, the Nepal Federations of Indigenous Nationalities, sought to ensure Indigenous peoples' right to self-determination and natural resources in the new constitution which was being drafted at the time of this writing. Between 19–27 May 2012, thousands of Indigenous people were in the street for a week-long movement. The Limbu students actively participated in the protest with Kirat Yakthung Chumlung, the national organization of Limbu Indigenous people. A trilingual banner (Nepali, Limbu and English) conveyed the students' slogan: *A practical [real] education in mother tongue is our campaign; Limbuwan in the Federal Republic Nepal.*

After each participation and observation, we sat together at a street corner and critically discussed the ideological meanings expressed in the movement's activities, connecting them to the broader sociopolitical context. Our dialogue focused on various codifications that we observed in the street. For Freire (1970), codifications, which mediate investigators in their critical analysis, can be an image, text, or oral description. For example, on the first day of the movement, in one 'street dialogue' we discussed the Limbu students' slogan and the protest in which Indigenous professors and activists were also present (Figure 9.2).

Discussing the slogan's meaning, the chairperson of the organization argued that mother tongue education is necessary to preserve Limbu culture, language, and identity. In responding to my question of how mother tongue education is a 'practical education,' she claimed that 'It's practical

Figure 9.2 Banner of the Limbu Students' Forum, May 2012: 'A practical [real] education in mother tongue is our campaign; Limbuwan in the Federal Republic Nepal' (photograph by Prem Phyak)

because the knowledge of mother tongue keeps us connected with our community' and helps us understand 'who we are and who our ancestors are.' During dialogue, I shared with the youth and other participants the significance of using students' home languages for equitable education (Cummins, 2007; García, 2009; Skutnabb-Kangas & Heugh, 2012). We critically examined how modern education has dispossessed Indigenous peoples from their culture, language and land. One youth criticized the fact that modern education privileges the accumulation of 'bookish knowledge' through individual competition while valorizing global languages and cultures; the same education system, the youth argued, ignores Indigenous peoples' knowledge about farming, subsistence, environment, weather, spirituality, learning/literacy and justice.

The youth not only participated in the movement but also engaged in praxis, fostering a critical awareness of their own oppression as they made plans for social transformation (Freire, 1970; Gegeo & Watson-Gegeo, 2013). Showing a greater awareness of their own action and ideology, the youth reimagined education from an Indigenous perspective, challenging a materialistic 'banking model of education' (Freire, 1970) in which learners are treated as passive consumers rather than generators of knowledge. While reimagining 'practical education' in the mother tongue, these youth defined education as an emancipatory tool to develop 'strong bonds of human beings with their lands and communities.' In Limbu, although there is no single word for education, *nisam/ni:tcham*, 'a complete knowledge or wisdom,' is used to describe the process of achieving knowledge.

As these youth claim, obtaining *ni:tcham* is to *ni:tchingma* – 'to be aware' or 'to become conscious.' Rather than focusing on the accumulation of market-driven knowledge, *ni:tcham* must contribute to *cho:tlung* – achieving 'a sense of completeness' or 'a sense of pride for the land.'

The Limbu youth's engagement in praxis cultivates their 'critical Indigenous awareness,' which Lee (2009) defines as 'an awareness of the historical and broad oppressive conditions that have influenced current realities of Indigenous people's lives' (2009: 318). These youth reject the linguistic nationalism and modernist ideology that delegitimize Indigenous languages and cultures and position Indigenous people as 'second-class citizens.' Muksam linked this linguistic discrimination with the history of internal colonization and argued that the Limbu people's 'collective identity' has been threatened since the end of Kipat. During the dialogue, all the youth expressed feeling 'alien in their own land' and committed to correcting the *bangyaieko itihas* (the distorted history) through activist work. Justifying the relevance of Limbuwan on their own slogan, Muksam challenged the 'racist and ethnic interpretations of Limbuwan' in dominant political discourses. The youth did not think that Limbuwan is linked only with Limbu ethnic identity, but associated it with the history of the land, which has been deliberately 'distorted' and 'hidden.' These youth believe that the new constitution must address their historical identities, ensure the 'right to self-determination,' and strengthen 'inclusive Nepali nationalism.'

Youth Challenging Neoliberalism and *Bikas*

Following the Indigenous movement, the Limbu youth engaged in uncovering neoliberal adversities in rural Indigenous communities. The notion of bikas or development, modernity and privatization were the main generative themes of our dialogue. These themes emerged from a 10-hour long workshop on language policy and Indigenous language with the Limbu youth and ethnographic observation of two villages in eastern Nepal. In my own village in the eastern hill of Nepal, bikas has brought unplanned construction of rugged roads that have no use at all. Besides elite capture and bureaucratic monopoly, a large portion of the budget goes to the owners of the excavator, the most famous machine used to build roads in the village. The Limbu youth contend that haphazard use of the excavator has resulted in landslides, deforestation, and environmental degradation. Most recently, temporary roads have been constructed to export timber from the village; local forests have been sold at the cheapest price to private mill owners in the town. Water sources – rivers, springs and wells – have dried, affecting the Indigenous peoples' livelihood. Since the government's bikas plans are mostly focused on urban development, the agrarian Indigenous people have not yet experienced any substantial changes.

Figure 9.3 Interaction with Limbu youth in their office in Kathmandu (photograph by Prem Phyak)

Foreign aid remains at the heart of the bikas plan. More than a quarter of the national budget includes developmental assistance from more than 40 bilateral/multilateral agencies (e.g. World Bank and IMF). National statistics show some socioeconomic development. However, due to the state's failure to address existing structural inequalities, asymmetrical power relations, and the exclusion of marginalized communities, the donor-driven bikas policies have become a 'failed development' (Pandey, 2012). These policies have not only reproduced existing social inequalities and promoted the 'elite capture' of social policies, but also 'tend to establish global policies and targets with little regard to local conditions' (Pandey, 2012: 95).

The Limbu youth have become more critical about neoliberal policies as they continue to engage in dialogue and understand how neoliberal ideologies are affecting their communities (Figure 9.3). Although the multinational agencies have focused on poverty reduction, the Limbu youth express their frustration that most Indigenous youth are forced to join labor markets in the Gulf, Malaysia, Qatar, South Korea, India, Kuwait, Israel and other foreign countries – even after earning a graduate degree. One youth, for example, maintained that, 'The Limbu youth don't focus on their study ... their educational degree does not give a job.' Another student told his friend's story: 'My friend couldn't continue his higher education due to poverty ... he just went to Malaysia ... he got a loan from a businessman to make his passport in Kathmandu and pay for visa fees and other costs to a manpower company.'

Statistics show that about 1500 Nepali youth join foreign labor markets every day (Amnesty International, 2011). Falling prey to what has been described by these Indigenous youth as 'mafia manpower' (recruiting agencies for foreign employment) that make false promises of better jobs and salaries, these migrant laborers experience ruthless 'corporate exploitation' abroad (see Amnesty International, 2011). Gibson and Pattisson (2014) report Nepali laborers' meager pay and dire working and living conditions in the multibillion-dollar integrated construction project for the 2022 FIFA World Cup in Qatar. At least 157 Nepali workers died in 2014 in Qatar alone and an equal number of migrant laborers died in other countries. While government estimates that foreign employment contributes 25% of the country's total gross domestic product, its sociopolitical, cultural and educational impacts on the lives of farmers, Indigenous people and the poor have not been discussed. As the Limbu youth portray, *khet-bari* (productive farmlands) are becoming barren due to lack of young people in the village. The Limbu youth expressed their frustration about the increasing difficulties of performing Indigenous cultural practices such as funerals and weddings in their village.

With this awareness, the Limbu youth became further engaged in dialogue on how neoliberalism has impacted Indigenous values. As Manju critiqued, foreign employment has promoted individualism, the break-up of families, and other casualties of modernity in Indigenous villages. As opposed to individualism, Limbu Indigenous communities are guided by *tangsing* – 'to cooperate or be together' – a traditional cultural practice in which all Limbus in the village come together in one place where their shamans cleanse their curses and provide power to succeed. As an organizing principle, Tangsing fosters cooperation and collectivism among Limbu people and serves as an emancipatory space in which community elders teach history, culture, language, morality, and life skills to younger generations. But as Abodh (and other youth) observed, the principle of tangsing is 'breaking down as our people are tempted to monetary gain and modern culture.' Most importantly, these youth demonstrated their critical awareness about the gap between modern education and Indigenous people's lived reality. Jalan, for example, related, 'Talking with you [Prem] and other people, I learned the educational relevance of *Mundhum*. But why aren't our schools [...], textbooks and teachers recognizing them? We're never taught about *tangsing* and *Mundhum*.' These youth have committed to teaching others the importance of Indigenous values in education.

While examining the impact of foreign employment, the Limbu youth were critical of the fact that migrant workers' families often move to town in pursuit of a 'quality education' for their children in private schools. Jalan contended that people wrongly believe that 'private schools are good as they teach in English.' Guided by an ideology that equates English with quality education, private schools reject Indigenous languages as the medium of instruction, thereby reproducing existing social divisions between rich and poor, urban and rural. The youth recognized that the general public unquestioningly embraced the symbolic capital of English as 'rich people's language,' necessary their children's upward social mobility.

Based on the same ideology, the Ministry of Education has encouraged public schools to adopt a policy of English as the medium of instruction, without considering its educational and social ramifications (Phyak, 2011, 2013). In dialogue sessions, the Limbu youth noted that the World Bank-supported policy of minimizing the state's role in public education gives power to a School Management Committee to oversee public schools. This contributes to the expansion of English as 'fashionable.' Because the School Management Committees reproduces dominant ideologies, the importance of Indigenous languages in education is diminished at the local level as well.

The 'uncritical celebration' of English-as-a-global-commodity in education has posed serious challenges to learning language and academic content for Indigenous children (Skutnabb-Kangas & Heugh, 2012). Limbu youth argue that the Indigenous children who do not speak Nepali well are further marginalized by English-only policies. Most importantly, these youth understand that official policies are *dhokebaj* (deceptive) in the neoliberal regime. Based on our interactions with a head teacher in a public school, Jalan called the state's mother-tongue education policy a *jhutho ashwasan* (a false promise) to Indigenous people, as the government does not provide teachers and resources to implement the policy. Another youth, Ram, criticized the state's indifference to Indigenous people's linguistic marginalization and historical oppression, and contended that public schools have discontinued teaching Limbu due to increased English language pressure. In our dialogues, these youth linked the displacement of Indigenous languages to ethnic discrimination. Since most public school head teachers are non-Indigenous language speakers, they do not provide space for Limbu in education.

Conclusion

With an increased critical awareness of hegemonic ideologies, the Limbu youth continue to engage pressing issues affecting Limbu Indigenous people through various forms of on-the-ground activist work. These youth have submitted memoranda to District Education Offices, organized a series of workshops and interaction programs, and lobbied teachers, parents and students to ensure space for the Limbu language in education. The youth continue to write essays on Indigenous issues for newspapers, and to collect oral tradition and other forms of Indigenous knowledge from Indigenous wisdom keepers.

Two major issues emerge from this language policy engagement by and with Limbu youth. First, the youth engaged in *critical Indigenous praxis*: 'people's own critical reflection on culture, history, knowledge, politics, economics, and the sociopolitical contexts in which they are living ... [and then] taking the next step to act on these critical reflections' (Gegeo & Watson-Gegeo, 2001: 59). Through their collaborative engagement in the sociolinguistic, educational, and political realities of Indigenous people's lives, and their interactions with multiple actors, the Limbu youth not only heightened their awareness of contested ideologies, but also acted as activists, challenging historical and contemporary inequalities. In the context of critical participatory dialogue, the youth interrogated official and de facto language policies, denaturalizing discriminatory ideologies of linguistic nationalism and neoliberalism. In this transformative process, the Limbu youth reclaimed their Indigenous identity (Davis, 2009; Henze & Davis, 1999) and positioned themselves as 'political and cultural actors' as opposed to 'language losers' (McCarty & Wyman, 2009; Messing, 2009).

Second, this engaged approach to language policy highlights the centrality of ideological clarification (Fishman, 1991) in denaturalizing oppressive language policies and practices. The Limbu youth's engagement in ideological analysis embraced what Kroskrity (2009) describes as the three major principles of social transformation: critical awareness, positionality and multiplicity. Through their explorations of multiple language ideologies as observed in language practices, their interactions with teachers and parents, and their participation in Indigenous movements, the youth collectively challenged commonsensical notions of language policy. Taking an activist stance, the youth demonstrated their commitment to transform historical and contemporary linguistic inequalities rooted in linguistic nationalism and neoliberalism. In this work the youth reimagined *language policy justice*. With this as a goal, they continue to seek meaningful participation in language policymaking processes.

Notes

(1) The youth conversations were held in Nepali. Bold-faced words are code-switched English words. Italicized words are in Nepali. The most frequently used Nepali words have not been translated.
(2) For example, Limbus pronounce *gham* [sun] as *kham* [envelope] and *parsi* [the day after tomorrow] as *pharsi* [pumpkin].

References

Amnesty International (2011) Nepal: Protect Nepalese migrants from 'false promises' of work abroad. Retrieved from https://www.amnesty.org/en/latest/news/2011/12/nepal-protect nepalese-migrants-false-promises-work-abroad/
Anderson, B. (1991) *Imagined Communities: Reflections on the Origin and Spread of Nationalism*. New York and London: Verso.
Bauman, R. and Briggs, C.L. (2003) *Voices of Modernity: Language Ideologies and the Politics of Inequality*. Cambridge: Cambridge University Press.
Blommaert, J. (ed.) (1999) *Language Ideological Debates*. Berlin: Mouton de Gruyter.

Blommaert, J. (2005) *Discourse: A Critical Introduction*. Cambridge: Cambridge University Press.

Blommaert, J. (2008) Notes on power. *Working Papers in Language Diversity* 7, 2–5.

Bourdieu, P. (1991) *Language and Symbolic Power*. Cambridge: Polity Press.

Caplan, L. (1970) *Land and Social Change in East Nepal: A Study of Hindu-Tribal Relations*. Berkeley: University of California Press.

Census (2011) *Nepal Living Standards Survey*. Kathmandu: Central Bureau of Statistics.

Cummins, J. (2007) Rethinking monolingual instructional strategies in multilingual classrooms. *Canadian Journal of Applied Linguistics* 10 (2), 221–240.

Dauenhauer, N.M. and Dauenhauer, R. (1998) Technical, emotional, and ideological issues in reversing language shift: Examples from Southeast Alaska. In L.A. Grenoble and L.J. Whaley (eds) *Endangered Languages: Language Loss and Community Response* (pp. 57–99). Cambridge: Cambridge University Press.

Davis, K. (2009) Agentive youth research: Towards individual, collective, and policy transformations. In T.G. Wiley, J.S. Lee and R.W. Rumberger (eds) *The Education of Language Minority Immigrants in the USA* (pp. 203–239). Bristol: Multilingual Matters.

Davis, K.A. (2014) Engaged language policy and practices. *Language Policy* 13 (2), 83–100.

Davis, K.A. and Phyak, P. (2015) In the face of neoliberal adversity: Engaging language education policy and practices. *L2 Journal* 7 (3), 146–166.

Davis, K.A. and Phyak, P. (2017) *Engaged Language Policy and Practices*. New York & London: Routledge.

Deutsch, M. (1974) Awakening the sense of injustice. In M. Lerner and M. Ross (eds) *The Quest for Justice: Myth, Reality, Ideal* (pp. 1–43). Montreal, QC: Holt, Rinehart and Winston.

Dorian, N. (1998) Western language ideologies and small-language prospects. In L.A. Grenoble and L.J. Whaley (eds) *Endangered Languages: Language Loss and Community Response* (pp. 3–21). Cambridge: Cambridge University Press.

Fine, M. and Weis, L. (2003) *Silenced Voices and Extraordinary Conversations: Re-imagining Schools*. New York, NY: Teachers College Press.

Fishman, J.A. (2001) Why is it so hard to save a threatened language? (A perspective on the cases that follow). In J.A. Fishman (ed.) *Can Threatened Languages Be Saved? Reversing Language Shift, Revisited: A 21st Century Perspective* (pp. 17–22). Clevedon: Multilingual Matters.

Freire, P. (1970) *Pedagogy of the Oppressed*. New York, NY: Continuum.

García, O. (2009) *Bilingual Education in the 21st Century: A Global Perspective*. Malden, MA: Wiley-Blackwell.

Gegeo, D.W. and Watson-Gegeo, K.A. (2001) 'How we know': Kwara'ae rural villagers doing Indigenous epistemology. *The Contemporary Pacific* 13 (1), 55–88.

Gegeo, D.W. and Watson-Gegeo, K.A. (2013) The critical villager revisited: Continuing transformations of language and education in Solomon Islands. In J.W. Tollefson (ed.) *Language Policies in Education: Critical Issues* (2nd edition, pp. 233–251). New York and London: Routledge.

Gibson, O. and Pattisson, P. (23 November 2014) Death toll among Qatar's 2022 World Cup workers revealed. Retrieved from http://www.theguardian.com/world/2014/dec/23/qatar-nepal-workers-world-cup-2022-death-toll-doha.

Gramsci, A. (1971) *Selections from the Prison Notebooks*. New York, NY: International Publishers.

Harvey, D. (2006) *Spaces of Global Capitalism: Towards a Theory of Unequal Geographical Development*. New York, NY: Verso.

Henze, R. and Davis, K.A. (1999) Authenticity and identity: Lessons from Indigenous language education. *Anthropology and Education Quarterly* 30 (1), 3–21.

hooks, b. (1994) *Teaching to Transgress: Education as the Practice of Freedom*. New York, NY: Routledge.

Kroskrity, P.V. (2009) Language renewal as sites of language ideological struggle: The need for 'ideological clarification.' In J. Reyhner and L. Lockard (eds) *Indigenous Language Revitalization: Encouragement, Guidance and Lessons Learned* (pp. 71–83): Flagstaff: Northern Arizona University Center for Excellence in Education.

Lawoti, M. (2010) *Federal State Building: Challenges in Framing the Nepali Constitution.* Kathmandu: Bhrikuti Academic Publications.

Lee, T.S. (2009) Language, identity, and power: Navajo and Pueblo young adults' perspectives and experiences with competing language ideologies. *Journal of Language, Identity, and Education* 8 (5), 307–320.

McCarty, T.L., Collins, J. and Hopson, R.K. (2011) Dell Hymes and the New Language Policy Studies: Update from an underdeveloped country. *Anthropology and Education Quarterly* 42 (4), 335–363.

McCarty, T.L., Romero-Little, M.E., Warhol, L. and Zepeda, O. (2009) Indigenous youth as language policy makers. *Journal of Language, Identity, and Education* 8 (5), 291–306.

McCarty, T.L. and Wyman, L.T. (2009) Indigenous youth and bilingualism – Theory, research, praxis. *Journal of Language, Identity, and Education* 8 (5), 279–290.

McGroarty, M. (2006) Neoliberal collusion or strategic simultaneity? On multiple rationales for language-in-education policies. *Language Policy* 5 (1), 3-13.

Messing, J.H. (2009) Ambivalence and ideology among Mexicano youth in Tlaxcala, Mexico. *Journal of Language, Identity, and Education* 8 (5), 350–364.

Ministry of Education (2010) *Manual for Implementing Multilingual Education.* Bhaktapur, Nepal: Department of Education.

Pandey, D.R. (2012) The legacy of Nepal's failed development. In S. von Einsiedel, D.M. Malone and S. Pradhan (eds) *Nepal in Transition: From People's War to Fragile Peace* (pp. 81–99). Cambridge: Cambridge University Press.

Pennycook, A. (2013) Language policies, language ideologies and local language practices. In L. Wee, R.B. Goh and L. Lim (eds) *The Politics of English: South Asia, Southeast Asia and the Asia Pacific* (pp. 1–18). Amsterdam: John Benjamins.

Phyak, P. (2011) Beyond the façade of language planning for Nepalese primary education: Monolingual hangover, elitism and displacement of local languages? *Current Issues in Language Planning* 12 (2), 265–287.

Phyak, P. (2013) Language ideologies and local languages as the medium-of-instruction policy: A critical ethnography of a multilingual school in Nepal. *Current Issues in Language Planning* 14 (1), 127–143.

Phyak, P. and Bui, T.T.N. (2014) Youth engaging language policy and planning: Ideologies and transformations from within. *Language Policy* 13 (2), 101–119.

Ricento, T. (ed.) (2015) *Language Policy and Political Economy: English in a Global Context.* Oxford and New York: Oxford University Press.

Sallabank, J. (2013) *Attitudes to Endangered Languages: Identities and Policies.* Cambridge: Cambridge University Press.

Silverstein, M. (1979) Language structure and linguistic ideology. In P.R. Clyne, W.F. Hanks and C.L. Hofbauer (eds) *The Elements: A Parasession on Linguistic Units and Levels* (pp. 193–247). Chicago, IL: Chicago Linguistic Society.

Skutnabb-Kangas, T. and Heugh, K. (eds) (2012) *Multilingual Education and Sustainable Diversity Work: From the Periphery to the Center.* New York, NY: Routledge.

Sonntag, S.K. (2007) Change and permanence in language politics in Nepal. In A.B.M. Tsui and J.W. Tollefson (eds) *Language Policy, Culture and Identity in Asian Contexts* (pp. 205–217). Mahwah, NJ: Lawrence Erlbaum.

Stoudt, B.G., Fox, M. and Fine, M. (2011) Awakening injustice in a new century. In P.T. Coleman (ed.) *Conflict, Interdependence, and Justice* (pp. 165–191). New York, NY: Springer.

Subba, C., Pyakurel, B., Bastola, T.S., Khajum Subba, M., Raut, N.K. and Karki, B. (2014) *A Study on Socio-economic Status of Indigenous Peoples in Nepal.* Kathmandu and Copenhagen: Lawyers' Association for Human Rights of Indigenous Peoples (LAHRIP) and International Work Group for Indigenous Affairs (IWGIA).

Thompson, J.B. (1991) Editor's introduction. In P. Bourdieu, *Language and Symbolic Power* (pp. 1–31). Cambridge: Polity Press.

Tollefson, J.W. (ed.) (2013) *Language Policies in Education: Critical Issues* (2nd edn). New York and London: Routledge.

Weinberg, M. (2013) Revisiting history in language policy: The case of medium of instruction in Nepal. *Working Papers in Educational Linguistics* 28 (1), 61–80.

Woolard, K.A. and Schieffelin, B.B. (1994) Language ideology. *Annual Review of Anthropology* 23, 55–82.

Wyman, L.T., McCarty, T.L. and Nicholas, S.E. (eds) (2014) *Indigenous Youth and Multilingualism: Language Identity, Ideology, and Practice in Dynamic Cultural Worlds*. New York, NY: Routledge.

10 Language Key Holders for Mexicano: The Case of an Intergenerational Community in Coatepec de los Costales, Mexico

Rosalva Mojica Lagunas

Despite having millions of speakers, Nahuatl is highly endangered. The dominant language of Coatepec, Guerrero, Mexico was historically Nahuatl, or 'Mexicano.' In the last 50 years, there has been a pronounced shift from Mexicano to Spanish. This study unravels the circumstances underlying this language shift through observation, in-depth interviews and archival analysis from a five-month ethnographic study. The analysis uses a conceptual framework that combines (1) a critical sociocultural approach to language policy; (2) Spolsky's (2004) definition of language policy as language practices, ideologies or beliefs, and management; (3) the ethnography of language policy; and (4) an Indigenous knowledge framework. The study finds that the 'key holders' of the language are the older generation, who hold the responsibility of sustaining Mexicano. Yet, a disconnect exists between the language ideologies of the older and younger generations, and a two-way receiving and transferring process is needed. This in-depth examination illuminates how and why language shift is occurring in Coatepec, and the possibilities for reversing the shift.

Introduction

Si se pierde náhuatl, el pueblo va a perder algo. Es la raíz de nuestro pueblo. El corazón. Nosotros [los jóvenes] necesitamos reflexionar y aprender a hablar, porque es nuestro idioma.

If Nahuatl disappears, the village will lose something. It's the root of our village. The heart. We [the youth] need to reflect and learn to speak it, because it's our language.

– Ana, 20 years old

I would like to introduce myself as a way of honoring the Indigenous knowledge that has been passed down to me (Wilson, 2009). My name is Rosalva Lagunas and I am a descendant of the Aztecs who once occupied the land that is now considered Mexico. My parents, Feliciano Lagunas and Sofia Mojica Lagunas, are native speakers of Mexicano. I grew up in the United States hearing the language from my parents and relatives, but I never had a real interest in learning the language until I started questioning where I came from and the knowledge that was passed down from generation to generation. I knew and felt something was missing. Recently, I rediscovered my ancestors' language, which was calling me to reclaim it in my heart, body and mind. I realized that the older generation would soon pass away and take the language with them. The language would no longer be heard in our family. At that moment, I decided to reclaim my language for myself, my family and my community of Coatepec.

This ethnographic study began with the roots of my family and led me into the academic world. As an Indigenous scholar, I am careful about how to represent my people in the most respectful and humble manner, and to represent their words so that their voices and testimonies will be heard (Denzin *et al.*, 2008; Smith, 2012; Wilson, 2009). I am honored to have learned from my ancestors and to be able to pass down their knowledge, which needs to be heard across the lands that Mother Earth has given us.

As an academic, I have learned how to navigate a world where I need to honor my ancestral ways of being on this land. As I continue, I am learning how to balance these worlds and spaces. It has been a learning process and a process of self-rediscovery and reflection. I have applied some of the research methods that I learned in Western academic institutions to what works best for the people of Coatepec. Doing research in an Indigenous community in Mexico, or any other country, is a humbling experience (Smith, 2012). I bring this up because it is important to acknowledge the negative relationship Indigenous people have had with research in the past. As an Indigenous researcher, I am aware of and sensitive to how I conduct research. 'Reclaiming a voice … has also been about reclaiming, reconnecting and reordering those ways of knowing which were submerged, hidden or driven underground' (Smith, 2012: 72). I continue to write and share this collaborative work undertaken with the people of Coatepec so that others can look to my findings for guidance as they continue their own work of language revitalization. I say collaborative work because it is work that I could not have done without my people. They have shared their knowledge with me. They have allowed me to enter their homes, interview them, take photographs and participate in their daily life style.

In the dimmed room, my father and uncles were conversing about my grandfather's funeral arrangements. I heard a musical tone that I grew up around, but never paid much attention to – they were speaking

Nahuatl. I was speaking with my cousins and siblings in English and we did not know how to speak our ancestral language. Our grandfather had passed away, and slowly the language was dying from our family – taking pieces of our knowledge as well. This phenomenon of language loss is occurring every day, and there is an essential need to save our Indigenous languages for the sake of our land and to preserve our knowledge.
(Lagunas, 2016)

According to global language archives, some Indigenous languages continue to have millions of speakers, others have small numbers of speakers, others have individuals who are the only speakers alive and some communities have no living speakers and their language is preserved only on paper and in recordings. Indigenous languages are always threatened with extinction if they are not the dominant language of governmental or educational institutions (Fishman, 1991, 2001; Hinton & Hale, 2001; Spolsky, 2009).

In this modern world, migration and globalization play an important role in language shift, and in such cases, it is much more difficult to sustain intergenerational transmission of Indigenous and other minoritized languages (see, e.g. King & Haboud, 2011). The primary reason people from my parents' natal village of Coatepec migrate to the United States is economic. People are searching and hoping for better wages with the goal of sending money to their families in Coatepec, perhaps to build a home, to pay off debt, or to take care of loved ones.

In this chapter, I look at a particular community, Coatepec de los Costales, located in Guerrero, Mexico. Nahuatl, the Indigenous language spoken in Coatepec, is often referred to as Mexicano (Hill & Hill, 1986), and I use these two terms interchangeably throughout the chapter. Although there are millions of Nahuatl speakers in Mexico, the language is highly endangered, especially in small communities such as Coatepec. In the last 50 years, there has been a pronounced shift from Mexicano to Spanish. This study seeks to unravel the circumstances surrounding this language shift through observation, in-depth interviews and archival analysis. Drawing from a larger ethnography study, I focus on how elders are at the core of language revitalization – they are the 'key holders' – and there is thus a need for relationship building between youth and elders for language revitalization to occur (Lee, 2009, 2014; McCarty *et al.*, 2006; Meek, 2007). The major theme to be examined is the importance of the elders' presence in a household.

A number of scholars have contributed to the study of Nahuatl language shift and revitalization in Mexico. Jane and Kenneth Hill's (1986) *Speaking Mexicano* is a classic ethnographic study that explores ethnic identity and the role of Spanish and Nahuatl in a central Mexican community. Flores Farfán (2006) investigated different modalities to revive languages and empower native speakers to speak their language. Messing and Rockwell (2006) conducted an ethnographic study in Tlaxcala,

Mexico exploring the usage of Mexicano in and out of schools. Messing (2007, 2009, 2014) continued the study of Mexicano in Tlaxcala, focusing on ambivalence in language ideologies amongst the youth. My work draws on their expertise while contributing to the larger field of Indigenous language reclamation.

Drawing from Spolsky's (2004) definition of language policy as language practices, ideologies, and management, and Fishman's (1991) Graded Intergenerational Disruption Scale (GIDS), I closely examined the mechanisms by which language shift has occurred among generations in Coatepec de Costales, specifically positioning the elders at the core of language revitalization. This study illuminates how and why language shift occurs and the possibilities for reversing language loss. This research is grounded in a conceptual framework that combines (1) a critical socio-cultural approach to language policy; (2) Spolsky's (2004) definition of language policy, (3) the ethnography of language policy (McCarty, 2011); and (4) research and practice in Indigenous knowledge systems (Brayboy *et al.*, 2012).

Brief Historical Background on Language Shift in Mexico

In the early 1500s, before the Spanish invasion, there were as many as 25 million Indigenous speakers in Mexico, and many Indigenous languages were spoken and heard across (what is today) Mexico (Heath, 1972). As Fishman and García (2010: 357) write, Latin America as a whole was home to approximately 170 linguistic families representing 2000 distinct languages. Indigenous languages were used in the political sphere, for economic trade, in storytelling, and to pass down ancestral knowledge to family members. The languages represented a way of being and seeing the world – they carried many stories, a means of ordering experiences, and a place on the land. Language shapes one's identity and creates a balance on earth with all living beings that occupy this land (Basso, 1996; Laduke, 1999).

This era ended in 1519–1521 with the Spanish invasion, which sought to strip the Indigenous people of their culture and language, similarly to Native Americans' experience in what is now the United States and Canada. According to Heath (1972), after the European invasion, only about one million Indigenous-language speakers remained. 'The Spaniards believed language and evangelization were the keys to making the natives "Spanish," in their understanding of the world' (Fitch, n.d.). People were forced to learn Spanish (Castilian) and assimilate to the colonizers' culture, an ideology that the Spanish Crown sought to define and compel the people to adopt. While Indigenous languages during this period 'were not displaced to the extent to which the Mexican colony had hoped,' the colonial process nonetheless 'limited the functionality and sociocultural force of these languages, especially Nahuatl, which was gradually being replaced by Castilian' (de León, 2017: 418).

With Mexican independence in 1821, the new government's goal was to unite the country under a single national identity (Olko & Sullivan, 2014). Spanish quickly became the majority language associated with prestige and success, and Indigenous languages were oppressed and minoritized. In post-revolutionary Mexico, people who spoke their Indigenous languages were punished and children were forbidden to speak their mother tongue at school. The process of language shift was heightened by devastating population loss among Indigenous peoples (de León, 2017). As Mexico began to heal from Spanish colonization, the identities of Indigenous peoples were erased 'from the Latin American social imaginary, and with that their cultural histories and language practices' (García et al., 2010: 354). Mexico was building a national identity with the perceived need to unite all people, which meant that Indigenous peoples would be forced to integrate into Mexico's new culture – a one language-one nation ideology. Many Indigenous languages and cultures were lost during this period, as Spanish went 'from being the minority language of the powerful elite to the vehicular language for much of the population and the officially sanctioned language of Latin American identity' (García et al., 2010: 358). With the loss of Indigenous languages, knowledge and cultural identity were also endangered (Woodbury, n.d.).[1]

Nahuatl (Mexicano)

Nahuatl (Mexicano) is part of the Uto-Aztecan language family. Most speakers are located in central Mexico in the states of Guerrero, Puebla, Morelos, Tlaxcala, Veracruz, Michoacan, Hidalgo, and Nayarit. The estimated number of speakers today ranges from 1.3 to 1.5 million (Archive of Indigenous Language of Latin America [AILLA], 2010; Baldauf & Kaplan, 2007; Coronel-Molina & McCarty, 2016). At the turn of the 20th century, Mexican national census data showed the number of Indigenous-language speakers as having declined as a percentage of the total population (de León, 2017). While the census statistics show variation across regions and language groups in Mexico, 'the overall tendency is increased subtractive bilingualism and language shift at a national level' (de León, 2017: 420). In the case of Nahuatl, historical events in Mexico have changed individuals' language ideologies and caused a language shift from Nahuatl to Spanish.

In December 2002, the Ley General de Derechos Lingüísticos de los Pueblos Indígenas (General Law of Linguistic Rights of the Indigenous Peoples) was passed. This law recognized the various Indigenous languages spoken in Mexico and is intended to protect people's rights to speak those languages. The Secretaria de Educación Publica (SEP) government recognized various Indigenous places and encouraged the people to preserve their languages by promoting bilingual and bicultural education, such as the Dirección General de Educación Indígena (DGEI).

Although Mexico has recognized Indigenous languages, Spanish continues to be the dominant language in all national institutions. The DGEI offers little support to Indigenous villages to preserve their languages, and there are not enough teachers who are trained to teach heritage languages (de León, 2017; Hamel, 2008).

For example, Cuayautitla, a preschool in Coatepec, the focus of this study, there is a preschool, Cuayautitla, which is considered an Indigenous school that promotes mother tongue learning. I interviewed one of the two teachers who taught at the preschool. The teacher informed me that they felt frustrated because they did not receive the support they needed to teach the students in Coatepec. The teachers' variety of Nahuatl was different from the Coatepec variety. The teacher also shared that the majority of the lessons were taught in Spanish and not in Nahuatl due to the lack of materials. For those reasons the teachers did not feel supported.

Despite recent government policies in support of Indigenous languages, the Indigenous peoples of Mexico, including Coatepec, knew that they needed to assimilate if they wanted to have a better life. They realized that they needed to speak Spanish in order to exchange and bargain goods in the city. People who spoke Spanish were able to communicate with the consumers and had more opportunities to sell and earn a better income. This was one of many of the covert signs that encouraged the ideology that Spanish correlates with success and money. There is an underlying ideology that the dominant language is the key to success (Hill & Hill, 1986; Messing, 2007). As time passed, many people began to prefer speaking Spanish and the use of Indigenous languages slowly began disappearing from family homes. This did not mean that the people did not respect their native tongue, but they realized that their mother tongue did not bring revenue into their homes. While economic pressures have been a major cause of language shift, there are many factors that contribute to language loss. I further describe these factors for Coatepec de los Costales below.

Coatepec de los Costales

Coatepec de los Costales is located in the state of Guerrero, Mexico, about 86 miles southwest of Mexico City (Figure 10.1). The population of Coatepec varies because there are often members migrating to the cities or the United States. As US immigration policies have become stricter, it is harder to find jobs and often family members come back to Coatepec. Many of the homes are abandoned, but the population escalates at times to up to 1500 members. Getting to and from Mexico City is fairly easy. There are buses and vans that commute back and forth, traveling once every 1.5 hours in the morning from 4:30 to 8:30am, and in the afternoons between 4:30 to 8:30pm. If residents want to go to the city during off-peak hours there are two additional transportation time schedules available.

Figure 10.1 Coatepec de los Costales, Guerrero, Mexico (photograph by Rosalva M. Lagunas)

The people of Coatepec are known for their artwork using maguey plant fibers called *morales* (Figure 10.2). This artistic knowledge is as endangered as the language. According to village residents, about 50 years ago, Mexicano could be heard everywhere in the village. In the past, as you walked down the dirt roads, you would pass a person and they would greet you in Mexicano; children playing games would tease and joke in Mexicano, and young children would talk to older people in Mexicano, a sign of respect. By the 1990s, this situation had begun to change. People started migrating to the nearest city, Iguala, and to Mexico City, and traveled back and forth to the United States. Some sent money home to help their family members. In the mid-1990s, the dirt roads were paved and schools were built. People started opening their own small shops, selling

Figure 10.2 Vicente making *morales* – an Indigenous artwork – from maguey fibers (photograph by Rosalva M. Lagunas)

soda, chips, basic dry foods, candles, and convenience store goods. People did not have to travel to the city and could go to these shops to buy practical items. Though small in scale at the time, capitalism was overtaking the village, and people started to associate money with a better lifestyle. To communicate with others and trade their goods in the city, they needed to speak Spanish. It was this motivation to learn Spanish that caused people to slowly shift from speaking Mexicano, as local language ideologies correlated money and power with Spanish speaking ability (Hill & Hill, 1986; Messing, 2009). There were few tangible positive outcomes related to speaking Mexicano, but there were negative outcomes to *not* speaking Spanish, related to getting ahead economically. People could not see how speaking Mexicano would lead them to a better life and greater income.

In the mid-1900s, educational administrators and teachers often compelled students to learn Spanish and encouraged them to speak it 'correctly,' which meant that students neglected their own language. Spanish was the language that was valued and recognized in educational institutions. Teachers taught a curriculum prescribed by the government, and were responsible for students learning Spanish at the cost of their Indigenous language. Language ideologies, management, and practices (Spolsky, 2004) were gradually shifting and Spanish became the dominant language of power and status. These ideologies were passed down from generation to generation, and thus we arrive at the consequences of language shift today.

In terms of Fishman's (1991) theoretical framework, Nahuatl in Coatepec may be positioned at stage 6 or 7 on the GIDS. There is still intergenerational transmission (stage 6), yet most Nahuatl speakers 'are a socially integrated and ethnolinguistically active population ... beyond child-bearing age' (stage 7) (Fishman, 1991: 89). Many factors have contributed to the shift in Coatepec de los Costales from a dominant Nahuatl speaking community to a community where elders are the only ones who fluently speak the language. Migration, education policies and capitalism are a few macro-level causes of language shift. In the next section I discuss one further cause of language loss underlying these macro-level factors: intergenerational language transfer.

Observable language practices in Coatepec

School

Coatepec is divided east and west of the *zócalo*, the village center, into two sides, Huayapa and Mazapa. This is a locally understood way to talk about location. Over a four-month period I observed and interviewed students and teachers during school hours at one elementary school located in the Huayapa side of the village. I also observed and developed relationships with the mothers who made lunch for their children. The school-teacher knew that I was a teacher in the United States, so when she introduced me she made sure that the students knew and called me *mae-stra*, as a sign of respect. School instruction was delivered only in Spanish, and parent meetings were in Spanish. Although one parent did not speak Spanish, there was no school official who could translate for her. School institutions value the Spanish language and promote English learning. The ideologies that determine power relations are visible in the curriculum and way that teachers talk about language. There is no space for Mexicano. Although some teachers did encourage students to learn their native language and tell stories of their pueblo, they did not help by giving them place and time in class. These activities were seen as something to do at home, outside of the school curriculum. The covert language status – that Spanish is the language of success – is present in local educational institutions, and there is no affirmation to students that their native tongue is valued in society. Therefore, they begin to internalize feelings of shame and believe that their mother tongue is impractical.

Community

As my stay continued, I was invited to several birthday parties and *convivios* (gatherings of family and friends to spend time together outside of any particular occasion), and during that time I participated in the events and observed the language practices that occurred. I listened to the languages that were spoken and those that were silenced. There were specific situations when one language was valued over the other. For example, when elders were present Mexicano was the language that was spoken and when they were not present, Spanish was the dominant language. The younger people spoke Spanish; if elders were not present, then Mexicano was not used. The elders' presence, in effect, served to 'manage' which language was spoken. Other people in attendance respected the elders, and if these others knew how to speak Mexicano they would switch to Mexicano in the elders' presence. One of the comments that elders made was that the younger generation had lost respect, but clearly the younger generation at these events respected their elders, although the respect may not have been expressed in the way that the elders wished.

Later in my stay in the pueblo, I attended federal government meetings, such as the *Tercer Edad* or *Oportunidades*. The goal of these meetings was to teach the people 'social skills,' and they were a requirement in order to receive government funds. For example, hygiene and nutrition classes were taught to the children in the pueblo. Government representatives encouraged mainstream ways of being and did not consider the people's ways as valuable. This is a covert way in which the government continues coercive assimilation of the people into their vision of a singular Mexico.

As a participant observer, I studied these everyday practices and interactions and how language played a role in various scenarios. I often asked myself which language was honored and given space, status and power. Spanish continued to dominate Mexicano in all these settings:

educational, governmental and public. Mexicano is not given the time, place, or status necessary to be revitalized or sustained.

Methods

During my six-month ethnographic study in Coatepec de los Costales, I took field notes, collected archives and conducted in-depth, audio-recorded interviews. The children, youth and adult interviews were conducted in Spanish. The elders' interviews were conducted in Nahuatl, and in such cases I had a translator to help carry out the interview. I interviewed four groups: children (6–12 years old), youth (13–18 years old), adults consisting mainly of females (19–59 years old) and elders (60+ years old).

An old white Catholic church is located in the zócalo, which divides the village into the two sides: Mazapa (west of the church) and Huayapa (east of the church). The participants were from both locations. Location plays an important role in language preservation, so it was important for me to include participants who lived in different parts of the village. I spent time in the zócalo observing people, writing field notes and interacting with the residents. Most of my observations were participant observation and I recorded my notes after the activity or event.

I also spent time with two families (one family, and the other participants I met who later became family to me) and observed language practices when they invited me into their homes as a member of their family. During my time there, I was able to build relationships and discuss issues occurring in the village. I am honored to have shared this time and space with these families who allowed me to view other ways of living in the village and how they negotiate a way of being and living.

Once I had collected all my data, I began transcribing my interviews. As I listened to and analyzed the interviews, I coded them and assigned them to categories. Larger themes were derived from the categories. The themes of shame, respect, counter-narrative and ambivalence are the core of my larger ethnographic study; similar themes have emerged from related research on language shift and revitalization looking specifically at youth and elders (Lee, 2009; McCarty et al., 2009; Meek, 2007; Messing, 2009; Moore, 2006; Nicholas, 2009). Drawing on Seidman's (2013) method of phenomenological data analysis, I crafted narrative profiles for a cross-section of participants in each age group, organizing these according to the three-part language policy framework of language practices, ideologies or beliefs and language management (Spolsky, 2004). The narrative profiles that follow exemplify crosscutting themes derived from the analysis of the interviews and observation data.

I coded my data to understand what I observed and recorded in my field notes, interviews, and document collection (Schwandt, 2007). Using the constant comparative method (Glaser & Strauss, 1967; Schwandt,

2007) these codes and categories were not static, but constantly changing as new patterns emerged. While I coded and categorized my data, I took an Indigenous epistemological stance to data analysis, focusing on the '4 Rs' of Critical Indigenous Research Methodologies (CIRM): relationality, responsibility, respect and reciprocity (Brayboy *et al.*, 2012). I intended 'to understand the complexity, resilience, contradiction, and self-determination of these communities, and [I was] driven by a desire to serve [my] community's interest' (Brayboy *et al.*, 2012: 432). During the coding process, I crafted profiles of the participants whom I had interviewed to give them a voice and help my readers develop a relationship with them through their stories and the complexities of their experiences.

Keeping all this in mind in the process of analyzing my data within a CIRM framework, my goal was to analyze the data and interpret the findings in order to serve the community and help them meet their needs. I made sure to use their voices and their experiences to re-tell stories of their life in the village. I regularly shared my notes with the participants to make sure that I was representing them in an accurate and a respectful manner. In the summer of 2015, I traveled back to Coatepec to share the findings and themes with participants.

Three major findings emerged from my analysis process. *La pena* (linguistic embarrassment or shame) was a major theme that was common across all generations. I delved into the various meanings of *la pena*, for it had slightly different connotations in each age category. At the same time, there was an ideology of the sacredness of our Indigenous language and how the members of Coatepec identify with their ancestral language. Specifically, I sought to carefully untangle youths' language ideologies. The juxtaposition of youth and elder ideologies may cause confusion about how individual community members view the Nahuatl language. Consequently, intergenerational language transmission suffers. I further discuss the relationship between the youth and elders below.

A second finding explores the relationship between language stigma versus respect. Contradictory narratives between the youth and elders were common, and these contradictions contribute to language shift. Many of the youth voiced the opinion that they did not speak the language but they believed that the language was beautiful. This related to the idea of 'growing into the language,' meaning that the youth believed they would not speak the language until they reached the age of responsibility.

Lastly, I discovered the importance of elders in the household and their responsibility for language maintenance and transmission to the next generation. The grandparents were the key to language preservation and the ones who managed the language.

The process of sharing and acknowledging the work as being collaborative was at the forefront of my study. I assured the participants that their voices would be represented in a respectful manner and as accurately as possible. As an Indigenous researcher doing work in my Indigenous community, it was important to share the findings before I continued to write. I write now so that their voices can be heard 'near and far' (as a dear friend would always remind me). Conducting research within an Indigenous community is humbling (Smith, 2012; Wilson, 2009).

Findings

From the four participant age categories, I have selected participants whose accounts provide an in-depth look into the major themes that emerged from the data analysis. In the following sections, I describe how language ideologies affect language learning for youth and the role of elders in the intergenerational language transmission and revitalization process. I begin with Omar, a boy who spoke Nahuatl to his friends but not to elders.

Language ideologies: La pena – 'They [elders] will make fun of me'

Omar is a 13-year-old boy who was in the sixth grade at the time of the study, and graduated from elementary school. Omar lives with his grandmother, mother, aunt, sisters, and brother north of the *zócalo*. He is considered the man of the house since he is the oldest male in the household. Omar attends school daily and then goes home to help gather wood or water from the *parota* (the village well and primary source of water). Later, after his chores, Omar hangs out with his friends. They mainly sit around and watch people walk back and forth or play soccer and basketball on the court located in the zócalo.

Omar stated that he speaks a little Mexicano, but is better able to understand than to speak. Omar's grandmother is a monolingual Mexicano speaker who communicates with her family and community members in Mexicano only. Omar has learned to communicate with his grandmother in Mexicano; therefore, he is able to understand and speak it. Omar has heard Mexicano growing up and is exposed to the language at home. Although he knows Mexicano, at times he does not speak it because of *la pena* [embarrassment]. In the following interview, I asked him what *la pena* means to him.[2]

> **Omar:** I don't like to speak it because then they [elders] make fun of me… if I say a word wrong. I don't want them to make fun of me, so I don't speak it at all. But I speak it with my friends.
> *No me gusta hablar [náhuatl] porque … si digo una palabra mal ellos se burlan. No quiero que se burlen de mí, entonces no hablo. Pero hablo con mis amigos.*

> **R:** You speak it with your friends? What do you guys talk about? If you can speak it, then why not speak it with others?
> *¿Lo hablas con tus amigos? ¿Y de qué hablan? Si puedes hablar Nahuatl, entonces por qué no lo hablas con otros?*

Omar: We laugh and joke around in Mexicano. Plus we don't speak it with girls...it's embarrassing. Just kids' stuff. No pressure, we can mess around. The elders would get mad.

Nos reímos y bromeamos en mexicano. Pero nunca con las mujeres ... es chistoso. Sólo cosas de nosotros. Sin presión, podemos jugar. Los mayores se enojan.

The embarrassment or *la pena* emerged as a theme across the generations. The elders believed that the youth were embarrassed to speak Mexicano and that they did not 'like' the language. The youth did not want to speak Mexicano because they did not want to be ridiculed by the elders. These counter-ideologies (Hill, 1992) were present and contributed to language shift in the community – a common theme in other research with Indigenous communities (Lee, 2009; McCarty *et al.*, 2009; Messing, 2009; Nicholas, 2009; Wyman, 2012). The youth expressed an interest in their language and a desire to learn their ancestral language, but most of those interviewed felt that the elders did not support them. They desired a safe place where they could speak and not be ridiculed. As Omar stated, he felt safe with his friends because they were all learning the language and they knew it was acceptable to make mistakes. A young girl stated:

My grandparents speak both languages. My grandparents want me to speak Nahuatl. They speak to me more in Nahuatl. I hear Spanish also, but it [Nahuatl] doesn't stick in my head. I understand and I answer in Spanish. But I know what they are saying.

Mis abuelos hablan los dos idiomas. Mis abuelos quieren que yo hable náhuatl. Me hablan más en náhuatl. Oigo español también, pero [náhuatl] no se queda en mi cabeza. Entiendo y respondo en español. Pero sé lo que están diciendo.

Although children and youth may not be ready to speak the language, they are listening to it every day if their grandparents are present in the household. The everyday repetition of the language is recorded in the youths' minds, and when they are comfortable they will be able to express themselves in their native tongue. The elders never directly mentioned that they were responsible in transferring the language to the younger generation, and yet, from the youths' accounts, it seems crucial for the elders to set an example of language reclamation. Some elders knew the importance of speaking the language to their grandchildren, in order for them to learn the language.

For instance, Omar's grandmother played an important role in maintaining his mother tongue. The grandmother, mother and the oldest sisters took care of the household and would communicate in Mexicano because the grandmother was present. The grandmother would ask her grandchildren to do chores and she managed how things were done in the household. She had great responsibility to run the household and the children respected and obeyed her. The grandmother diligently decided to speak only Mexicano and she did not try to speak in Spanish. For example, when she attended school meetings she would have her daughter translate for her. The daughter was embarrassed, but the grandmother sat there until the meeting was over. This was also the case when she attended *Oportunidades* meetings.

I never had the chance to ask the grandmother about why she chose not to speak Spanish, but she was one of the youngest adult monolingual speakers in the pueblo. Her consistency and dedication to her language helped her family preserve their language. Her two daughters, who live in the same household, speak Mexicano; one of them speaks limited Spanish, while the other is bilingual. The 18-year-old struggled learning Spanish in school and had difficulty learning in the mainstream educational institution, where instruction was in Spanish. Teachers presumed she had a learning disability, but it is likely language was the factor. As an experienced teacher of a second language, I know the importance of valuing and teaching in the native tongue. If the curriculum was taught in her native tongue, she might have been successful in acquiring the skills that were required. Some teachers did not understand that language was impeding her learning, and some of her classmates teased her.

This family encountered negative experiences as native Mexicano speakers, so they learned how to manage living in the community. They would speak Mexicano at home, but at school and in the community they spoke only Spanish – to the point that they would deny being able to speak Mexicano. This is an example of how negative connotations can lead to linguistic shame and, in turn, language loss. This particular family continues to hold on to their language because of the grandmother's commitment to language maintenance. The grandmother did not allow external factors to contribute to the language she would pass down to her children and grandchildren.

The grandmother is the key holder to language maintenance within the family. She has influenced her daughters to continue speaking their native tongue. Despite the pressure of official language policies, this family continues to exercise the right to preserve their language. Several times a day, they negotiate language choices and ways to maintain their Indigeneity. In the household, their language is valued and honored.

Growing into a language: Respect – 'It's not time, once I get older I will speak it'

> Si hablamos el idioma [náhuatl], tenemos que aprender a cuidar y respetarlo.
>
> If we speak that language [Nahuatl], we need to learn to take care of it and respect it.
>
> – Xochitl, 21 years old

Carmela, a 15-year-old girl, lives with her mother and father. Carmela is 5'1', thin, with short black hair, and tanned, brown skin. Her daily duties are to attend school, clean her room, and attend to the family's little store and *molino* (mill). Their mini-store is a room in the house where they sell detergent, soap, sugar and rice, and they use the *molino* to grind maize for customers. Carmela deals with customers and community members daily. She lives on the Mazapa side, east of the zócalo on the main road. She is in the ninth grade and goes to Tonolapa, a nearby village, to attend school. She does not speak Mexicano, but she can understand it. Her mother speaks a little Mexicano, as does her father. In the store, she interacts with many customers who are elders and speak to her in Mexicano.

I interviewed Carmela at her store/home. During the interview, there were a few customers who came to purchase products and others to have their maize ground. The interview continued with interruptions, and at the same time I was able to observe language practices and management as the customers entered the store.

R: You said that you don't speak Mexicano? Why is that?
¿Dijiste que no hablas mexicano? ¿Porqué?

C: Well...my parents never taught me. But I will speak it later.
Bueno ... mis padres nunca me enseñaron. Pero lo voy hablar más tarde.

R: What do you mean that you will speak it later?
¿Qué quieres decir que vas a hablar más tarde?

C: Well, you know once I get older. It's not cool to speak it as a teen.
Bueno, tu sabes que cuando tenga mas años. No esta en moda de hablar, como joven.

R: How will you speak it if you don't speak it right now?
¿Cómo vas hablar lo si no lo hablas ahora?

C: I have this friend that is young and he didn't speak it. Now he's married and he speaks it. He's older and mature and he can speak it.
Tengo un amigo que es joven y no lo habló. Pero ahora está casado y lo habla. Es mayor y ya maduro y ahora puede hablarlo.

Carmela didn't speak Mexicano as a sign of respect to the elders. A common theme throughout the interviews with youth was that they had great respect for their Indigenous language and for the elders. They believed that the language was beautiful and sacred – a gift that their ancestors had left them. Many youth admitted that they understood and spoke a little, but were afraid to let their voices be heard. They felt as teenagers that they did not have the knowledge to speak the language. As adults, they would have more responsibilities, including the responsibility to protect and use their language.

Carmela was not the only youth who had the same ideologies. I observed other youth who stated that they did not speak the language, but their grandparents spoke to them and they would listen. Perhaps some were not ready to let their voices be heard, or they did not desire to position themselves in a vulnerable space where they could be targeted and teased by the elders (Lee, 2009; Messing, 2009).

During the interview, Carmela and other participants stated that Nahuatl is a language for older people. 'The older generation speaks Nahuatl, younger people don't,' said a 20-year-old female. Likewise, a 42-year-old woman said, 'I speak it with the older people.' And a 24-year-old woman said, 'I only hear it from my father-in-law and grandparents.' Most of the younger participants said that they hear their grandparents speak it. The older people spoke Nahuatl, and the younger people did not want to speak it until they were ready, as sort of a rite of passage. The language is something sacred that one must be ready to appreciate, and when one is older she/he will understand the value of speaking the language.

'The language will never die' connects to the notion of 'I will grow into the language.' Most of the participants believed that the language would survive and always be present in the village, within their families, and in their surroundings. They never thought of the concept of their language being gone from their community. It was a strange and ridiculous idea. The youths interviewed asserted that they will speak the language, and therefore it would be alive or there would be someone who would speak it. (See Meek, 2007, for a discussion of similar youth language ideologies.) The youth are also clearly key holders who can sustain the language, but the effort requires collaboration with the elders to continue creating spaces to practice and speak.

Key holders – The grandparents or elders

Through my observations and stay in Coatepec, I realized that language maintenance in the village is possible, and Mexicano would survive if grandparents are present in the household. The grandparents mostly spoke Mexicano and were the managers of the language spoken in their homes. In Coatepec, the grandparents or elders are treated with the highest respect in the entire village. An elder may be walking down the street struggling with a pail of maize, and a person at any stage in life, whether a child, youth, or adult, will offer to help carry the maize. If there is a community meeting and an elder is looking for a place to sit, someone will offer him or her a seat, similar to the etiquette on a bus. Although the elder may be a stranger, people are taught about respect and how to treat others through family ways of knowing and being. Therefore, if an elder joins a conversation and converses in Mexicano, the language will switch from Spanish to Mexicano.

As a community member, I observed many of these language practices in various situations. On one occasion, the women of the pueblo gathered at a woman's house to prepare food for an offering. I woke up early with the sunrise, and went with my mother and aunt to the señora's house. It was time to make tamales, and a typical reunion of women always meant sharing and gossiping about the latest scandals and activities in the village. *Did you hear about the girl who took off with that guy? ... The X's son is going to el norte ...* I would listen and once in a while would whisper to my aunt or mother for clarification. The conversation was all in Spanish, but as soon as an elder came in and commented in Mexicano, the entire conversation changed to Mexicano. All the women began speaking Mexicano. Other women who did not speak it well or were embarrassed to speak the language shared a little in Mexicano, perhaps saying words and phrases, or maybe a sentence or two. Yet the conversation was virtually all Mexicano, with some Spanish. The power of the elders to manage the language is a sign of hope for keeping the language alive if all of the community members continue to work together.

Similarly, my observations of the family households showed that Mexicano was alive and fluently spoken if the grandparents lived with the family. The grandparents spoke in Mexicano, so there was space in the house for Mexicano and the children would listen to it as they grew up. The grandparents would communicate with the parents in Mexicano, which encouraged the parents to maintain their language, and, although the parents may not have spoken to their children in Mexicano, the grandparents did. As mentioned above, the children would listen and obey their grandparents' out of respect, which created a safe space to hear and use the language in an informal manner.

As I conducted my fieldwork, I also reflected on how the findings were similar to my family's situation. When my grandfather passed away, he took some of the linguistic knowledge with him. My parents raised us speaking Spanish and I have wondered why they chose not to teach us Mexicano. My grandparents never lived with us, but we lived close by, and during family events they managed the language that was spoken. They spoke in Nahuatl, as it was the best way for them to express themselves. After my grandparents passed away, less of the language was heard at our family events and reunions in the US and Mexico. I realized the importance of the elders and the influence they have on language maintenance. They cannot be held solely responsible for sustaining Mexicano, though, because relationships and collaboration with the youth and children are necessary.

These reflections led to the realization that it is my responsibility to maintain our language within our family, which is why I decided to convene a language revitalization class at my parents' home. At the beginning it was my parents and me, and then three friends joined. With hope, persistence, time and sustainability (Hinton, 2001) we will be able to revitalize the language within my family, for me, for my future children and our future generations.

Figure 10.3 Three generations of strong *cihuāmeh* – meaning women in Nahuatl. From left to right, Rosalva Mojica Lagunas, her grandmother Guadalupe Mojica Cabrera and her mother Sofia Mojica Lagunas (photograph by Rosalva Mojica Lagunas)

Conclusion

Mexicano is an Indigenous language that will no longer be heard in Coatepec if it is not nurtured and cared for through use. The Coatepec people respect and love their language, but this ethnographic study suggests that they do not fully appreciate the danger of their language disappearing from their community and homes. Community members across generations need to meet and discuss these issues, asking the following questions: *How can we include the elders in school settings as language teachers? How can they begin a language program in the village?* To begin a language revitalization project, the community members need to lead the way and be at the forefront of the project. As a researcher and community member, my role is to support this effort and offer my knowledge to them as we continue this journey together to benefit all people.

In similar cases, communities have not been as fortunate in maintaining native speakers of their languages. According to Fishman's (1991) GIDS, the people of Coatepec are at a stage where they still have fluent speakers, but slowly the speakers will pass away and, like my grandparents, take a little piece of Indigenous knowledge. Elders and youth, together, are at the core of language revitalization. Language learning flourishes when it begins at home through everyday sociocultural practices. The role of grandparents is essential in this process because they are the key holders of language preservation. They possess the knowledge and the stories that were passed down to them, and they are poised to pass this knowledge to future generations (Figure 10.3).

As I continue this work of language revitalization, I realize the importance of the elders in my community of Coatepec and within my family in the United States. They are at the core of language maintenance. As a young adult it is my responsibility to join them to continue this journey together to honor our past generations and our future ones. I also hope this work will contribute to the larger field of language revitalization and language planning and policy.

Notes

(1) For more on the history of language policies in Mexico from the colonial period to the 21st century (in particular, educational language policies), see de León (2017) and Hamel (2008).
(2) All names are pseudonyms. Original interviews with the youth discussed here were conducted in Spanish.

References

Archive of Indigenous Language of Latin America [AILLA] (2010) Reference TBI.
Baldauf, R. and Kaplan, R. (2007) *Language Planning and Policy*. Clevedon: Multilingual Matters.
Basso, K. (1996) *Wisdom Sits in Places: Landscape and Language among the Western Apache*. Albuquerque: University of New Mexico Press.
Brayboy, B.M.J., Gough, H., Leonard, B., Roehl, R. and Solyom, J. (2012) Reclaiming scholarship: Critical Indigenous research methodologies. In S. Lapan, M. Quartaroli and F. Riemer (eds) *Qualitative Research: An Introduction to Methods and Designs* (pp. 423–450). San Francisco, CA: Jossey-Bass.
Coronel-Molina, S.M. and McCarty, T.L. (2016) Introduction. In S.M. Coronel-Molina and T.L. McCarty (eds) *Indigenous Language Revitalization in the Americas* (pp. 1–11). New York, NY: Routledge.
de León, L. (2017) Indigenous language policy and education in Mexico. In T.L. McCarty and S. May (eds) *Language Policy and Political Issues in Education* (3rd edition, pp. 415–433). Cham, Switzerland: Springer International.
Denzin, N., Lincoln, Y. and Smith, T. (2008) *Handbook of Critical and Indigenous Methodologies*. Thousand Oaks, CA: SAGE.
Fishman, J.A. (1991) *Reversing Language Shift: Theoretical and Empirical Foundations of Assistance to Threatened Languages*. Clevedon: Multilingual Matters.
Fishman, J.A. (ed.) (2001) *Can Threatened Languages be Saved? Reversing Language Shift, Revisited: A 21st Century Perspective*. Clevedon: Multilingual Matters.
Fishman, J.A. and García, O. (2010) *Handbook of Language and Ethnic Identity*. New York, N.Y: Oxford University Press.
Fitch, N. (n.d) The conquest of Mexico: An annotated bibliography. Retrieved from http://faculty.fullerton.edu/nfitch/nehaha/conquestbib.htm
Flores Farfán, J.A. (2006) Intervention in indigenous education. Culturally-sensitive materials for bilingual Nahuatl speakers. In M. Hidalgo (ed.) *The Mexican Indigenous Languages at the Dawn of the 21st* (pp. 301–324). Berlin: Mouton de Gruyter.
Glaser, B. and Strauss, A. (1967) *The Discovery of Grounded Theory*. Chicago, IL: Aldine.
Hamel, R. (2008) Indigenous language policy and education in Mexico. In S. May and N.H. Hornberger (eds) *Encyclopedia of Language and Education, Vol. 1: Language Policy and Political Issues in Education* (2nd edition, pp. 301–312). New York, NY: Springer.
Heath, S. (1972) *Telling Tongues*. New York, NY: Teachers College Press.

Hill, J. (1992) 'Today there is no respect': Nostalgia, 'respect' and oppositional discourse in Mexicano (Nahuatl) language ideology. *Pragmatics* 2 (3), 263-280.

Hill, J. and Hill, K. (1986) *Speaking Mexicano*. Tucson: University of Arizona Press.

Hinton, L. and Hale, K. (eds) (2001) *The Green Book of Language Revitalization in Practice*. San Diego, CA: Academic Press.

Hinton, L. (2001) Language revitalization: An overview. In L. Hinton and K. Hale (eds) *The Green Book of Language Revitalization in Practice* (pp. 3–18). San Diego, CA: Academic Press.

King, K.A. and Haboud, M. (2011) International migration and Quichua language shift in the Ecuadorian Andes. In T.L. McCarty (ed.) *Ethnography and Language Policy* (pp. 139–159). New York, NY: Routledge.

Laduke, W. (1999) *All our Relations: Native Struggles for Land and Life*. Cambridge, MA: South End Press.

Lagunas, R.M. (2016) Intergenerational Language Ideologies, Practices, and Management: An Ethnographic Study in a Nahuatl Community. Unpublished PhD dissertation, Arizona State University, Mary Lou Fulton Teachers College, Tempe, AZ.

Lee, T.S. (2009) Language, identity, and power: Navajo and Pueblo young adults' perspectives and experiences with competing language ideologies. *Journal of Language, Identity, and Education* 8 (5), 307–320.

Lee, T.S. (2014) Critical language awareness among Native youth in New Mexico. In L.T. Wyman, T.L. McCarty and S.E. Nicholas (eds) *Indigenous Youth and Multilingualism: Language Identity, Ideology, and Practice in Dynamic Cultural Worlds* (pp. 130–148). New York, NY: Routledge.

McCarty, T. L. (ed.) (2011) *Ethnography and Language Policy*. New York, NY: Routledge.

McCarty, T.L., Romero, M.E. and Zepeda, O. (2006) Reclaiming the gift: Indigenous youth counter-narratives on Native language loss and revitalization. *American Indian Quarterly* 30 (1 & 2), 28–48.

McCarty, T.L., Romero-Little, M., Warhol, L. and Zepeda, O. (2009) Indigenous youth as language policy makers. *Journal of Language, Identity, and Education* 8 (5), 291–306.

Meek, B. (2007) Respecting the language of elders: Ideological shift and linguistic discontinuity in a Northern Athapascan Community. *Journal of Linguistic Anthropology* 17 (1) 23–43.

Messing, J. (2007) Ideologies of public and private usages of language in Tlaxcala, Mexico. *International Journal of the Sociology of Language* 187/188, 211–227.

Messing, J. (2009) Ambivalence and ideology among Mexicano youth in Tlaxcal, Mexico. *Journal of Language, Identity, and Education*, 8 (5), 350–364.

Messing, J. (2014) 'I didn't know you knew Mexicano!' Shifting ideologies, identities, and ambivalence among former youth in Tlaxcala, Mexico. In L.T. Wyman, T.L. McCarty and S.E. Nicholas (eds) *Indigenous Youth and Multilingualism: Language Identity, Ideology, and Practice in Dynamic Cultural Worlds* (pp. 111–129). New York, NY: Routledge.

Messing, J. and Rockwell, E. (2006) Local language promoters and new discursive spaces: Mexicano in and out of schools in Tlaxcala, In M. Hidalgo (ed.) *The Mexican Indigenous Languages at the Dawn of the 21st Century* (pp. 249–280). Berlin: Mouton de Gruyter.

Moore, R. (2006) Disappearing, Inc.: Glimpsing the sublime in the politics of access to endangered languages. *Language and Communication* 26, 296–315.

Nicholas, S.E. (2009) 'I live Hopi, I just don't speak it' – The critical intersection of language, culture, and identity in the lives of contemporary Hopi youth. *Journal of Language, Identity, and Education*, 8 (5), 321–334.

Olko, J. and Sullivan, J. (2014) Toward a comprehensive model for Nahuatl language research and revitalization. *Annual Meeting of the Berkeley Linguistics Society* 40, 369–397.

Schwandt, T. (2007) *The Sage Dictionary of Qualitative Inquiry*. Los Angeles, CA: SAGE.

Seidman, I.E. (2013) *Interviewing as Qualitative Research: A Guide for Researchers in Education and the Social Sciences*. New York, NY: Teachers College Press.

Smith, L. (2012) *Decolonizing Methodologies: Research and Indigenous Peoples* (2nd edn). London: Zed Books.

Spolsky, B. (2004) *Language Policy*. Cambridge: Cambridge University Press.

Spolsky, B. (2009) *Language Management*. Cambridge: Cambridge University Press.

Wilson, S. (2009) *Research Is Ceremony: Indigenous Research Methods*. Winnipeg, MB: Fernwood.

Woodbury, A. (n.d) What is an endangered language? Retrieved from https://www.linguisticsociety.org/sites/default/files/Endangered_Languages.pdf

Wyman, L. (2012) *Youth Culture, Language Endangerment and Linguistic Survivance*. Bristol: Multilingual Matters.

Author Index

Subject Index